Jim Henson's
BENEATH THE
DARK CRYSTAL™

ADAM
SMITH

ALEXANDRIA
HUNTINGTON

VOLUME ONE

Published by
ARCHAIA™

Jim Henson's
BENEATH THE
DARK CRYSTAL ™

Written by **Adam Smith**
Illustrated by **Alexandria Huntington**
Lettered by **Jim Campbell**

Cover and Chapter Break Art by **Benjamin Dewey**

Series Designer **Marie Krupina**
Collection Designer **Jillian Crab**
Assistant Editor **Gavin Gronenthal**
Editor **Cameron Chittock**

Special Thanks to **Brian Henson, Lisa Henson, Jim Formanek, Nicole Goldman, Carla DellaVedova, Karen Falk, Blanca Lista, Shane Mang, the entire Jim Henson Company team, Wendy Froud, Brian Froud, David Williams, and Sierra Hahn.**

Ross Richie CEO & Founder
Joy Huffman CFO
Matt Gagnon Editor-in-Chief
Filip Sablik President, Publishing & Marketing
Stephen Christy President, Development
Lance Kreiter Vice President, Licensing & Merchandising
Phil Barbaro Vice President, Finance & Human Resources
Arune Singh Vice President, Marketing
Bryce Carlson Vice President, Editorial & Creative Strategy
Scott Newman Manager, Production Design
Kate Henning Manager, Operations
Spencer Simpson Manager, Sales
Sierra Hahn Executive Editor
Jeanine Schaefer Executive Editor
Dafna Pleban Senior Editor
Shannon Watters Senior Editor
Eric Harburn Senior Editor
Whitney Leopard Editor
Cameron Chittock Editor
Chris Rosa Editor
Matthew Levine Editor
Sophie Philips-Roberts Assistant Editor
Gavin Gronenthal Assistant Editor
Michael Moccio Assistant Editor
Gwen Waller Assistant Editor
Amanda LaFranco Executive Assistant
Jillian Crab Design Coordinator
Michelle Ankley Design Coordinator
Kara Leopard Production Designer
Marie Krupina Production Designer
Grace Park Production Design Assistant
Chelsea Roberts Production Design Assistant
Samantha Knapp Production Design Assistant
Elizabeth Loughridge Accounting Coordinator
Stephanie Hocutt Social Media Coordinator
José Meza Event Coordinator
Holly Aitchison Digital Sales Coordinator
Megan Christopher Operations Assistant
Rodrigo Hernandez Mailroom Assistant
Morgan Perry Direct Market Representative
Cat O'Grady Marketing Assistant
Breanna Sarpy Executive Assistant

JIM HENSON'S BENEATH THE DARK CRYSTAL Volume One, March 2019. Published by Archaia, a division of Boom Entertainment, Inc. ™ & © 2019 The Jim Henson Company. JIM HENSON's mark & logo, BENEATH THE DARK CRYSTAL, mark & logo, and all related characters and elements are trademarks of The Jim Henson Company. Originally published in single magazine form as BENEATH THE DARK CRYSTAL No. 1-4. ™ & © 2018 The Jim Henson Company. All rights reserved. Archaia™ and the Archaia logo are trademarks of Boom Entertainment, Inc., registered in various countries and categories. All characters, events, and institutions depicted herein are fictional. Any similarity between any of the names, characters, persons, events, and/or institutions in this publication to actual names, characters, and persons, whether living or dead, events, and/or institutions is unintended and purely coincidental.

BOOM! Studios, 5670 Wilshire Boulevard, Suite 400, Los Angeles, CA 90036-5679.

Printed in China. First Printing.

ISBN: 978-1-68415-323-7
eISBN: 978-1-64144-176-6

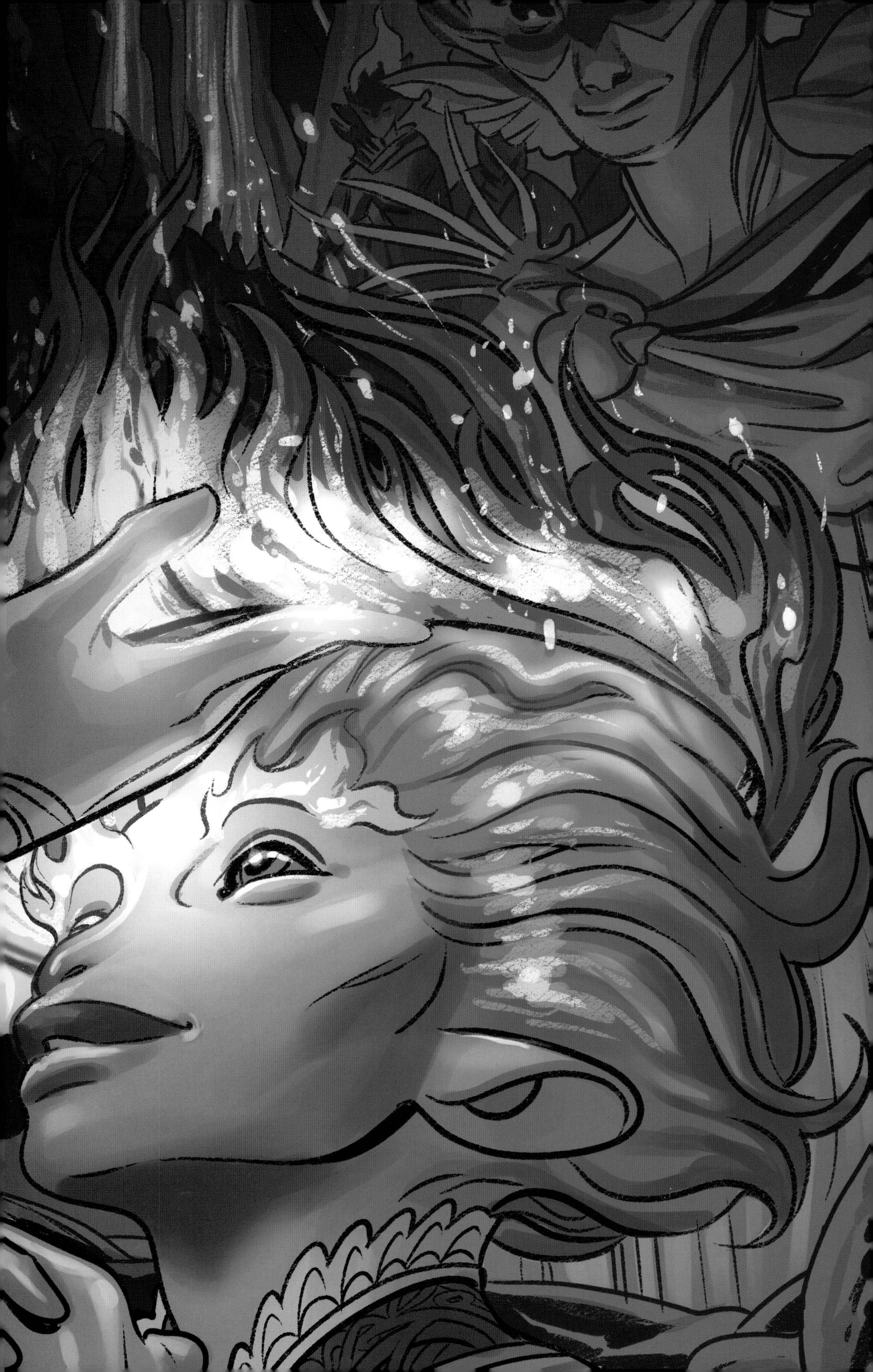

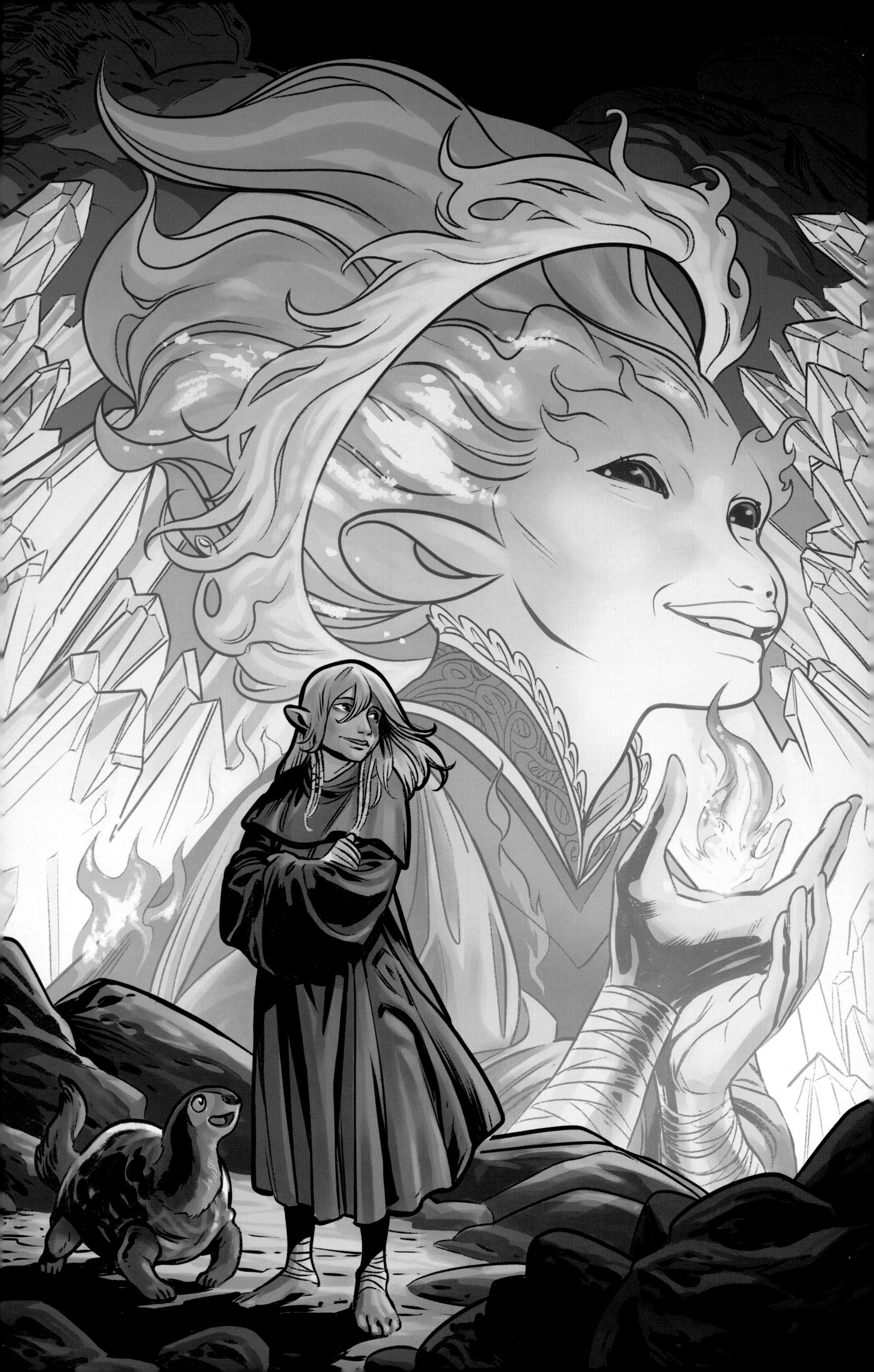

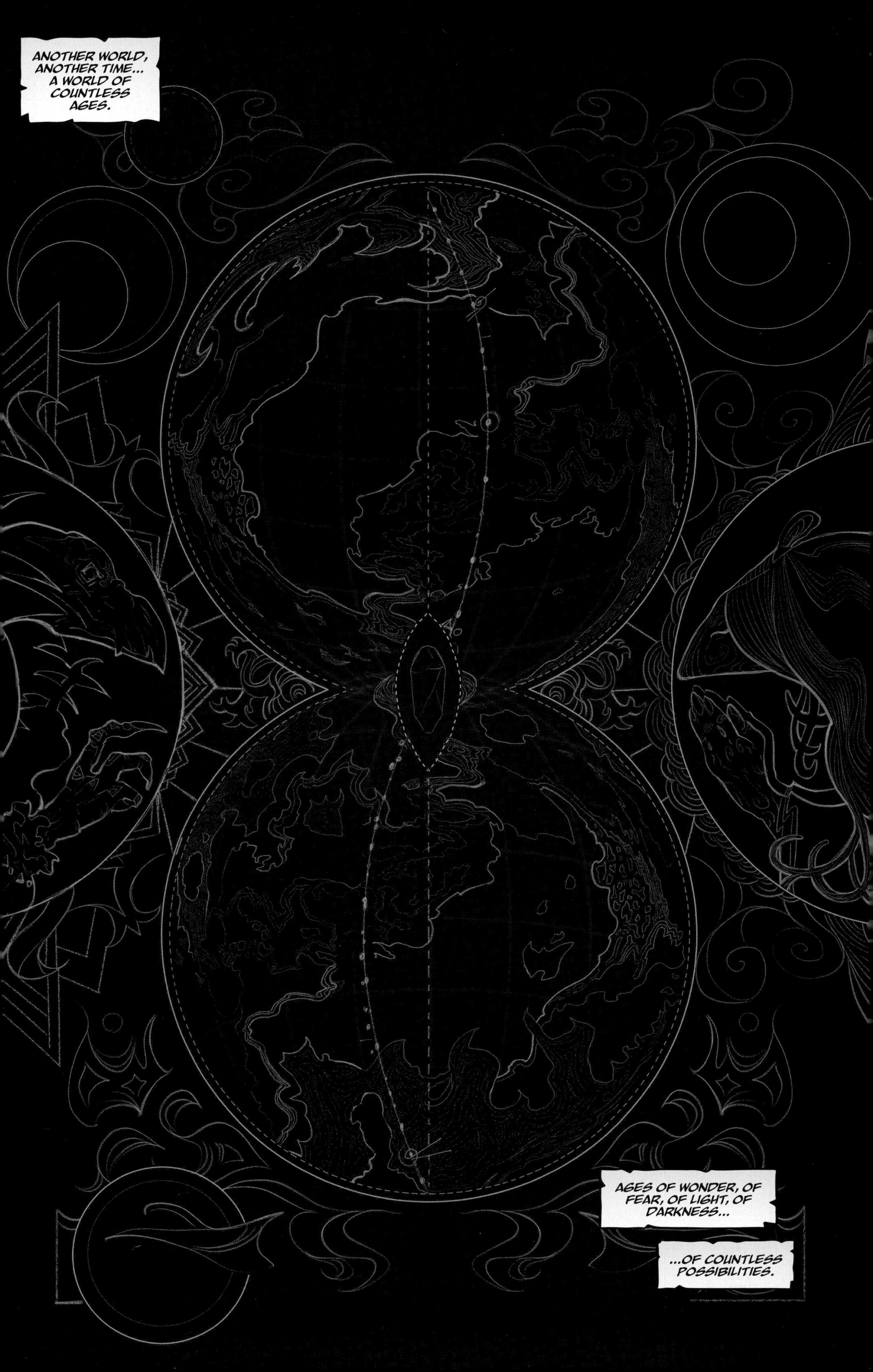
ANOTHER WORLD, ANOTHER TIME... A WORLD OF COUNTLESS AGES.
AGES OF WONDER, OF FEAR, OF LIGHT, OF DARKNESS...
...OF COUNTLESS POSSIBILITIES.

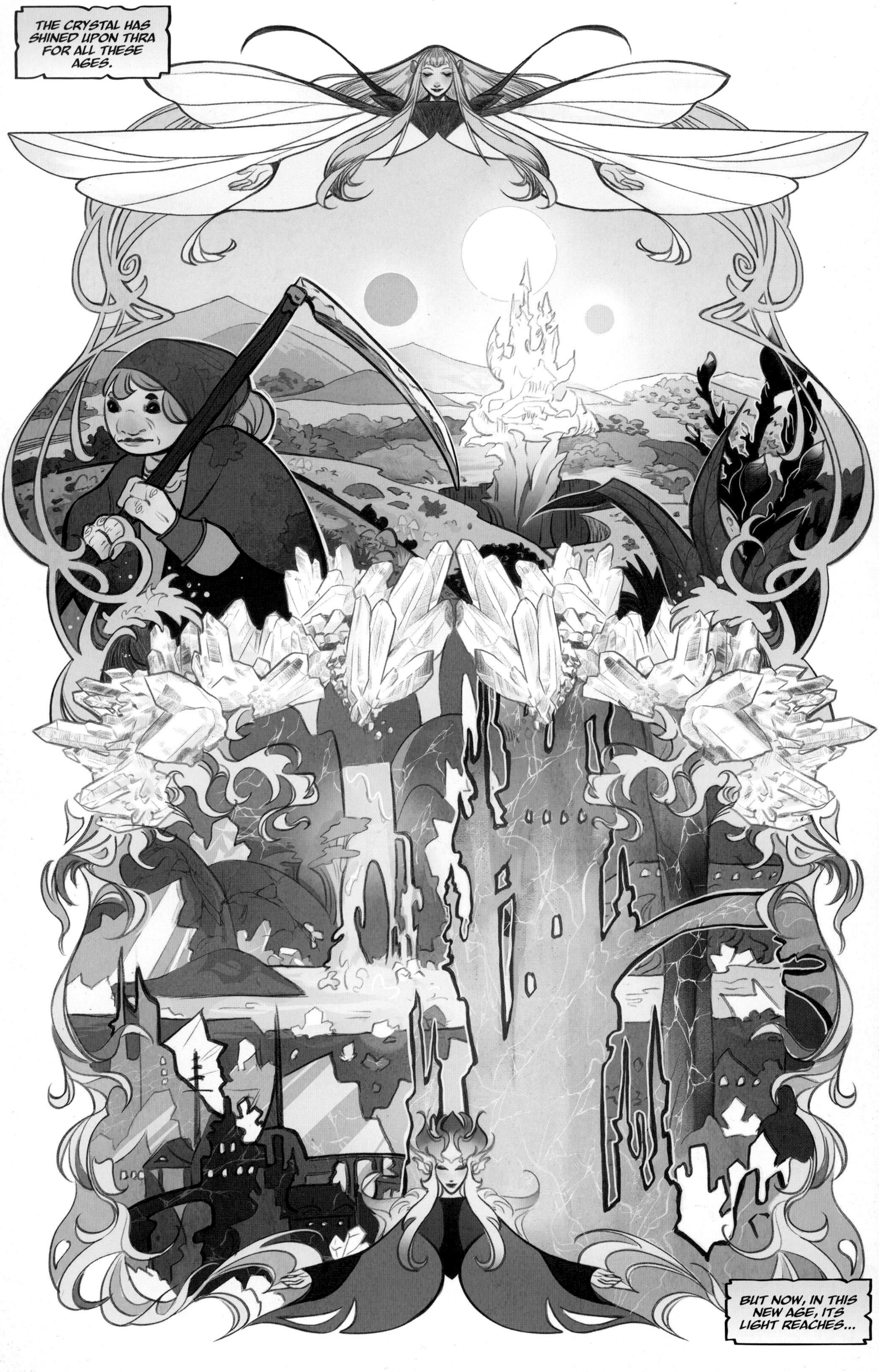
THE CRYSTAL HAS SHINED UPON THRA FOR ALL THESE AGES.
BUT NOW, IN THIS NEW AGE, ITS LIGHT REACHES...

BENEATH THE DARK CRYSTAL ™

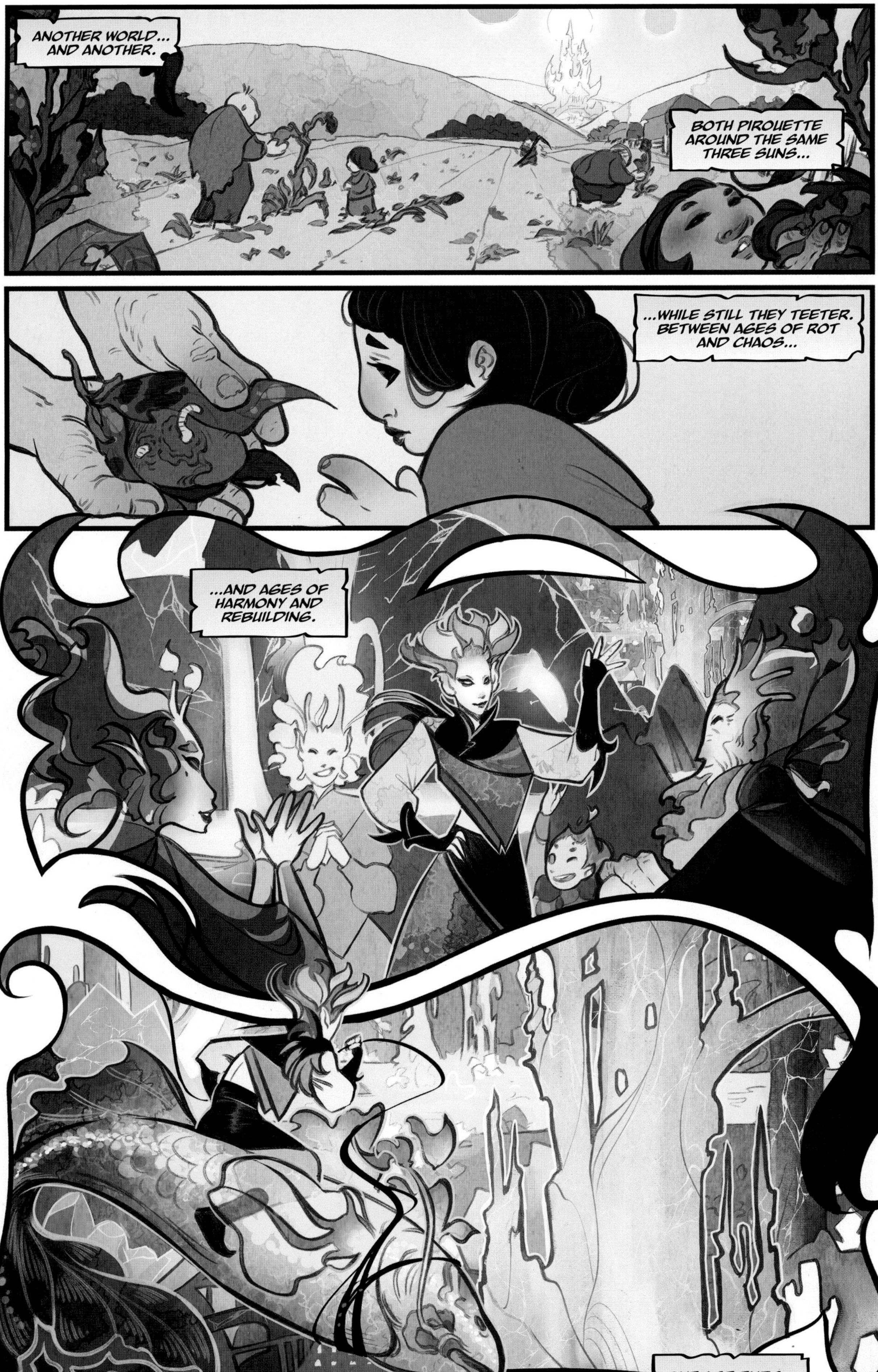
ANOTHER WORLD... AND ANOTHER.
BOTH PIROUETTE AROUND THE SAME THREE SUNS...
...WHILE STILL THEY TEETER. BETWEEN AGES OF ROT AND CHAOS...
...AND AGES OF HARMONY AND REBUILDING.
ONE AGE ENDS... AND FALLS TO THE NEXT...

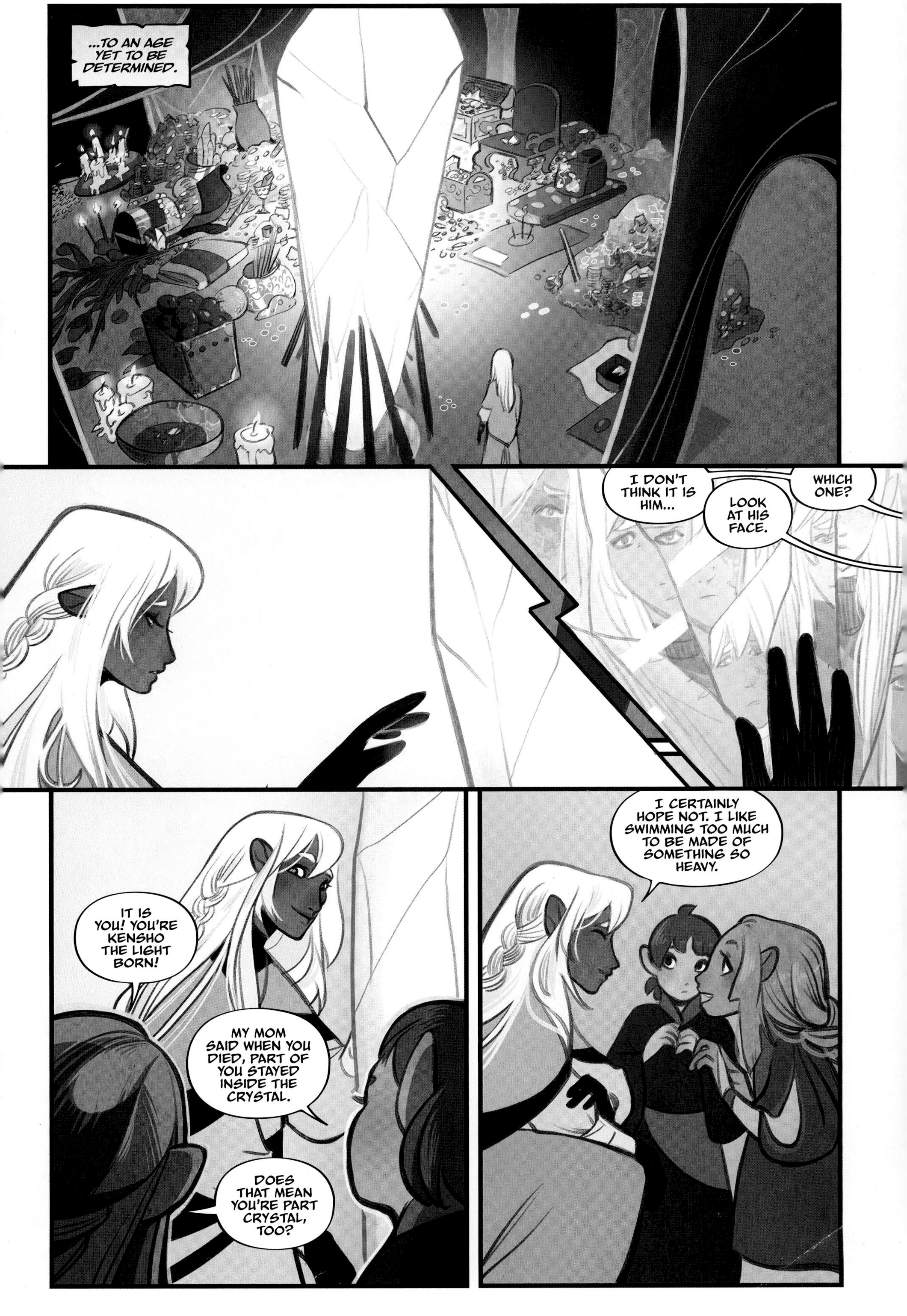
...TO AN AGE YET TO BE DETERMINED.
I DON'T THINK IT IS HIM...
WHICH ONE?
LOOK AT HIS FACE.
IT IS YOU! YOU'RE KENSHO THE LIGHT BORN!
MY MOM SAID WHEN YOU DIED, PART OF YOU STAYED INSIDE THE CRYSTAL.
DOES THAT MEAN YOU'RE PART CRYSTAL, TOO?
I CERTAINLY HOPE NOT. I LIKE SWIMMING TOO MUCH TO BE MADE OF SOMETHING SO HEAVY.

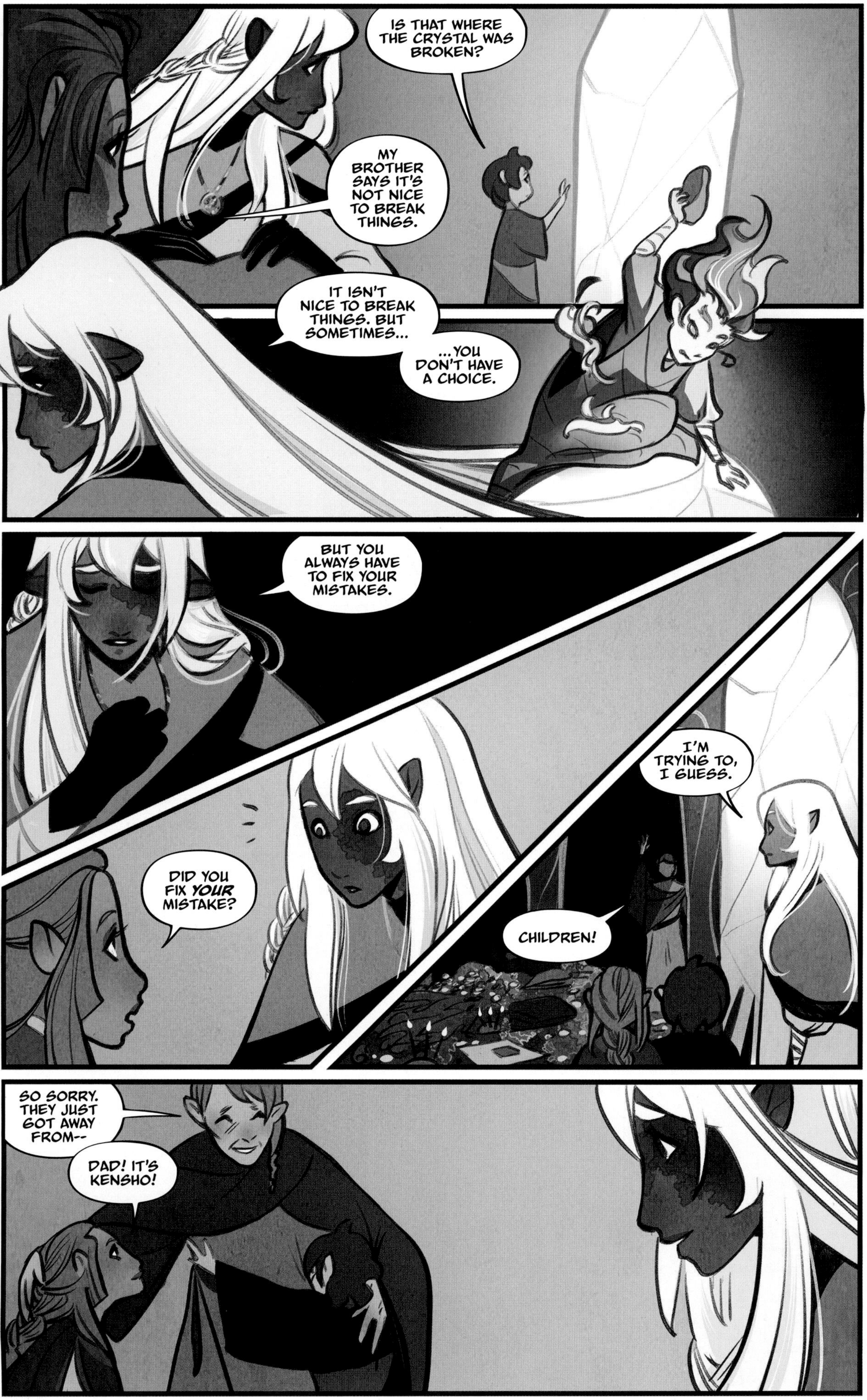
IS THAT WHERE THE CRYSTAL WAS BROKEN?
MY BROTHER SAYS IT'S NOT NICE TO BREAK THINGS.
IT ISN'T NICE TO BREAK THINGS. BUT SOMETIMES...
...YOU DON'T HAVE A CHOICE.
BUT YOU ALWAYS HAVE TO FIX YOUR MISTAKES.
DID YOU FIX *YOUR* MISTAKE?
I'M TRYING TO, I GUESS.
CHILDREN!
SO SORRY. THEY JUST GOT AWAY FROM--
DAD! IT'S KENSHO!

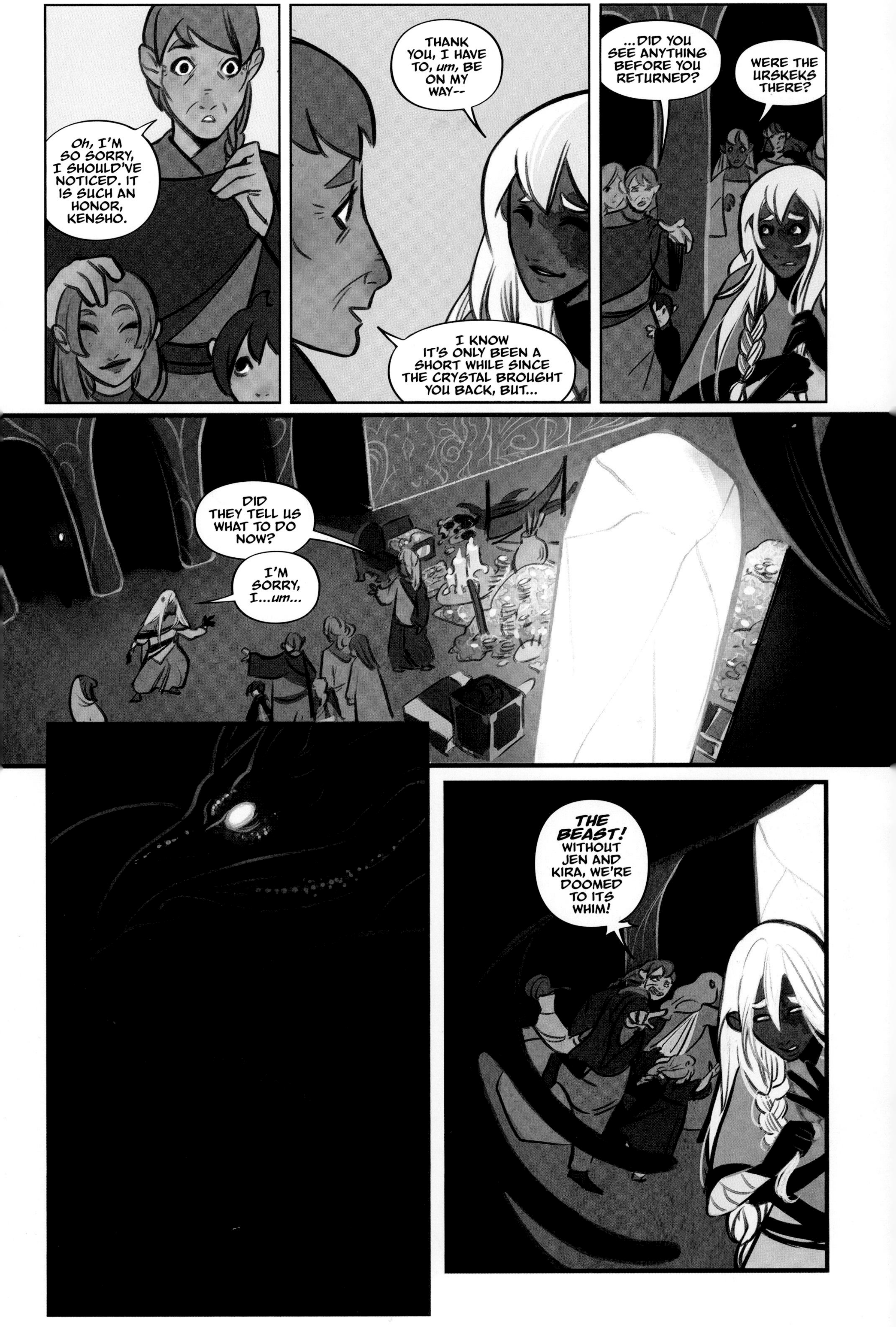
Oh, I'M SO SORRY, I SHOULD'VE NOTICED. IT IS SUCH AN HONOR, KENSHO.
THANK YOU, I HAVE TO, um, BE ON MY WAY--
I KNOW IT'S ONLY BEEN A SHORT WHILE SINCE THE CRYSTAL BROUGHT YOU BACK, BUT...
...DID YOU SEE ANYTHING BEFORE YOU RETURNED?
WERE THE URSKEKS THERE?
DID THEY TELL US WHAT TO DO NOW?
I'M SORRY, I...um...
THE BEAST! WITHOUT JEN AND KIRA, WE'RE DOOMED TO ITS WHIM!

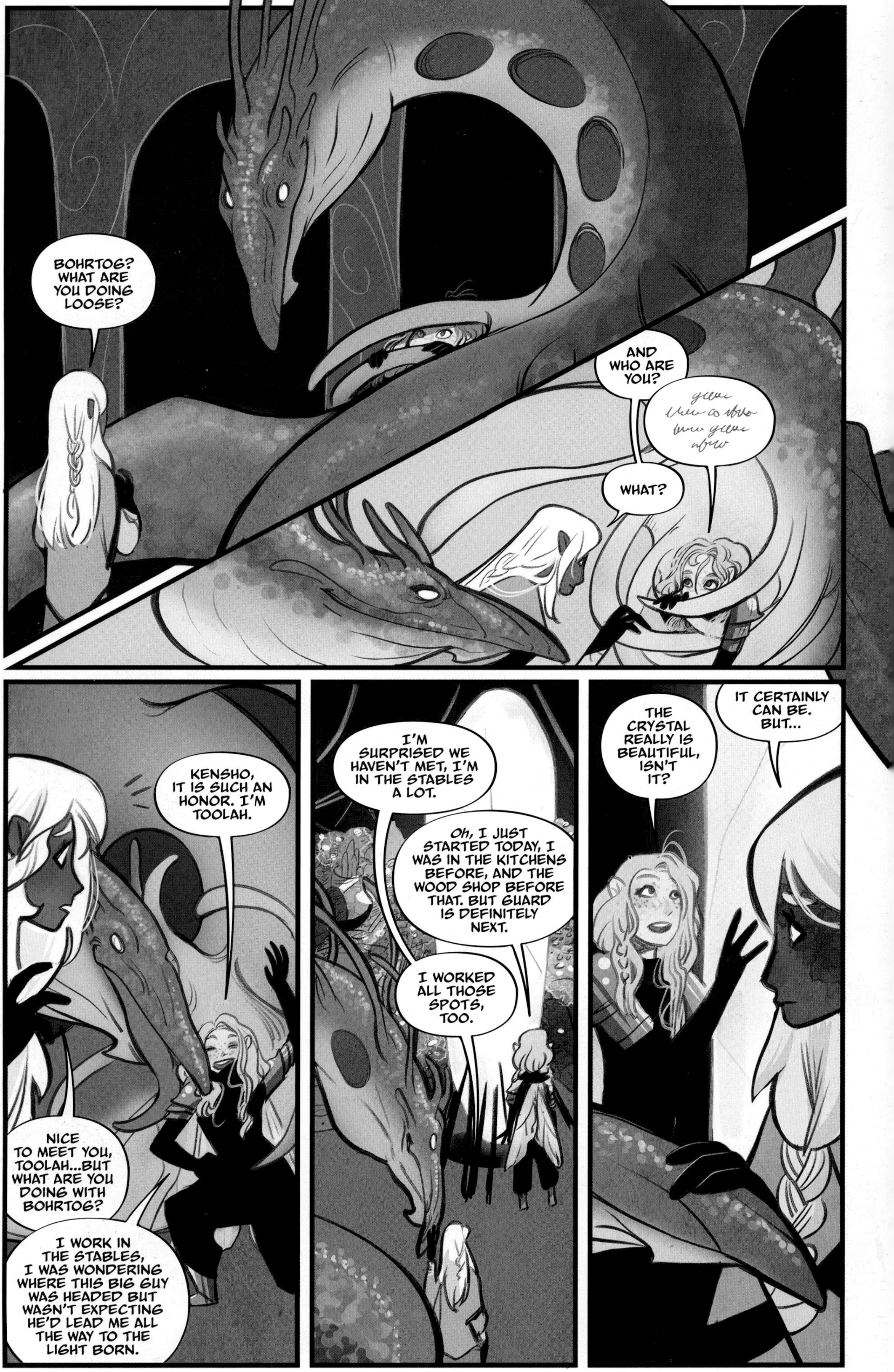
BOHRTOG? WHAT ARE YOU DOING LOOSE?
AND WHO ARE YOU?
WHAT?
KENSHO, IT IS SUCH AN HONOR. I'M TOOLAH.
NICE TO MEET YOU, TOOLAH...BUT WHAT ARE YOU DOING WITH BOHRTOG?
I WORK IN THE STABLES, I WAS WONDERING WHERE THIS BIG GUY WAS HEADED BUT WASN'T EXPECTING HE'D LEAD ME ALL THE WAY TO THE LIGHT BORN.
I'M SURPRISED WE HAVEN'T MET, I'M IN THE STABLES A LOT.
Oh, I JUST STARTED TODAY, I WAS IN THE KITCHENS BEFORE, AND THE WOOD SHOP BEFORE THAT. BUT GUARD IS DEFINITELY NEXT.
I WORKED ALL THOSE SPOTS, TOO.
THE CRYSTAL REALLY IS BEAUTIFUL, ISN'T IT?
IT CERTAINLY CAN BE. BUT...

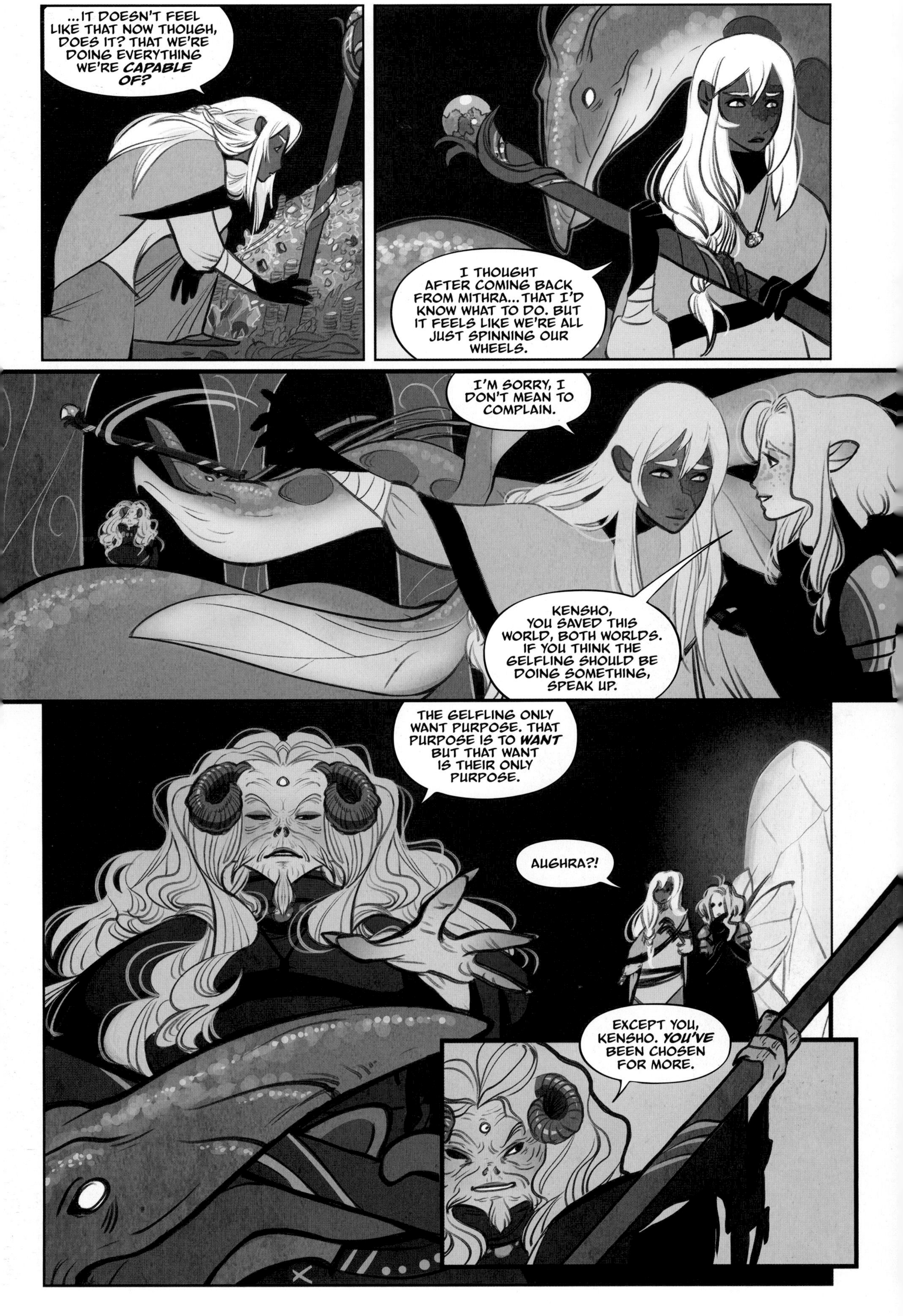
...IT DOESN'T FEEL LIKE THAT NOW THOUGH, DOES IT? THAT WE'RE DOING EVERYTHING WE'RE CAPABLE OF?
I THOUGHT AFTER COMING BACK FROM MITHRA...THAT I'D KNOW WHAT TO DO. BUT IT FEELS LIKE WE'RE ALL JUST SPINNING OUR WHEELS.
I'M SORRY, I DON'T MEAN TO COMPLAIN.
KENSHO, YOU SAVED THIS WORLD, BOTH WORLDS. IF YOU THINK THE GELFLING SHOULD BE DOING SOMETHING, SPEAK UP.
THE GELFLING ONLY WANT PURPOSE. THAT PURPOSE IS TO WANT BUT THAT WANT IS THEIR ONLY PURPOSE.
AUGHRA?!
EXCEPT YOU, KENSHO. YOU'VE BEEN CHOSEN FOR MORE.

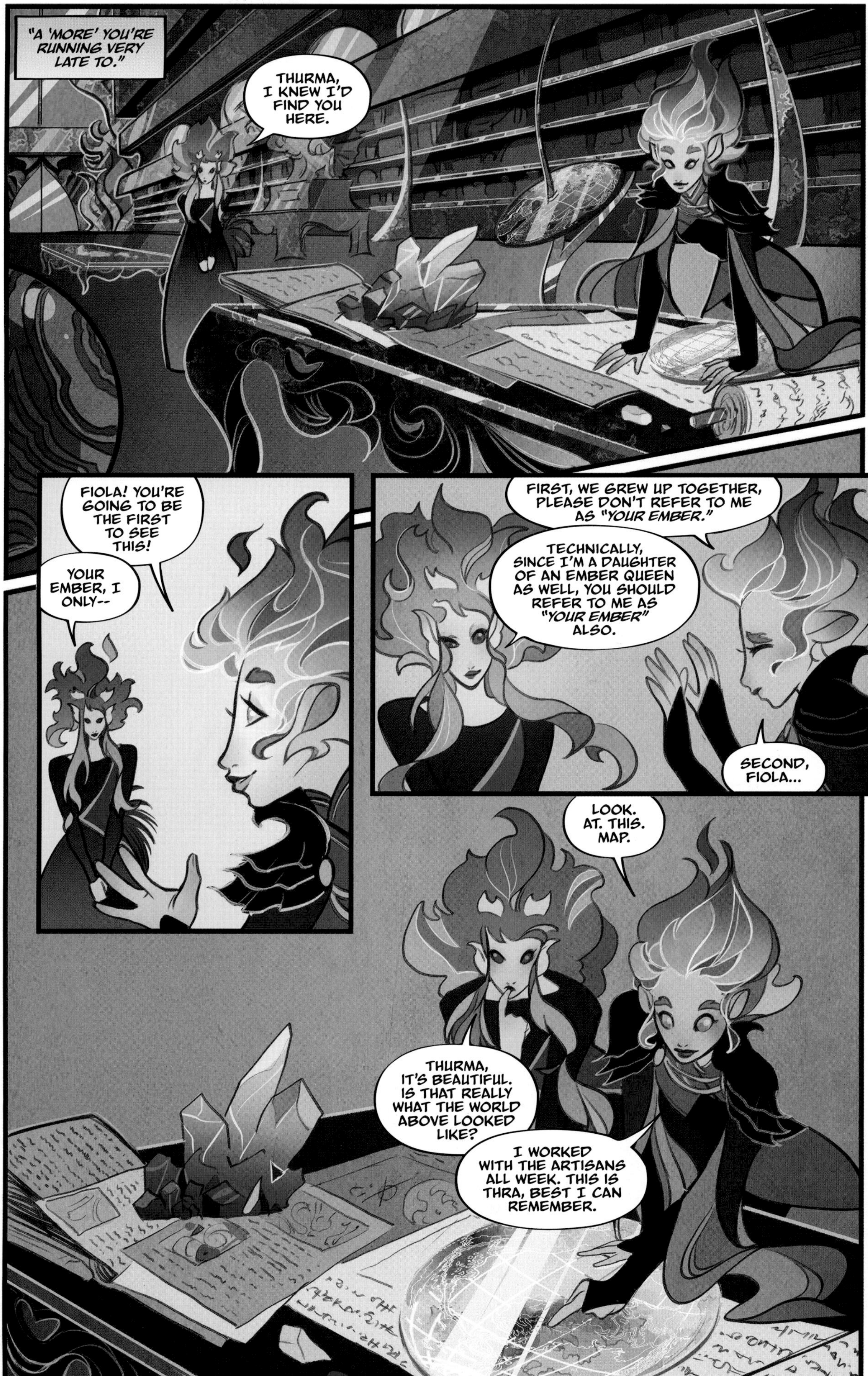
"A 'MORE' YOU'RE RUNNING VERY LATE TO."
THURMA, I KNEW I'D FIND YOU HERE.
FIOLA! YOU'RE GOING TO BE THE FIRST TO SEE THIS!
YOUR EMBER, I ONLY--
FIRST, WE GREW UP TOGETHER, PLEASE DON'T REFER TO ME AS "YOUR EMBER."
TECHNICALLY, SINCE I'M A DAUGHTER OF AN EMBER QUEEN AS WELL, YOU SHOULD REFER TO ME AS "YOUR EMBER" ALSO.
SECOND, FIOLA...
LOOK. AT. THIS. MAP.
THURMA, IT'S BEAUTIFUL. IS THAT REALLY WHAT THE WORLD ABOVE LOOKED LIKE?
I WORKED WITH THE ARTISANS ALL WEEK. THIS IS THRA, BEST I CAN REMEMBER.

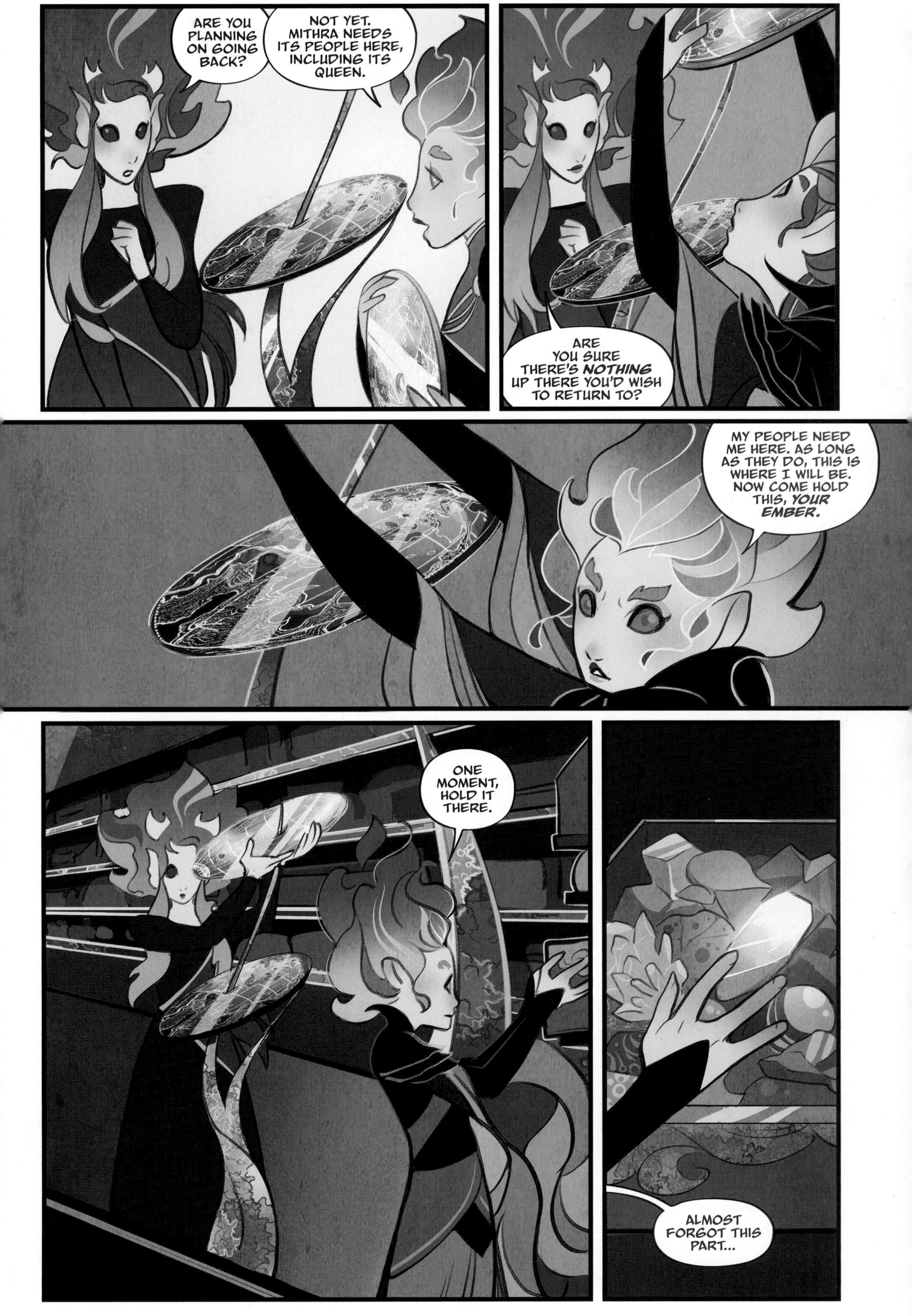
ARE YOU PLANNING ON GOING BACK?
NOT YET. MITHRA NEEDS ITS PEOPLE HERE, INCLUDING ITS QUEEN.
ARE YOU SURE THERE'S *NOTHING* UP THERE YOU'D WISH TO RETURN TO?
MY PEOPLE NEED ME HERE. AS LONG AS THEY DO, THIS IS WHERE I WILL BE. NOW COME HOLD THIS, *YOUR EMBER.*
ONE MOMENT, HOLD IT THERE.
ALMOST FORGOT THIS PART...

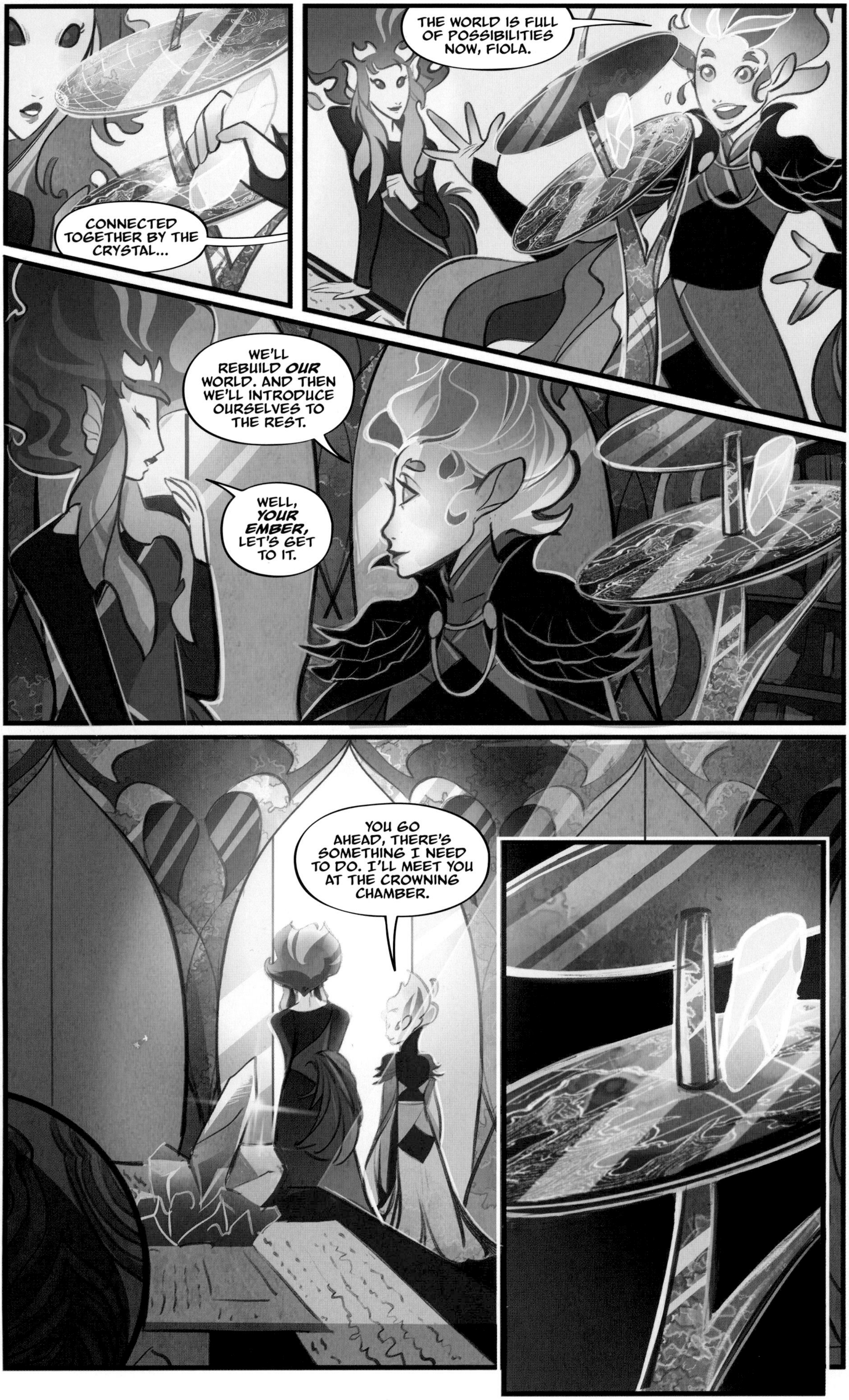
CONNECTED TOGETHER BY THE CRYSTAL...
THE WORLD IS FULL OF POSSIBILITIES NOW, FIOLA.
WE'LL REBUILD *OUR* WORLD. AND THEN WE'LL INTRODUCE OURSELVES TO THE REST.
WELL, *YOUR EMBER,* LET'S GET TO IT.
YOU GO AHEAD, THERE'S SOMETHING I NEED TO DO. I'LL MEET YOU AT THE CROWNING CHAMBER.

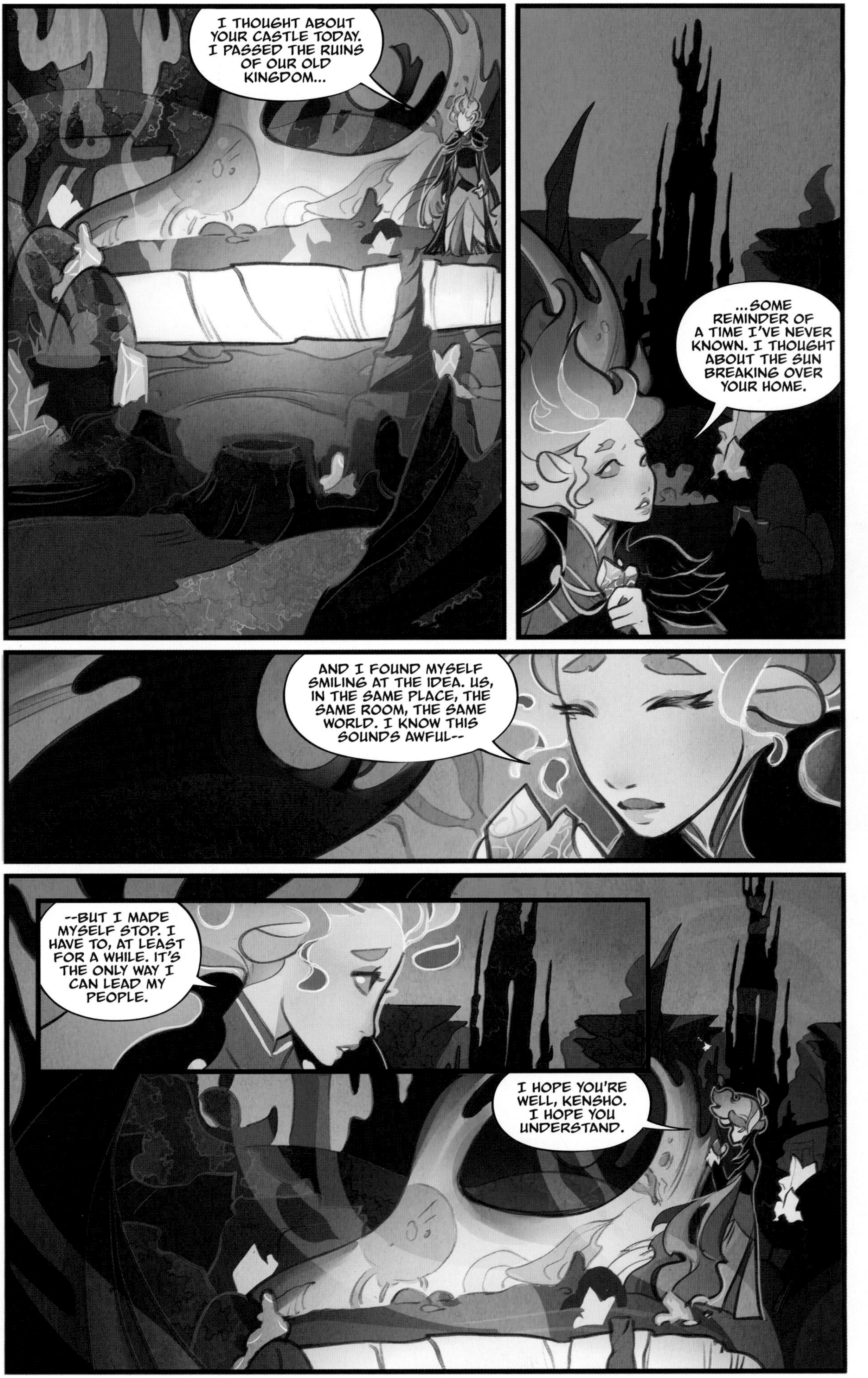
I THOUGHT ABOUT YOUR CASTLE TODAY. I PASSED THE RUINS OF OUR OLD KINGDOM...
...SOME REMINDER OF A TIME I'VE NEVER KNOWN. I THOUGHT ABOUT THE SUN BREAKING OVER YOUR HOME.
AND I FOUND MYSELF SMILING AT THE IDEA. US, IN THE SAME PLACE, THE SAME ROOM, THE SAME WORLD. I KNOW THIS SOUNDS AWFUL--
--BUT I MADE MYSELF STOP. I HAVE TO, AT LEAST FOR A WHILE. IT'S THE ONLY WAY I CAN LEAD MY PEOPLE.
I HOPE YOU'RE WELL, KENSHO. I HOPE YOU UNDERSTAND.

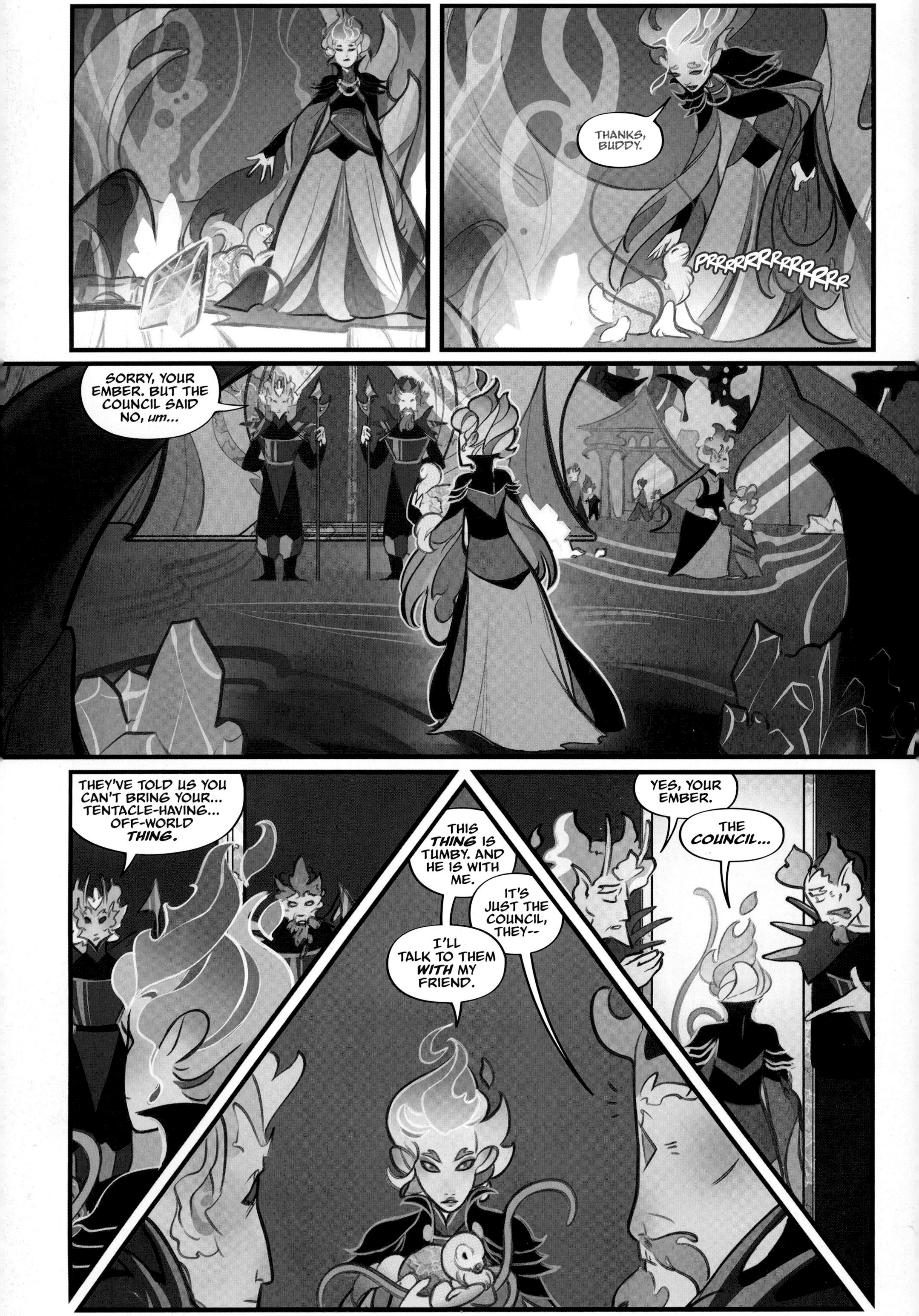
THANKS, BUDDY.
PRRRRRRRRRRRRRR
SORRY, YOUR EMBER. BUT THE COUNCIL SAID NO, *um*...
THEY'VE TOLD US YOU CAN'T BRING YOUR... TENTACLE-HAVING... OFF-WORLD ***THING.***
THIS ***THING*** IS TUMBY. AND HE IS WITH ME.
IT'S JUST THE COUNCIL, THEY--
I'LL TALK TO THEM ***WITH*** MY FRIEND.
YES, YOUR EMBER.
THE ***COUNCIL...***

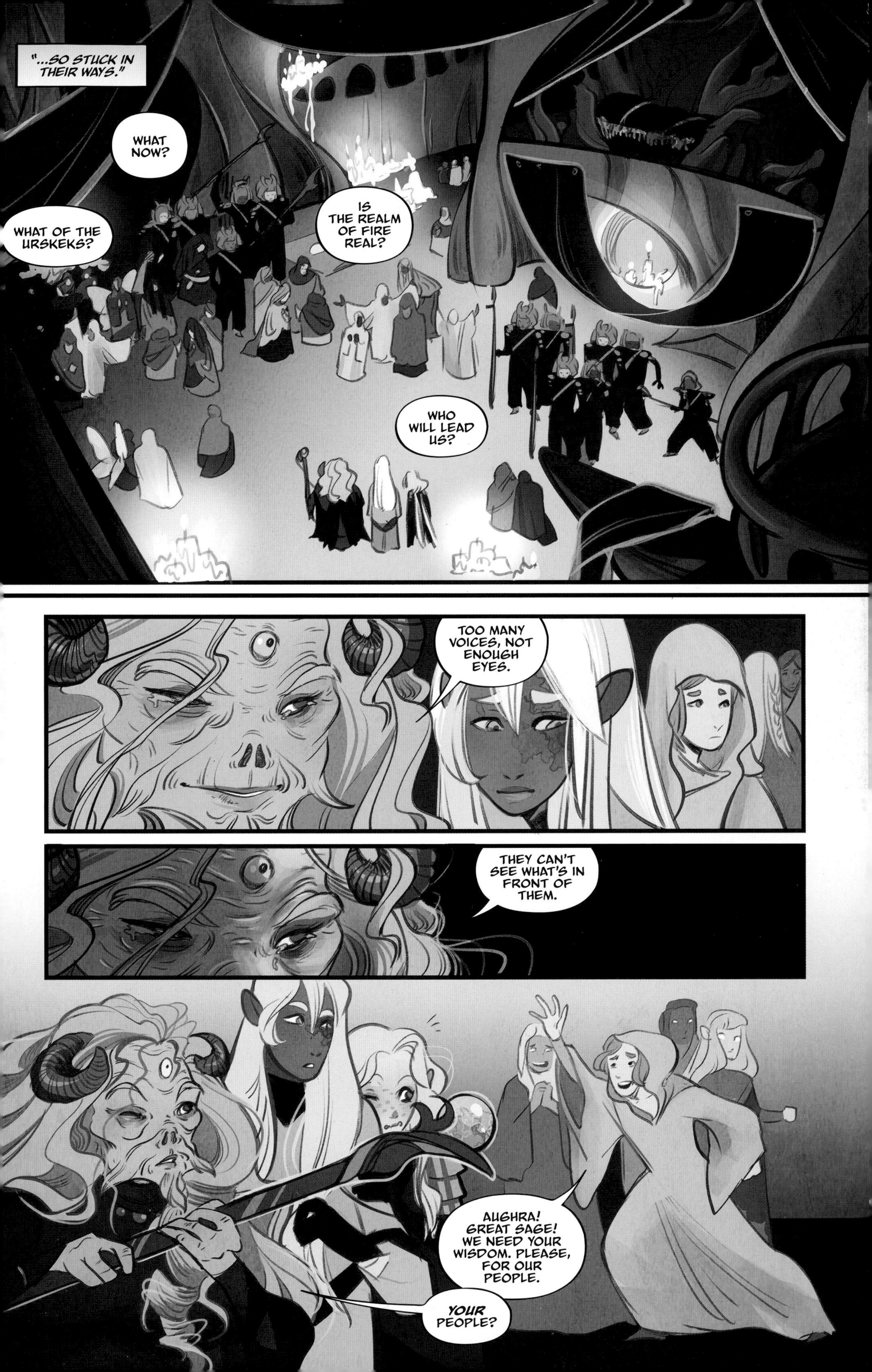
"...SO STUCK IN THEIR WAYS."
WHAT NOW?
WHAT OF THE URSKEKS?
IS THE REALM OF FIRE REAL?
WHO WILL LEAD US?
TOO MANY VOICES, NOT ENOUGH EYES.
THEY CAN'T SEE WHAT'S IN FRONT OF THEM.
AUGHRA! GREAT SAGE! WE NEED YOUR WISDOM. PLEASE, FOR OUR PEOPLE.
YOUR PEOPLE?

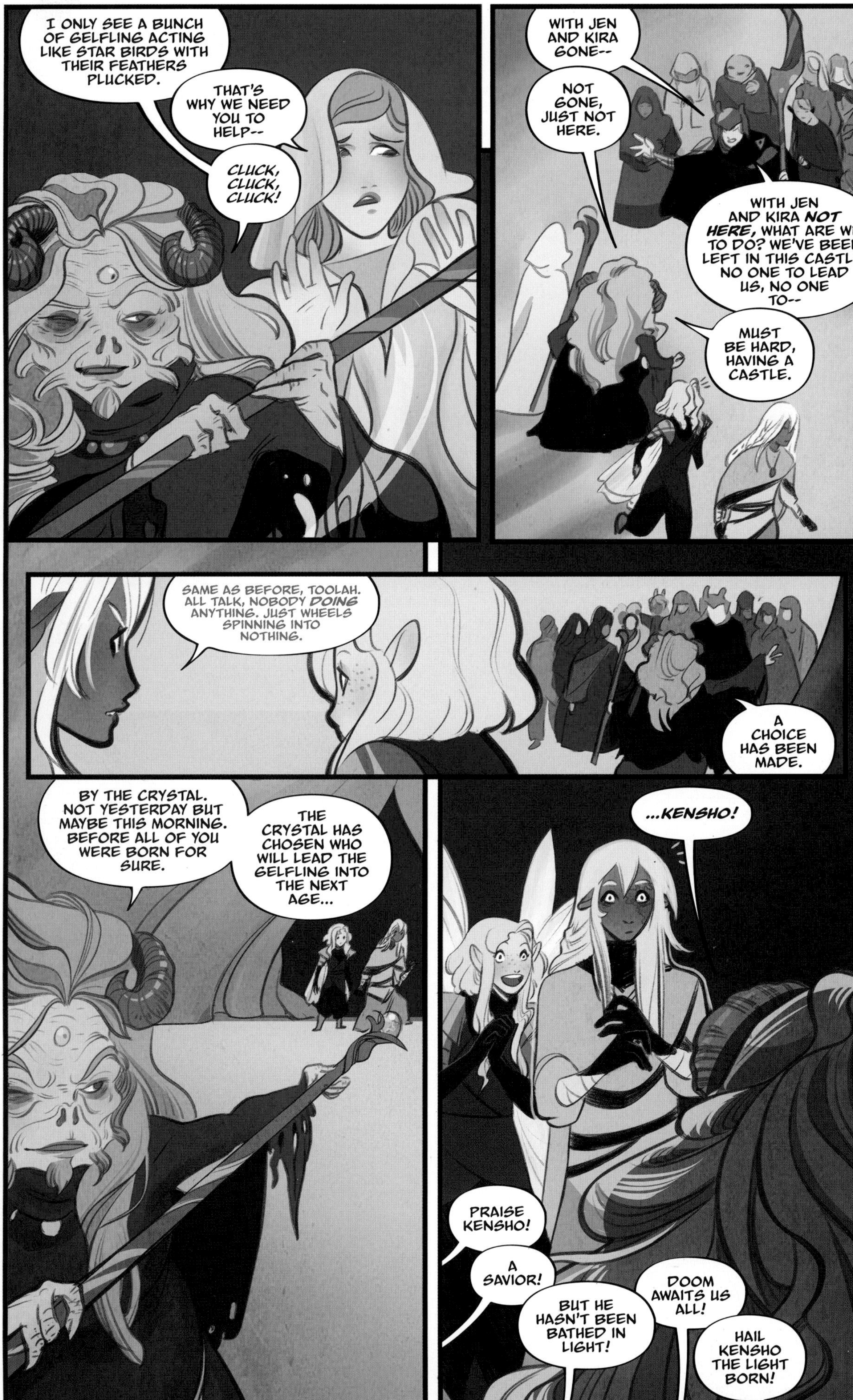
I ONLY SEE A BUNCH OF GELFLING ACTING LIKE STAR BIRDS WITH THEIR FEATHERS PLUCKED.
THAT'S WHY WE NEED YOU TO HELP--
CLUCK, CLUCK, CLUCK!
WITH JEN AND KIRA GONE--
NOT GONE, JUST NOT HERE.
WITH JEN AND KIRA NOT HERE, WHAT ARE WE TO DO? WE'VE BEEN LEFT IN THIS CASTLE, NO ONE TO LEAD US, NO ONE TO--
MUST BE HARD, HAVING A CASTLE.
SAME AS BEFORE, TOOLAH. ALL TALK, NOBODY DOING ANYTHING. JUST WHEELS SPINNING INTO NOTHING.
A CHOICE HAS BEEN MADE.
BY THE CRYSTAL. NOT YESTERDAY BUT MAYBE THIS MORNING. BEFORE ALL OF YOU WERE BORN FOR SURE.
THE CRYSTAL HAS CHOSEN WHO WILL LEAD THE GELFLING INTO THE NEXT AGE...
...KENSHO!
PRAISE KENSHO!
A SAVIOR!
BUT HE HASN'T BEEN BATHED IN LIGHT!
DOOM AWAITS US ALL!
HAIL KENSHO THE LIGHT BORN!

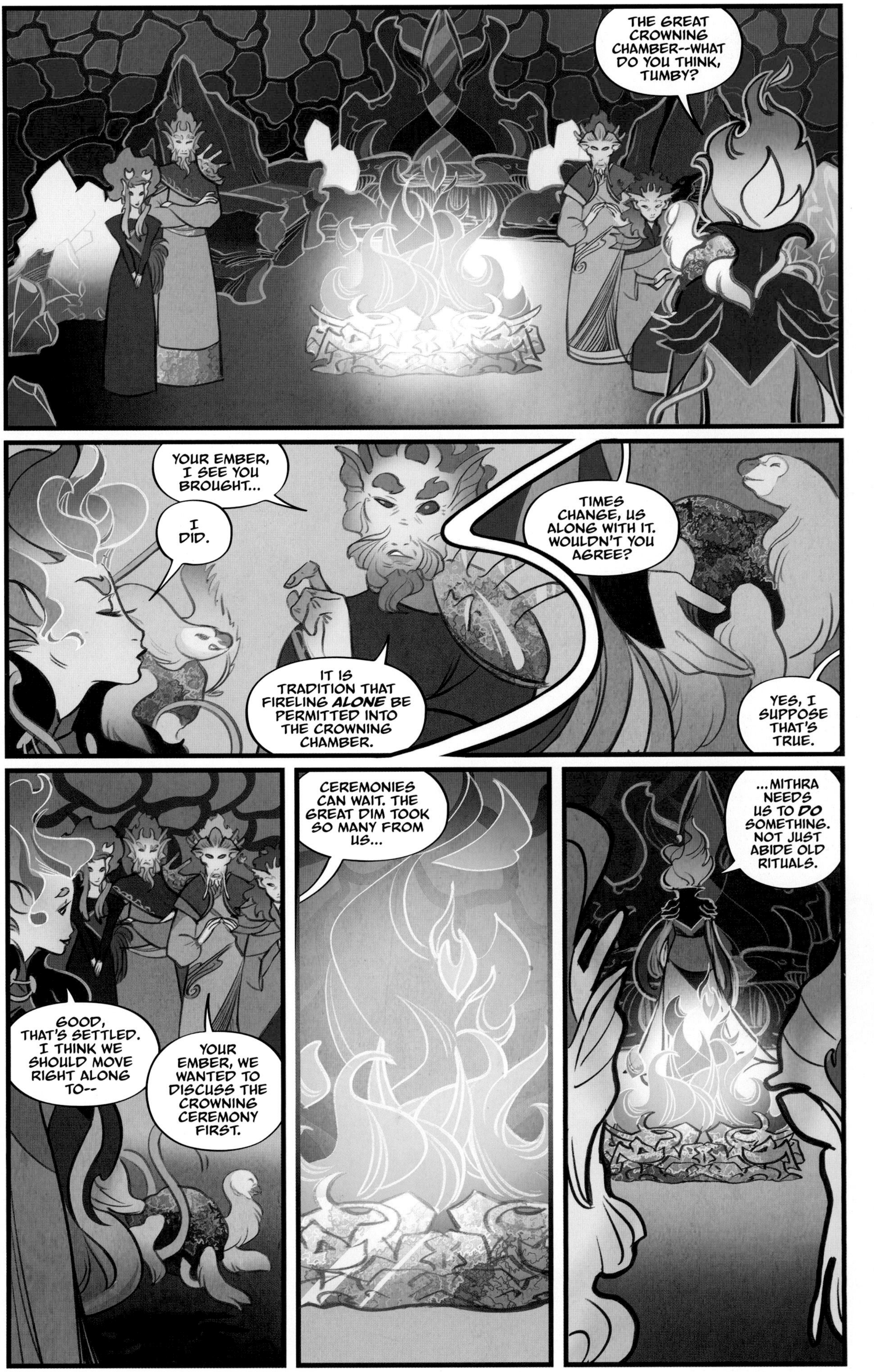
THE GREAT CROWNING CHAMBER--WHAT DO YOU THINK, TUMBY?
YOUR EMBER, I SEE YOU BROUGHT...
I DID.
IT IS TRADITION THAT FIRELING *ALONE* BE PERMITTED INTO THE CROWNING CHAMBER.
TIMES CHANGE, US ALONG WITH IT. WOULDN'T YOU AGREE?
YES, I SUPPOSE THAT'S TRUE.
GOOD, THAT'S SETTLED. I THINK WE SHOULD MOVE RIGHT ALONG TO--
YOUR EMBER, WE WANTED TO DISCUSS THE CROWNING CEREMONY FIRST.
CEREMONIES CAN WAIT. THE GREAT DIM TOOK SO MANY FROM US...
...MITHRA NEEDS US TO *DO* SOMETHING. NOT JUST ABIDE OLD RITUALS.

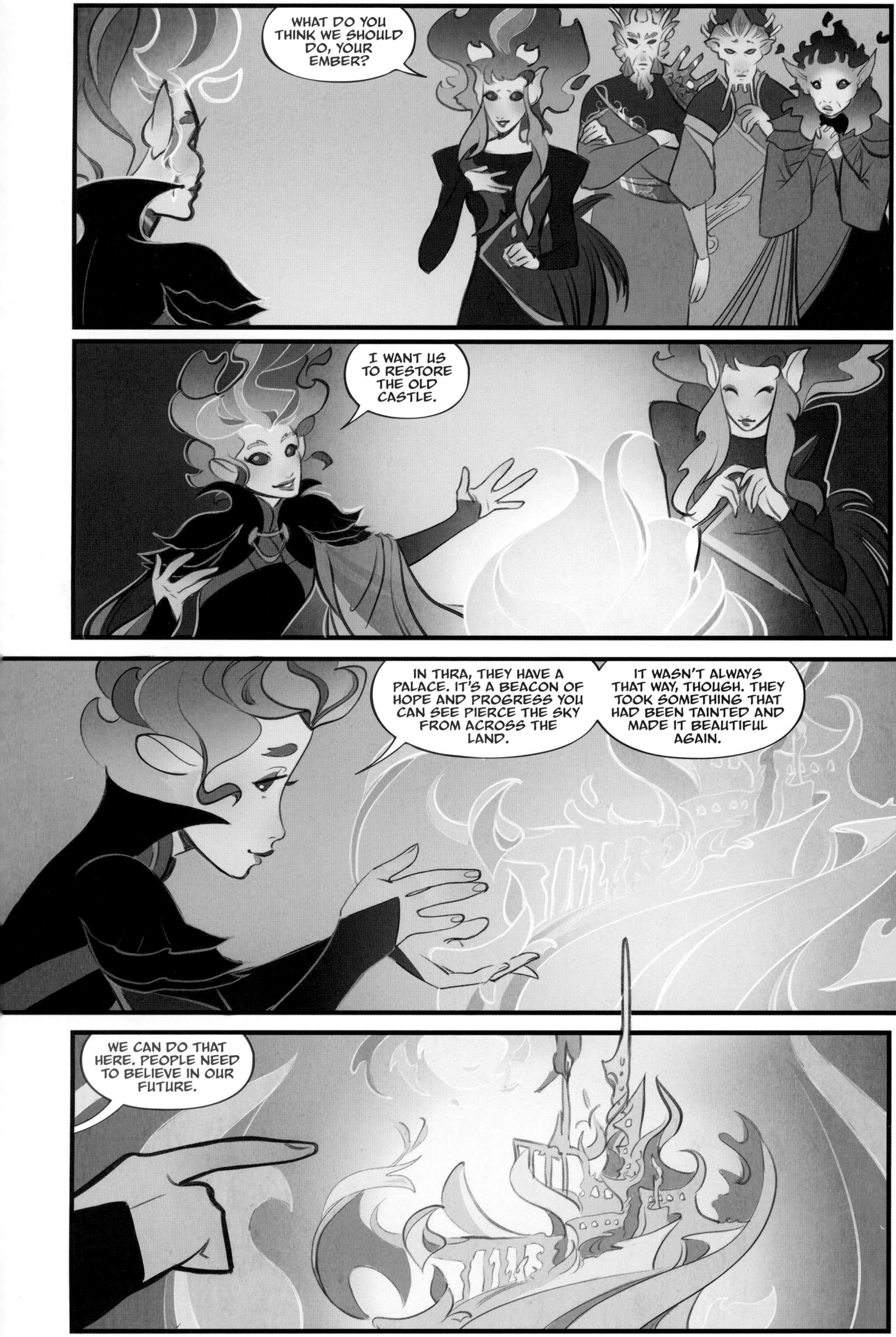
WHAT DO YOU THINK WE SHOULD DO, YOUR EMBER?
I WANT US TO RESTORE THE OLD CASTLE.
IN THRA, THEY HAVE A PALACE. IT'S A BEACON OF HOPE AND PROGRESS YOU CAN SEE PIERCE THE SKY FROM ACROSS THE LAND.
IT WASN'T ALWAYS THAT WAY, THOUGH. THEY TOOK SOMETHING THAT HAD BEEN TAINTED AND MADE IT BEAUTIFUL AGAIN.
WE CAN DO THAT HERE. PEOPLE NEED TO BELIEVE IN OUR FUTURE.

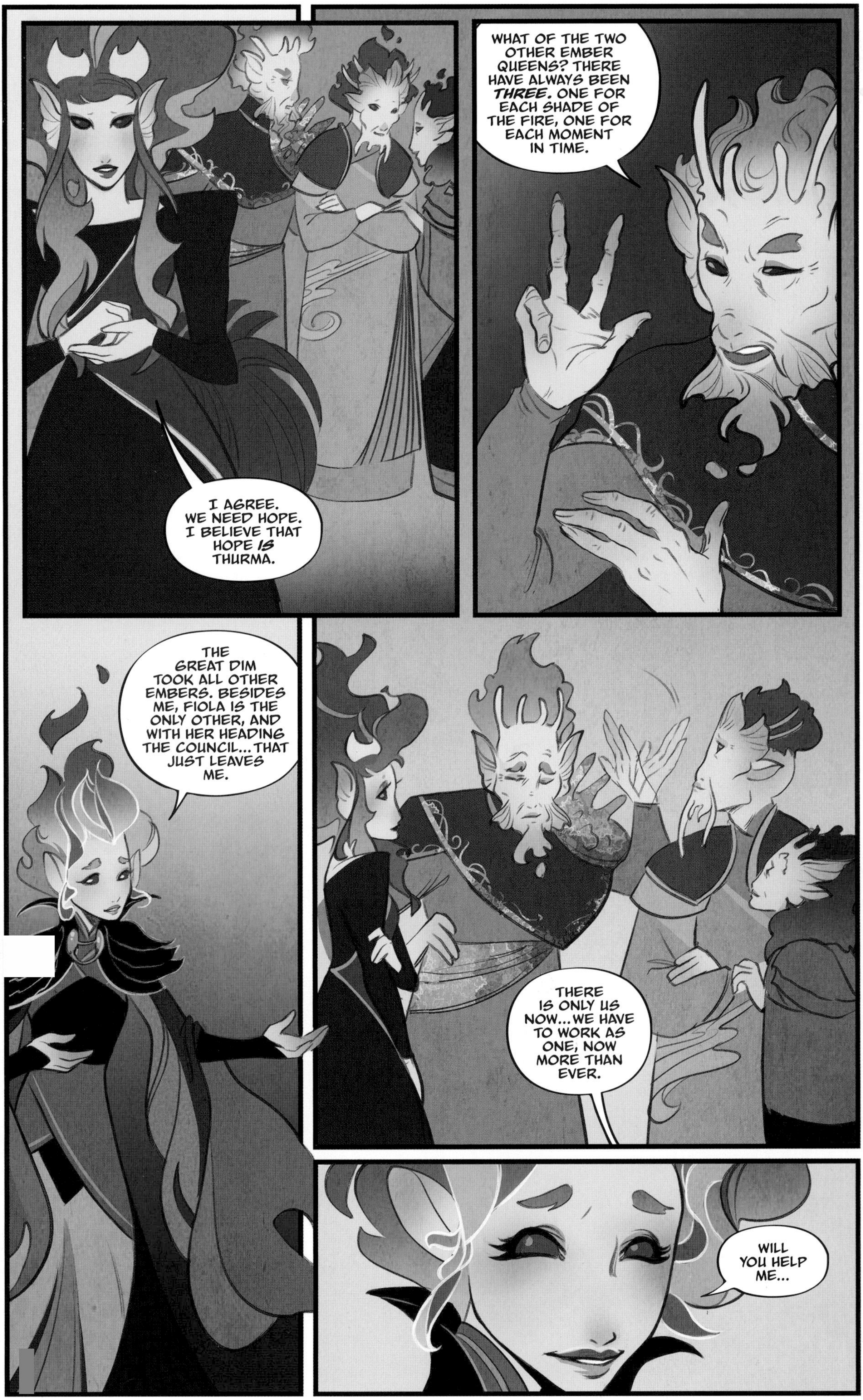
I AGREE. WE NEED HOPE. I BELIEVE THAT HOPE *IS* THURMA.
WHAT OF THE TWO OTHER EMBER QUEENS? THERE HAVE ALWAYS BEEN *THREE.* ONE FOR EACH SHADE OF THE FIRE, ONE FOR EACH MOMENT IN TIME.
THE GREAT DIM TOOK ALL OTHER EMBERS. BESIDES ME, FIOLA IS THE ONLY OTHER, AND WITH HER HEADING THE COUNCIL... THAT JUST LEAVES ME.
THERE IS ONLY US NOW... WE HAVE TO WORK AS ONE, NOW MORE THAN EVER.
WILL YOU HELP ME...

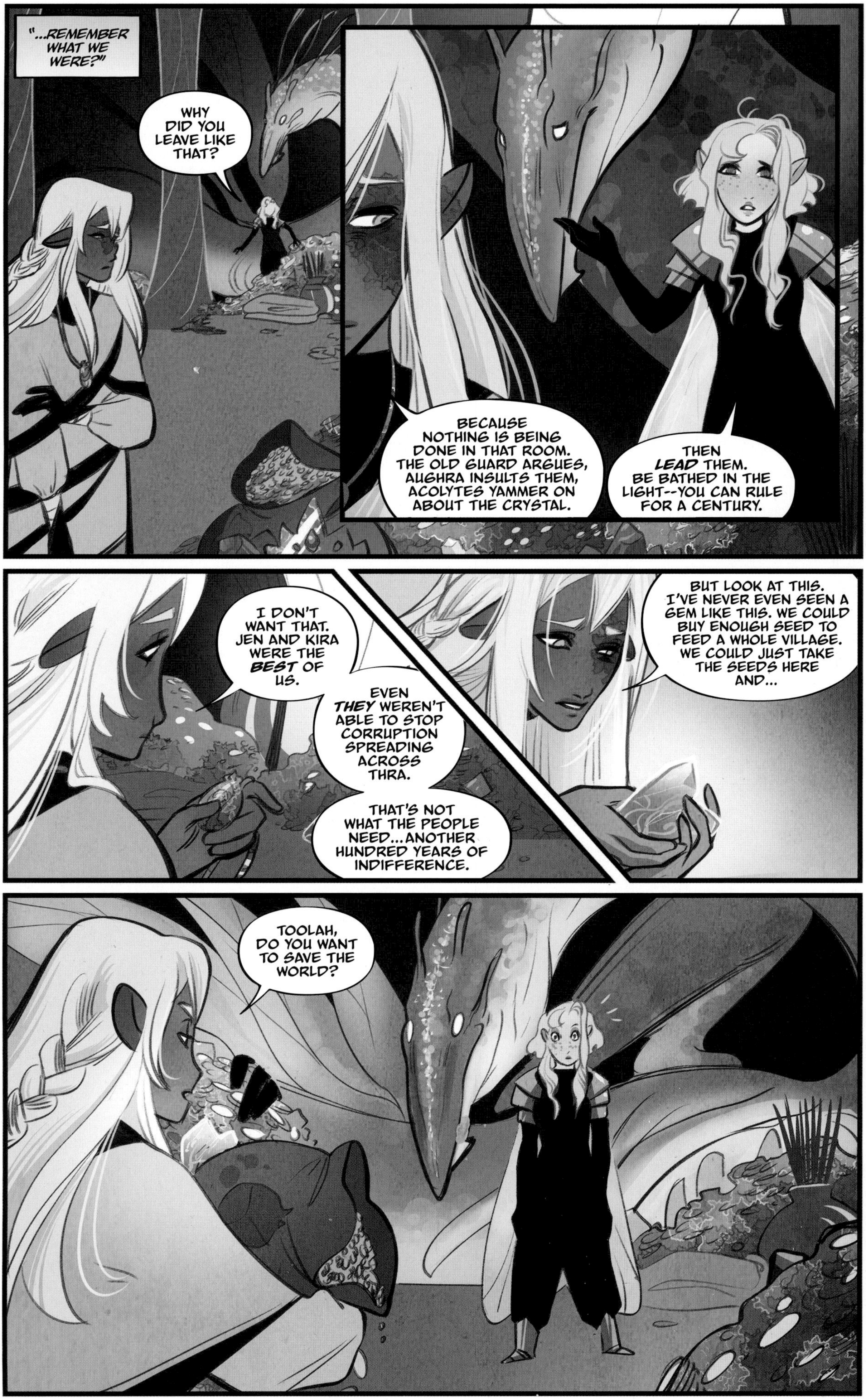
"...REMEMBER WHAT WE WERE?"
WHY DID YOU LEAVE LIKE THAT?
BECAUSE NOTHING IS BEING DONE IN THAT ROOM. THE OLD GUARD ARGUES, AUGHRA INSULTS THEM, ACOLYTES YAMMER ON ABOUT THE CRYSTAL.
THEN LEAD THEM. BE BATHED IN THE LIGHT--YOU CAN RULE FOR A CENTURY.
I DON'T WANT THAT. JEN AND KIRA WERE THE BEST OF US.
EVEN THEY WEREN'T ABLE TO STOP CORRUPTION SPREADING ACROSS THRA.
THAT'S NOT WHAT THE PEOPLE NEED...ANOTHER HUNDRED YEARS OF INDIFFERENCE.
BUT LOOK AT THIS. I'VE NEVER EVEN SEEN A GEM LIKE THIS. WE COULD BUY ENOUGH SEED TO FEED A WHOLE VILLAGE. WE COULD JUST TAKE THE SEEDS HERE AND...
TOOLAH, DO YOU WANT TO SAVE THE WORLD?

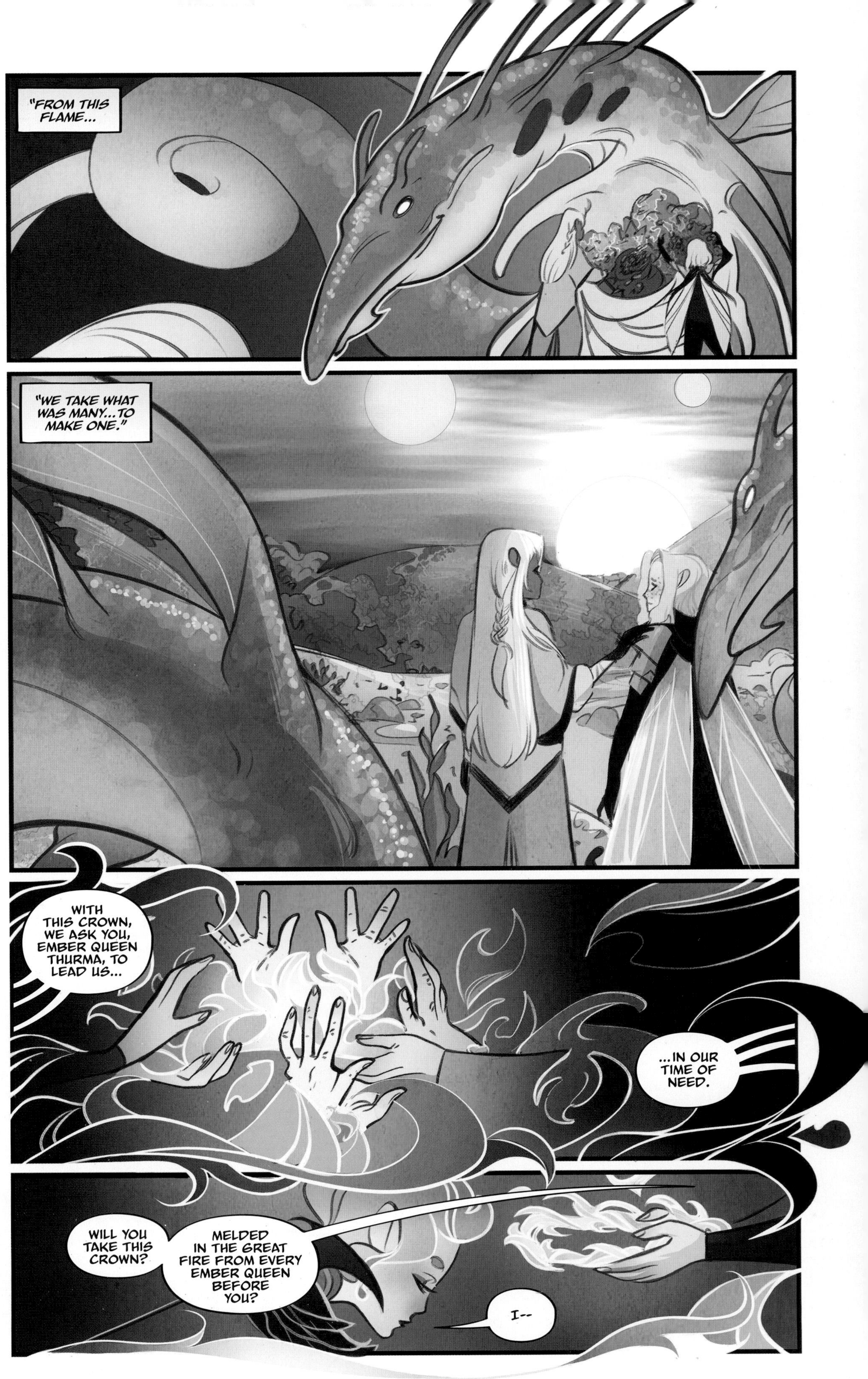
"FROM THIS FLAME...
"WE TAKE WHAT WAS MANY...TO MAKE ONE."
WITH THIS CROWN, WE ASK YOU, EMBER QUEEN THURMA, TO LEAD US...
...IN OUR TIME OF NEED.
WILL YOU TAKE THIS CROWN?
MELDED IN THE GREAT FIRE FROM EVERY EMBER QUEEN BEFORE YOU?
I--

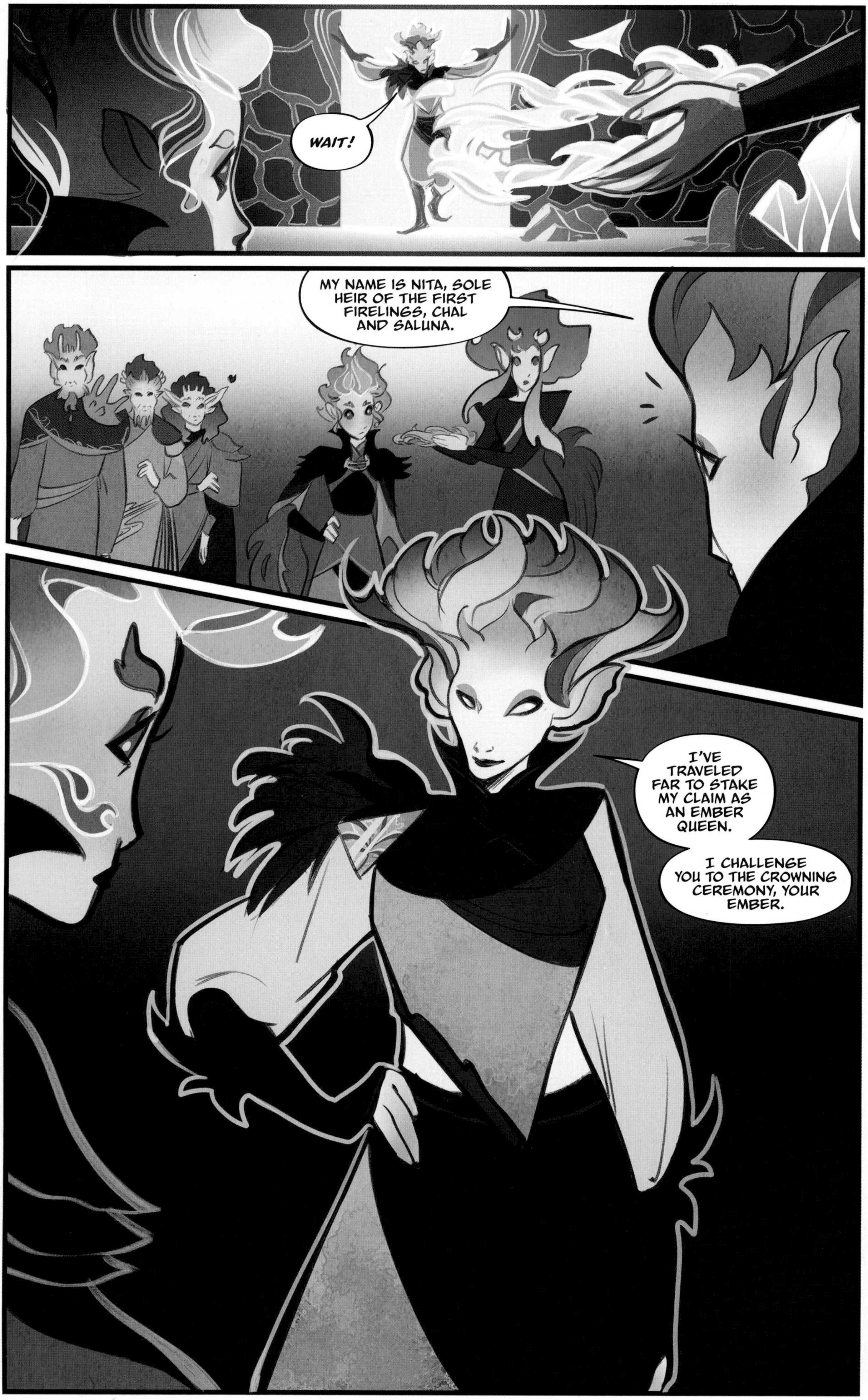
WAIT!
MY NAME IS NITA, SOLE HEIR OF THE FIRST FIRELINGS, CHAL AND SALUNA.
I'VE TRAVELED FAR TO STAKE MY CLAIM AS AN EMBER QUEEN.
I CHALLENGE YOU TO THE CROWNING CEREMONY, YOUR EMBER.

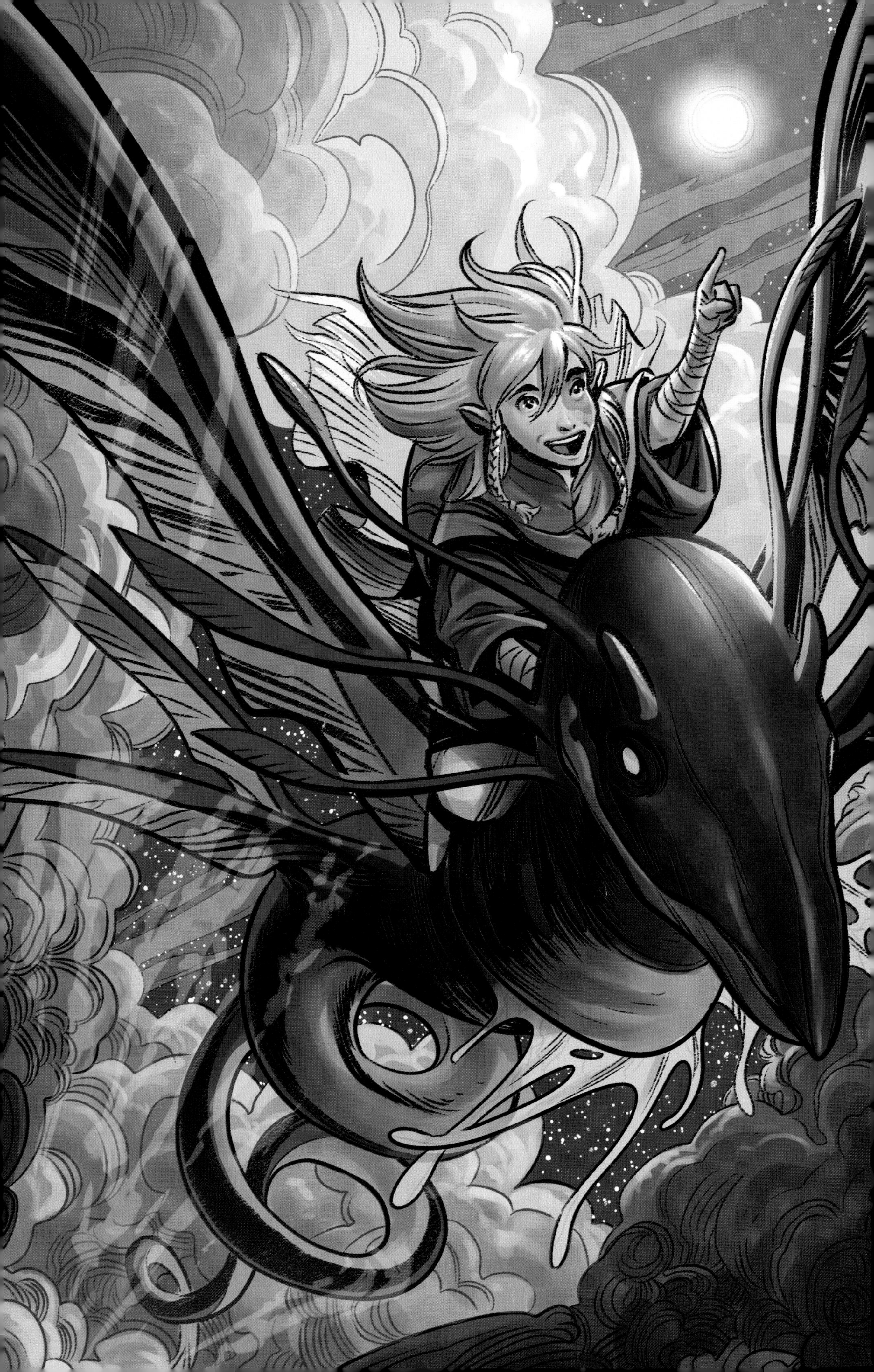

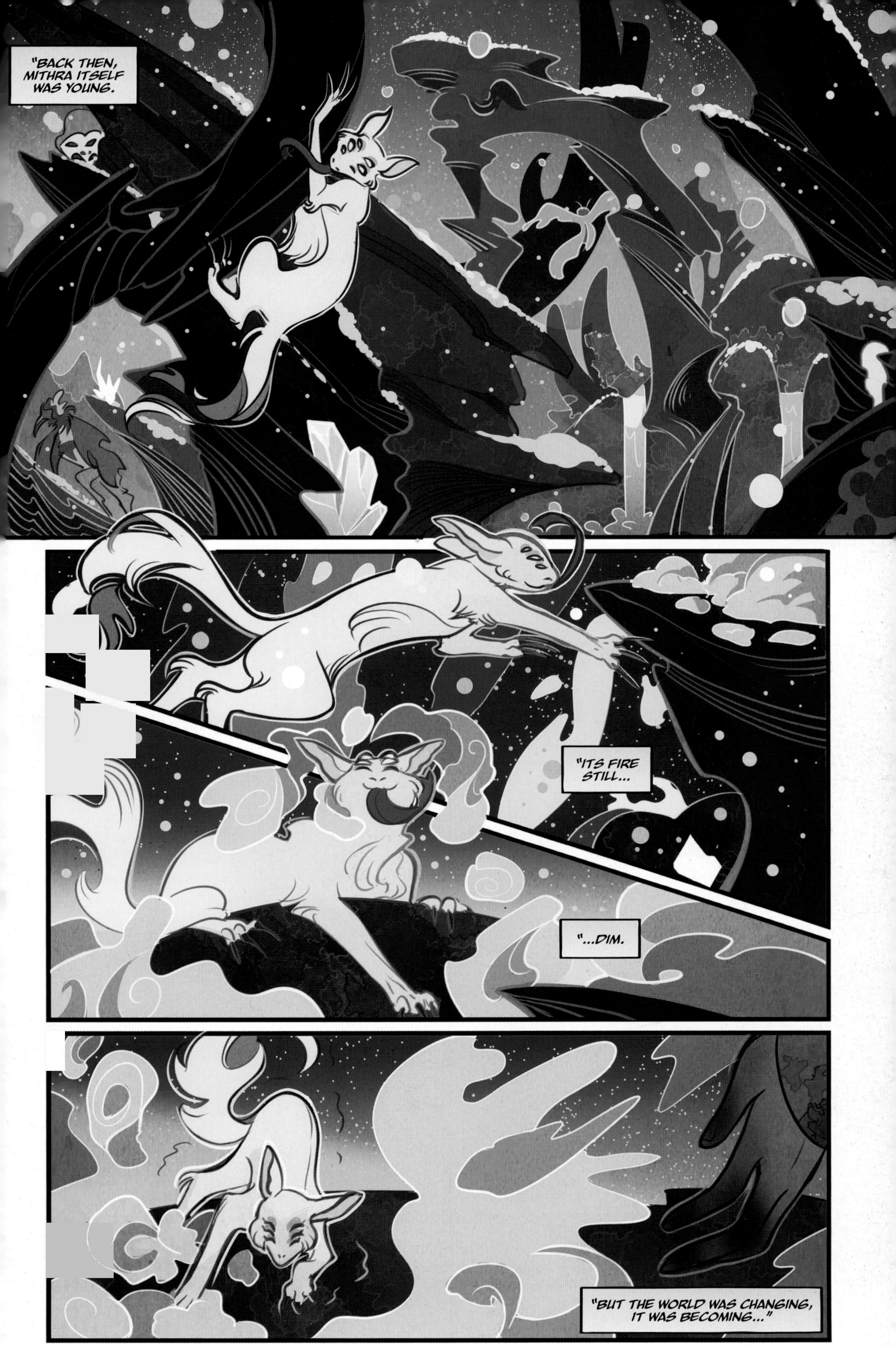
"BACK THEN, MITHRA ITSELF WAS YOUNG.
"ITS FIRE STILL...
"...DIM.
"BUT THE WORLD WAS CHANGING, IT WAS BECOMING..."

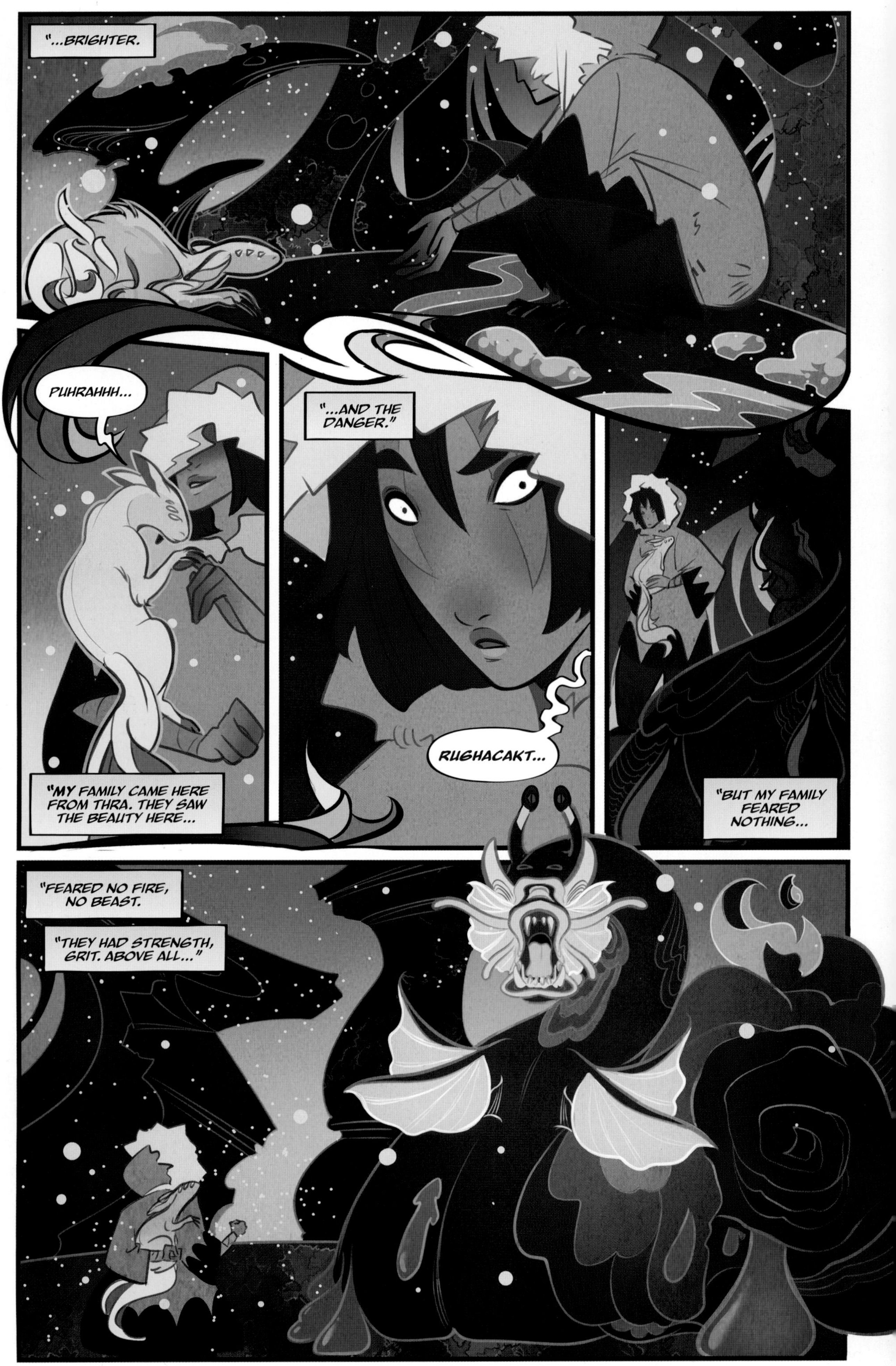
"...BRIGHTER.
PUHRAHHH...
"MY FAMILY CAME HERE FROM THRA. THEY SAW THE BEAUTY HERE...
"...AND THE DANGER."
RUGHACAKT...
"BUT MY FAMILY FEARED NOTHING...
"FEARED NO FIRE, NO BEAST.
"THEY HAD STRENGTH, GRIT. ABOVE ALL..."

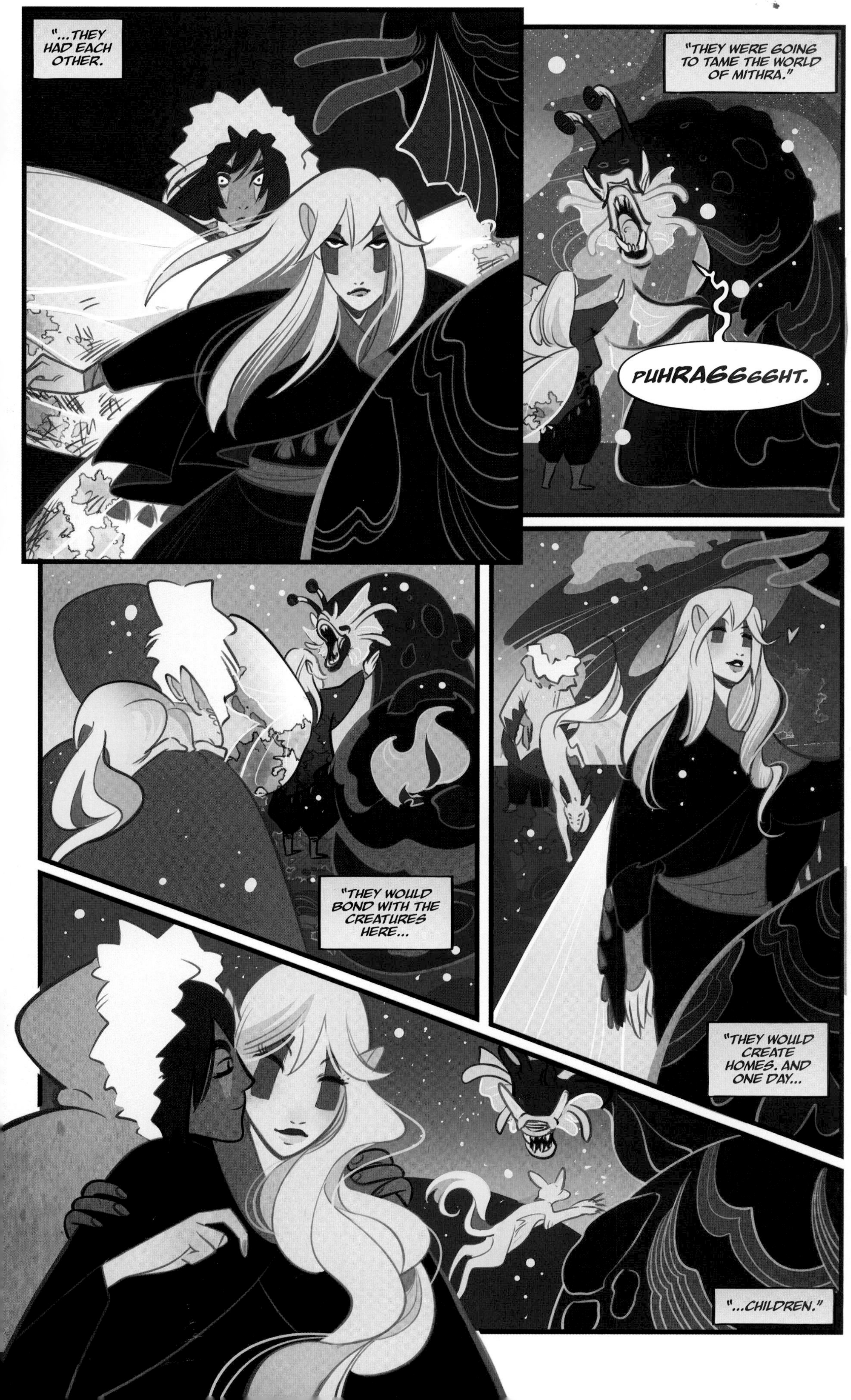
"...THEY HAD EACH OTHER.
"THEY WERE GOING TO TAME THE WORLD OF MITHRA."
PUHRAGGGGGHT.
"THEY WOULD BOND WITH THE CREATURES HERE...
"THEY WOULD CREATE HOMES. AND ONE DAY...
"...CHILDREN."

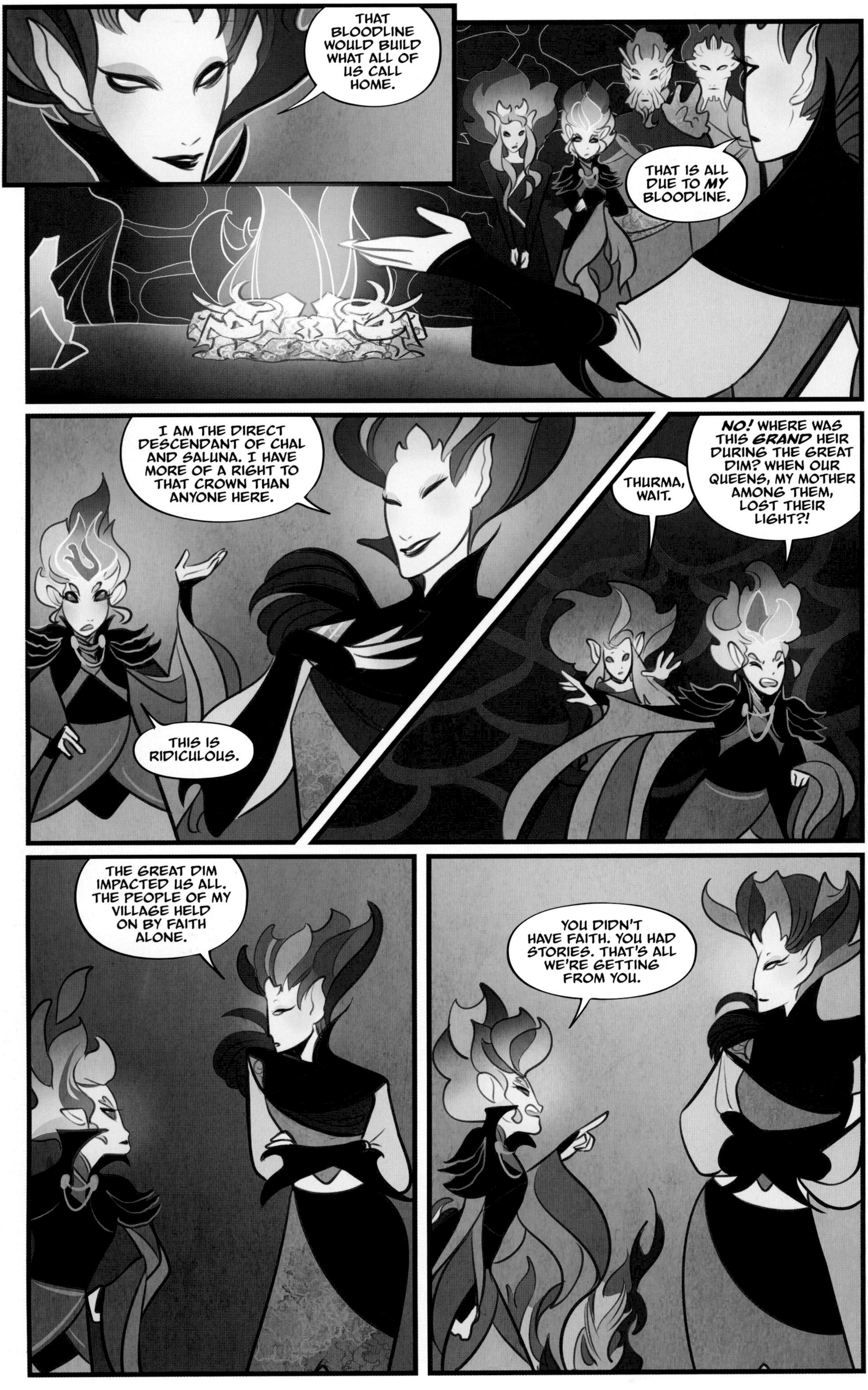
THAT BLOODLINE WOULD BUILD WHAT ALL OF US CALL HOME.
THAT IS ALL DUE TO *MY* BLOODLINE.
I AM THE DIRECT DESCENDANT OF CHAL AND SALUNA. I HAVE MORE OF A RIGHT TO THAT CROWN THAN ANYONE HERE.
THIS IS RIDICULOUS.
THURMA, WAIT.
NO! WHERE WAS THIS ***GRAND*** HEIR DURING THE GREAT DIM? WHEN OUR QUEENS, MY MOTHER AMONG THEM, LOST THEIR LIGHT?!
THE GREAT DIM IMPACTED US ALL. THE PEOPLE OF MY VILLAGE HELD ON BY FAITH ALONE.
YOU DIDN'T HAVE FAITH. YOU HAD STORIES. THAT'S ALL WE'RE GETTING FROM YOU.

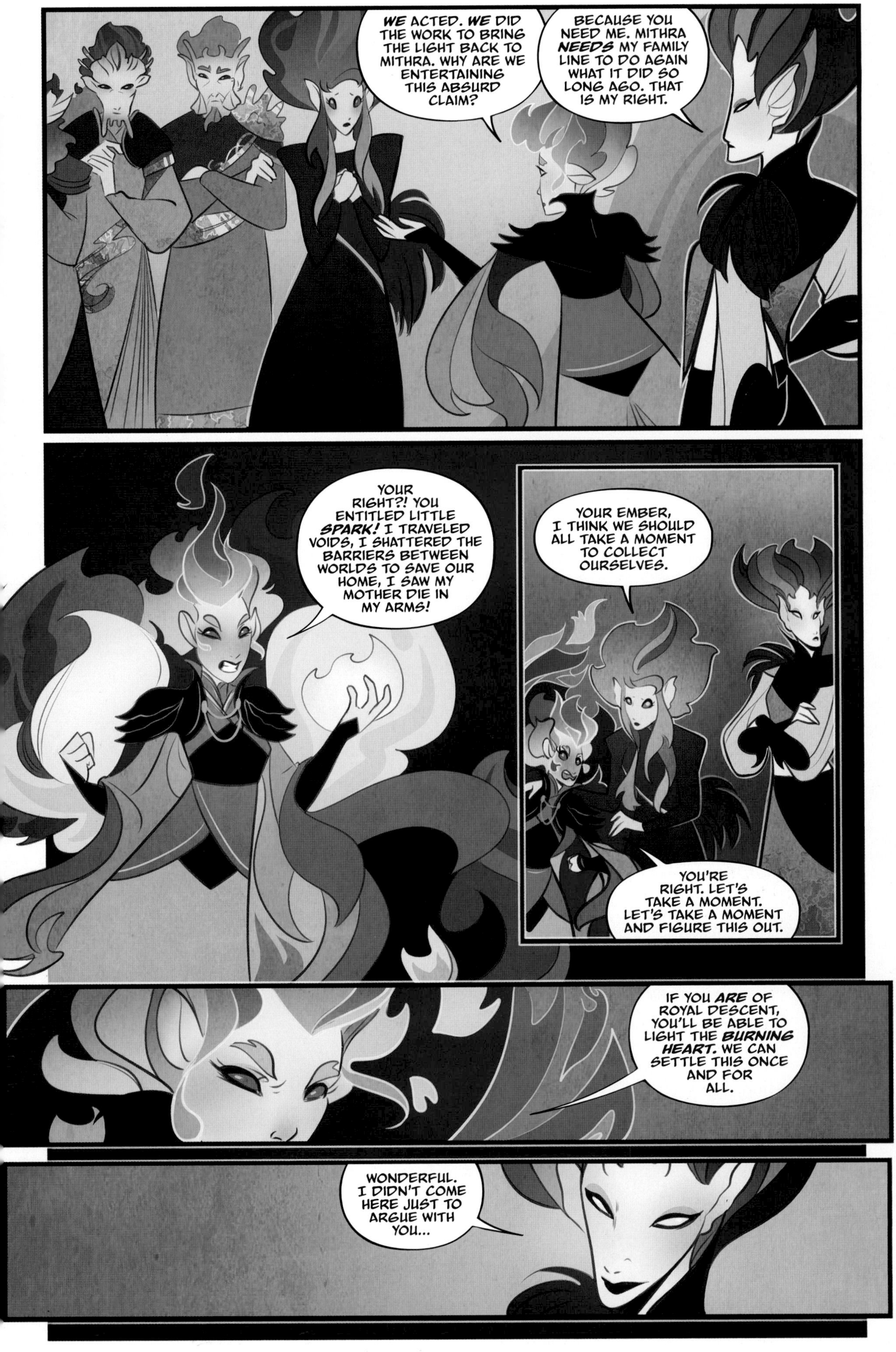
WE ACTED. WE DID THE WORK TO BRING THE LIGHT BACK TO MITHRA. WHY ARE WE ENTERTAINING THIS ABSURD CLAIM?
BECAUSE YOU NEED ME. MITHRA NEEDS MY FAMILY LINE TO DO AGAIN WHAT IT DID SO LONG AGO. THAT IS MY RIGHT.
YOUR RIGHT?! YOU ENTITLED LITTLE SPARK! I TRAVELED VOIDS, I SHATTERED THE BARRIERS BETWEEN WORLDS TO SAVE OUR HOME, I SAW MY MOTHER DIE IN MY ARMS!
YOUR EMBER, I THINK WE SHOULD ALL TAKE A MOMENT TO COLLECT OURSELVES.
YOU'RE RIGHT. LET'S TAKE A MOMENT. LET'S TAKE A MOMENT AND FIGURE THIS OUT.
IF YOU ARE OF ROYAL DESCENT, YOU'LL BE ABLE TO LIGHT THE BURNING HEART. WE CAN SETTLE THIS ONCE AND FOR ALL.
WONDERFUL. I DIDN'T COME HERE JUST TO ARGUE WITH YOU...

"...LET'S SEE MY GREAT HALL."

IT IS... BEAUTIFUL.

AND SACRED TO OUR PEOPLE, NITA.

I'D PREFER *"YOUR EMBER"* TO NITA.

AND I AM AWARE OF THE PURPOSE OF THIS HALL. IT WAS MY FAMILY THAT LIT THE FIRST FLAME.

COME ON, THURMA. I'LL LIGHT THE BURNING HEART FOR YOU.

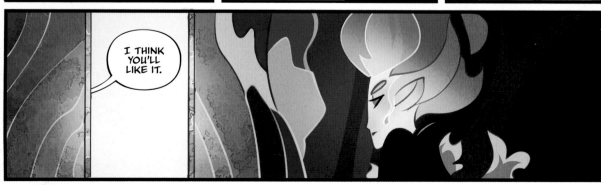

I THINK YOU'LL LIKE IT.

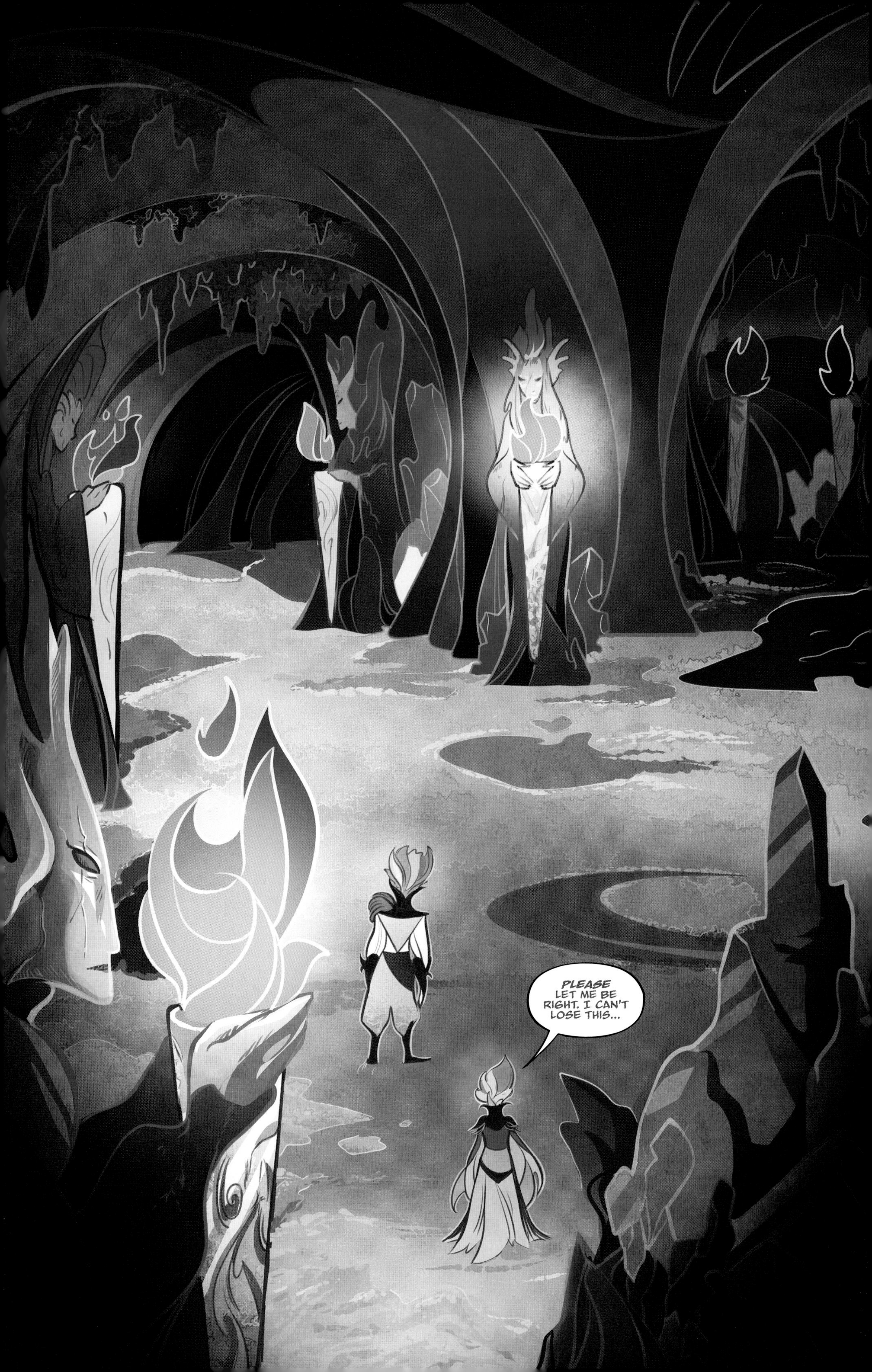
PLEASE LET ME BE RIGHT. I CAN'T LOSE THIS...

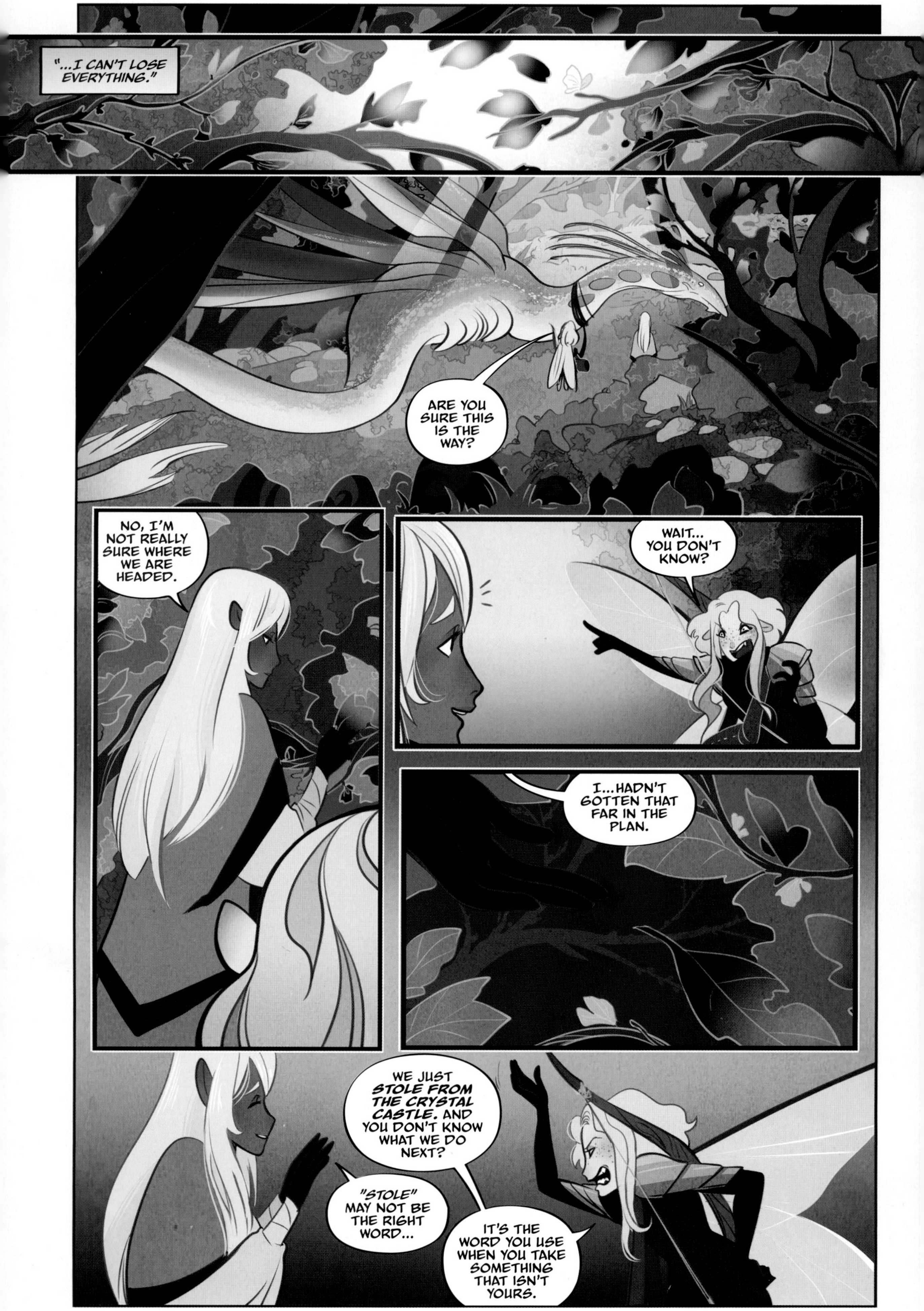
"...I CAN'T LOSE EVERYTHING."
ARE YOU SURE THIS IS THE WAY?
NO, I'M NOT REALLY SURE WHERE WE ARE HEADED.
WAIT... YOU DON'T KNOW?
I...HADN'T GOTTEN THAT FAR IN THE PLAN.
WE JUST STOLE FROM THE CRYSTAL CASTLE. AND YOU DON'T KNOW WHAT WE DO NEXT?
"STOLE" MAY NOT BE THE RIGHT WORD...
IT'S THE WORD YOU USE WHEN YOU TAKE SOMETHING THAT ISN'T YOURS.

WHAT WE TOOK, WE'RE JUST RETURNING TO THE PEOPLE. THOSE OFFERINGS SHOULD NEVER HAVE BEEN MADE AND NOW--

AND NOW WE'RE *FUGITIVES.* BOHRTOG HERE IS MORE OR LESS A WALKING TREASURE CHEST OF CRIME!

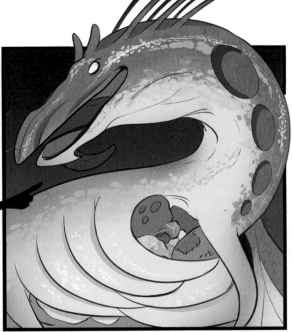

YOU MESSED IT UP, TOOLAH. YOU WERE FINALLY ON THE PATH TO BEING A ROYAL GUARD AND YOU GOT SWEPT UP IN *THIS.*

MAYBE I CAN GO BACK...RETURN THE *STOLEN* GOODS.

THIS LEAF FELL FROM THE TREE, RIGHT?

YOU PULLED THAT LEAF OFF. SOME MIGHT SAY YOU STOLE IT.

BUT WHEREVER THIS LEAF IS TAKEN, IT'S STILL A PART OF THE TREE. IT'S STILL A PART OF THRA.

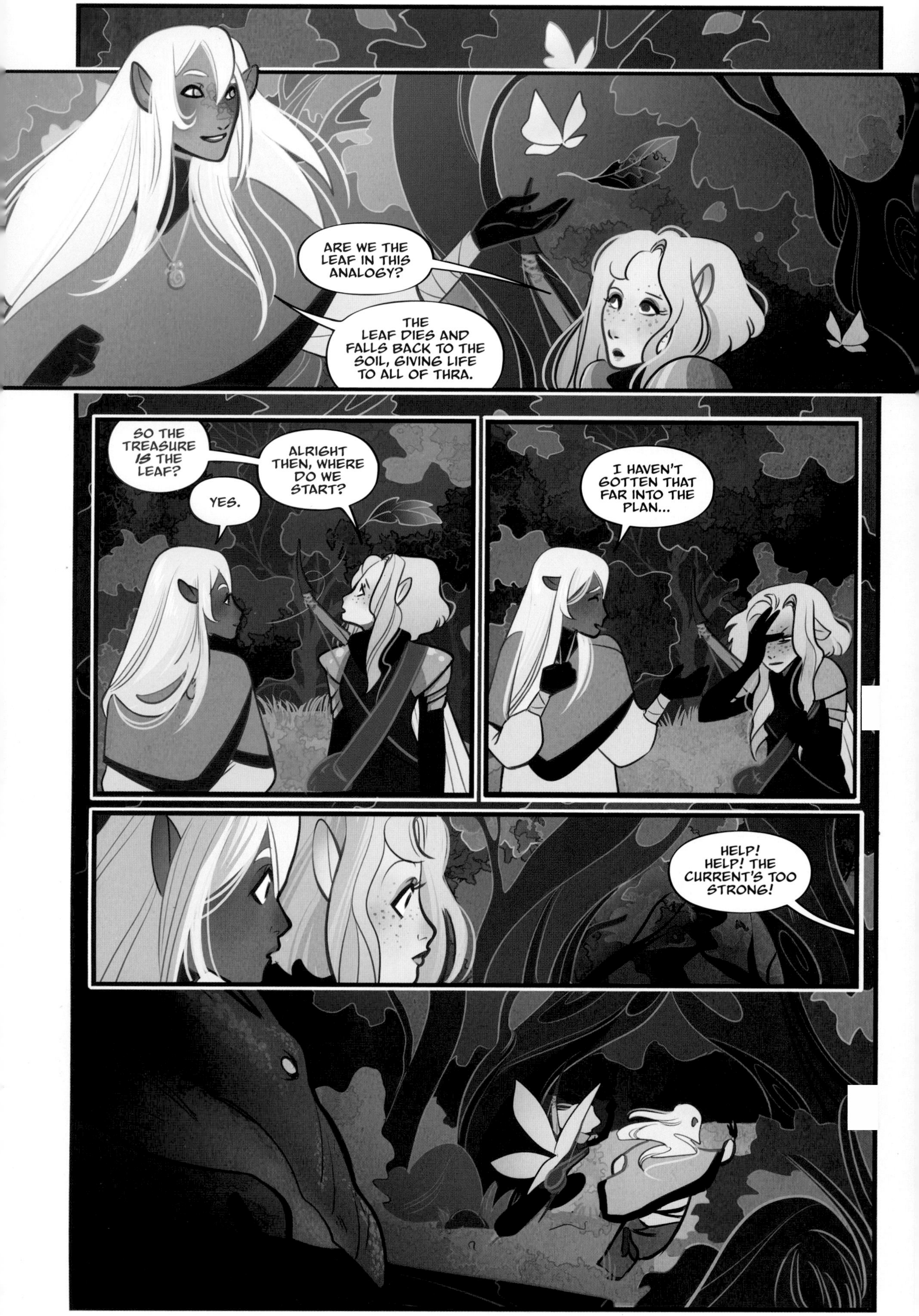
ARE WE THE LEAF IN THIS ANALOGY?
THE LEAF DIES AND FALLS BACK TO THE SOIL, GIVING LIFE TO ALL OF THRA.
SO THE TREASURE *IS* THE LEAF?
YES.
ALRIGHT THEN, WHERE DO WE START?
I HAVEN'T GOTTEN THAT FAR INTO THE PLAN...
HELP! HELP! THE CURRENT'S TOO STRONG!

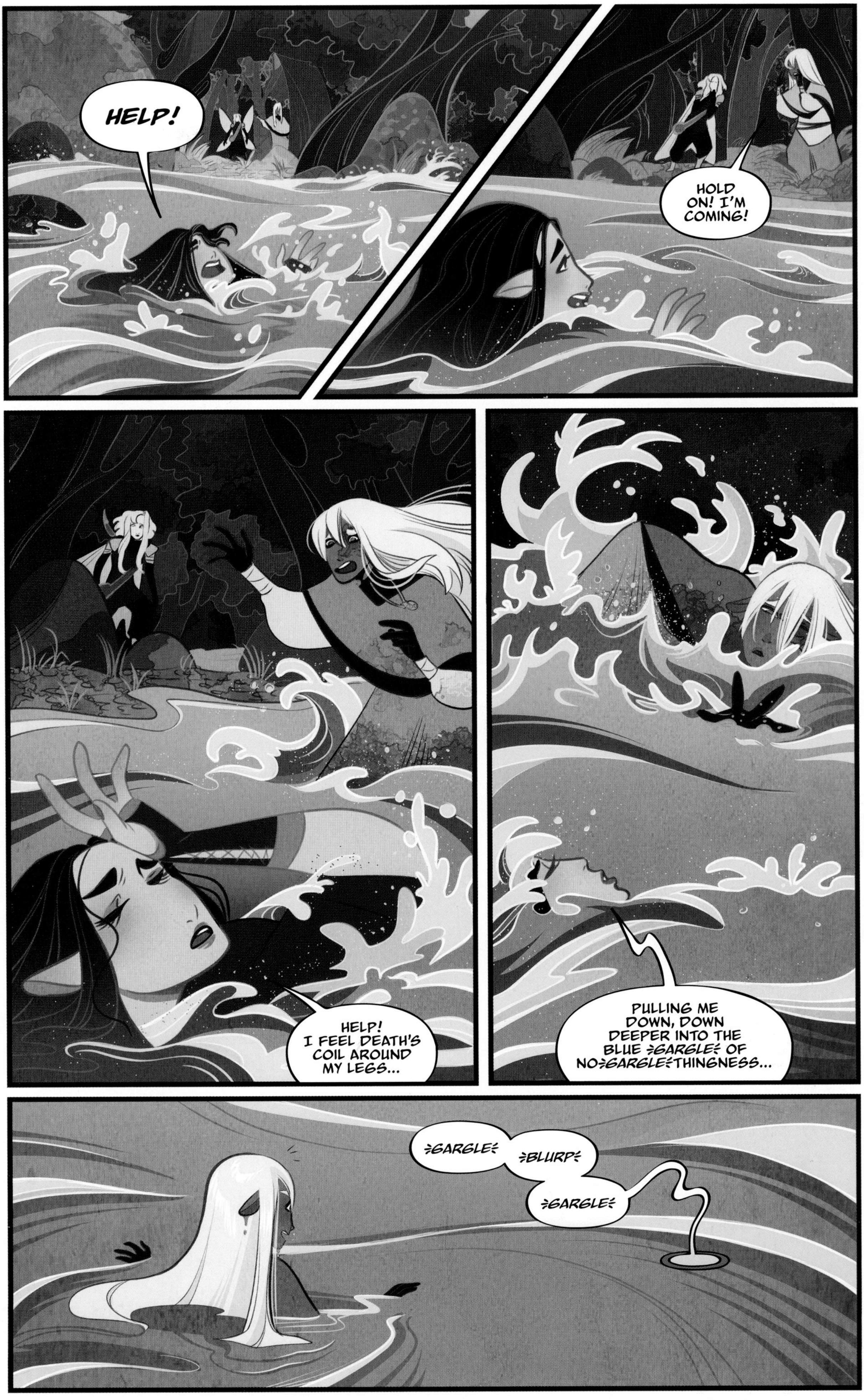
HELP!
HOLD ON! I'M COMING!
HELP! I FEEL DEATH'S COIL AROUND MY LEGS...
PULLING ME DOWN, DOWN DEEPER INTO THE BLUE ≠GARGLE≠ OF NO≠GARGLE≠THINGNESS...
≠GARGLE≠
≠BLURP≠
≠GARGLE≠

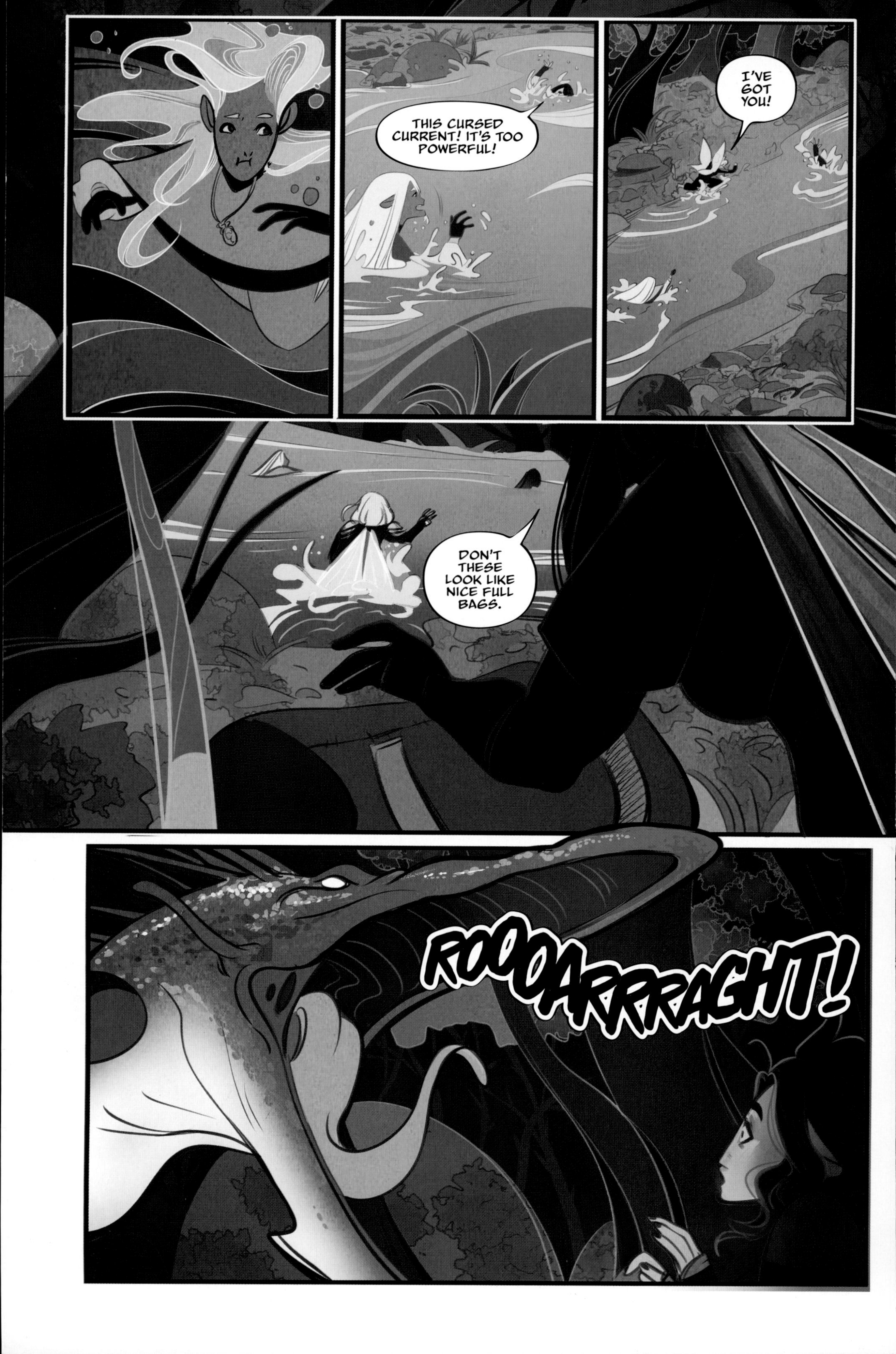
THIS CURSED CURRENT! IT'S TOO POWERFUL!
I'VE GOT YOU!
DON'T THESE LOOK LIKE NICE FULL BAGS.
ROOOARRRAGHT!

HELP!

?

HELP! CALL YOUR BEAST OFF!

HOW'D SHE GET BACK TO THE SHORE SO QUICKLY?

MY GUESS IS, SHE *DIDN'T.*

I THINK SHE HAD SOME HELP...

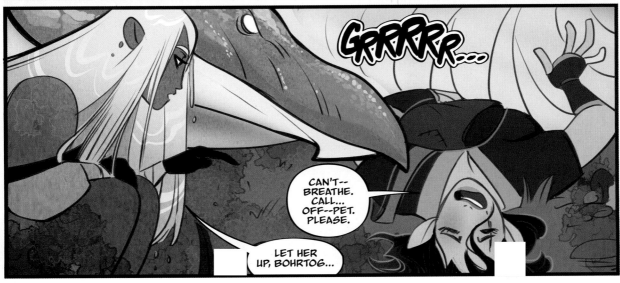

GRRRRR...

CAN'T-- BREATHE. CALL... OFF--PET. PLEASE.

LET HER UP, BOHRTOG...

"...THIS ONE HAS SOME EXPLAINING TO DO."

WAS THAT HER? IT'S BEAUTIFUL IN A WAY, WHAT YOUR MOTHER DID FOR YOU.

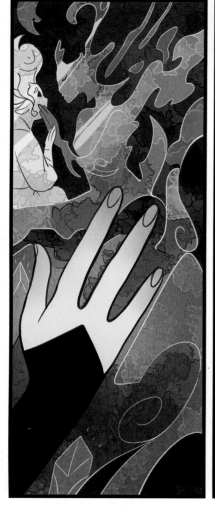

DO YOU REGRET HER *FIRE* DIMMED SO YOURS COULD SHINE BRIGHTER?

ENOUGH!

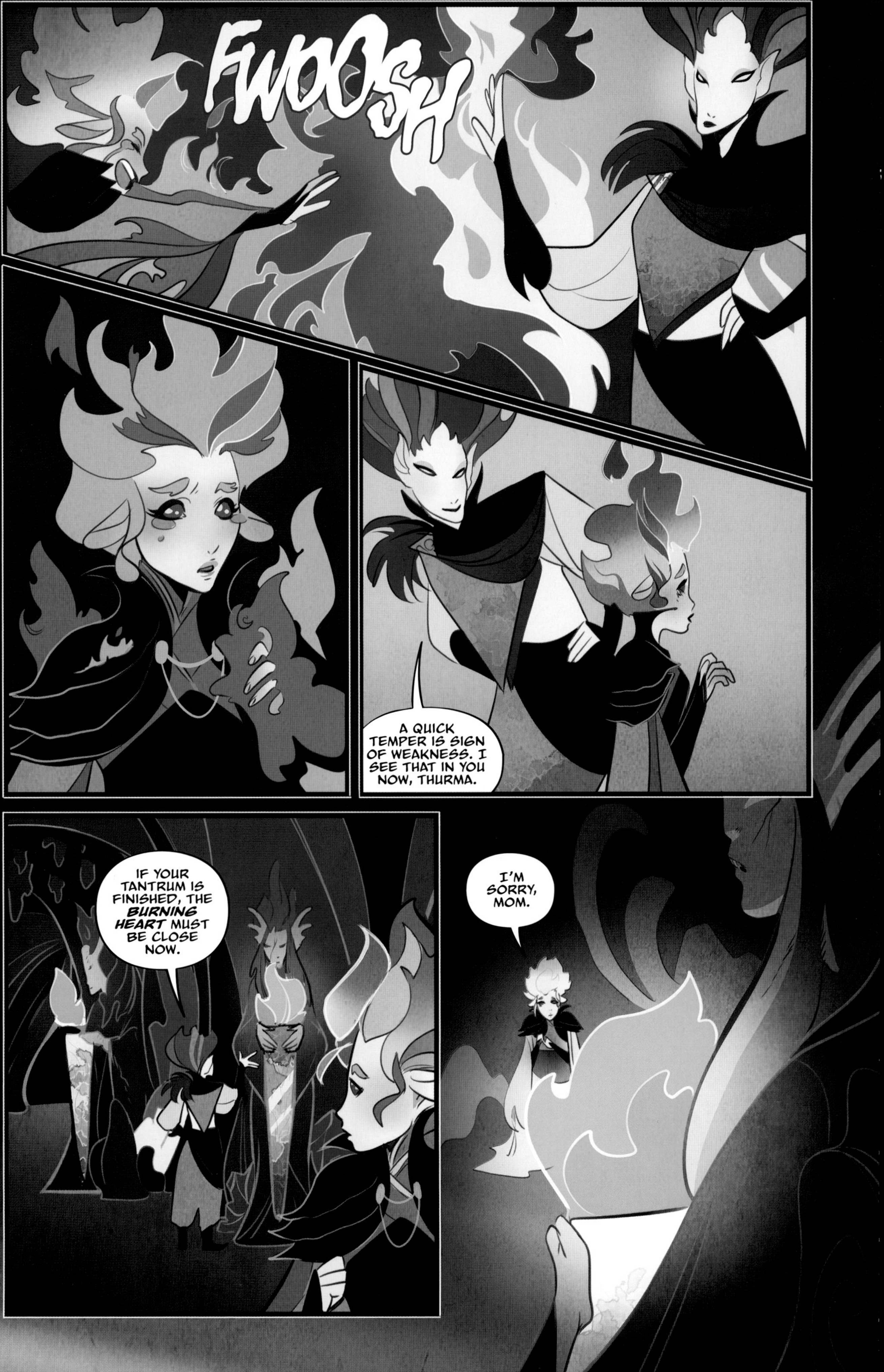
FWOOSH
A QUICK TEMPER IS SIGN OF WEAKNESS. I SEE THAT IN YOU NOW, THURMA.
IF YOUR TANTRUM IS FINISHED, THE BURNING HEART MUST BE CLOSE NOW.
I'M SORRY, MOM.

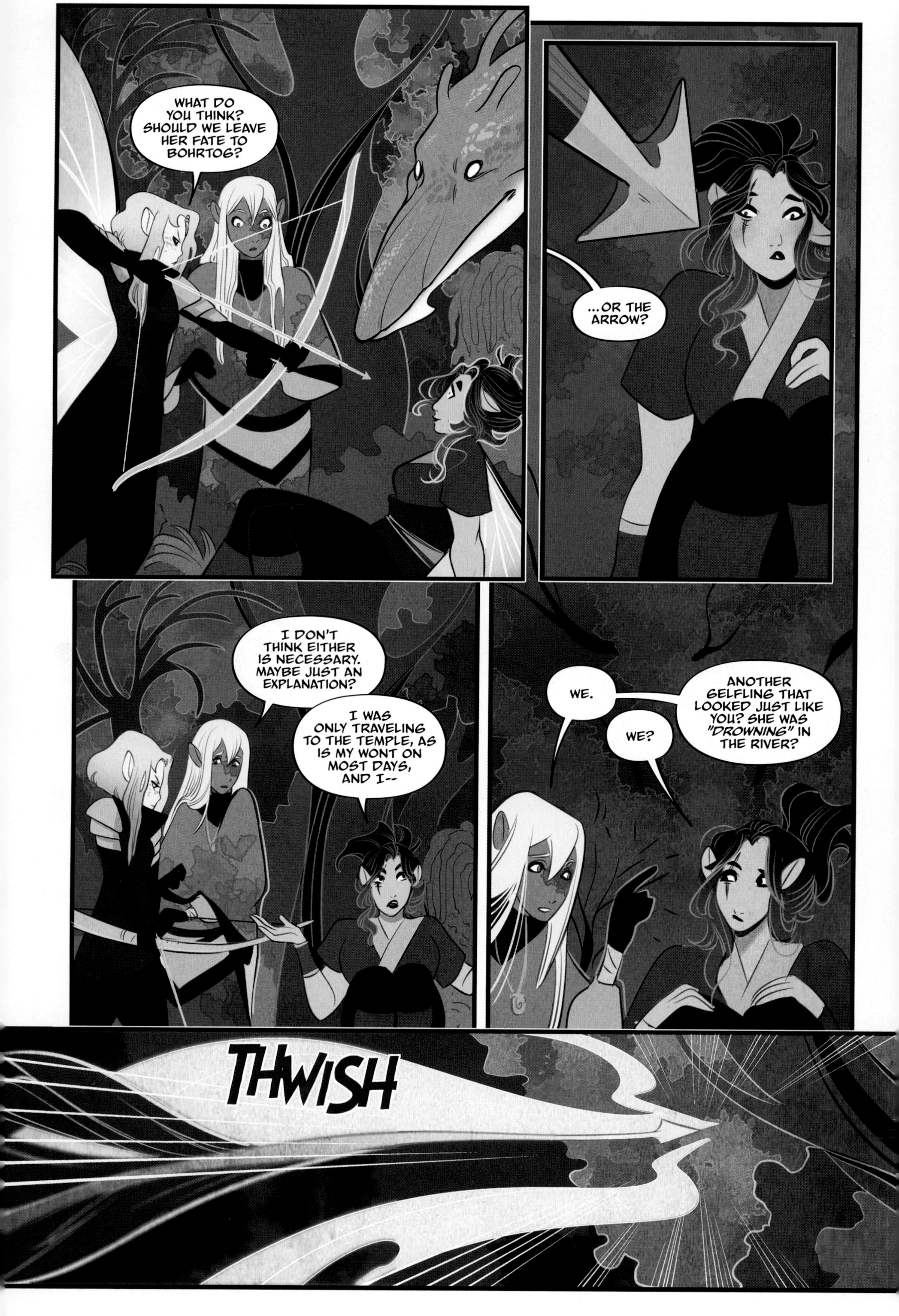
WHAT DO YOU THINK? SHOULD WE LEAVE HER FATE TO BOHRTOG?
...OR THE ARROW?
I DON'T THINK EITHER IS NECESSARY. MAYBE JUST AN EXPLANATION?
I WAS ONLY TRAVELING TO THE TEMPLE, AS IS MY WONT ON MOST DAYS, AND I--
ANOTHER GELFLING THAT LOOKED JUST LIKE YOU? SHE WAS "DROWNING" IN THE RIVER?
WE?
WE.
THWISH

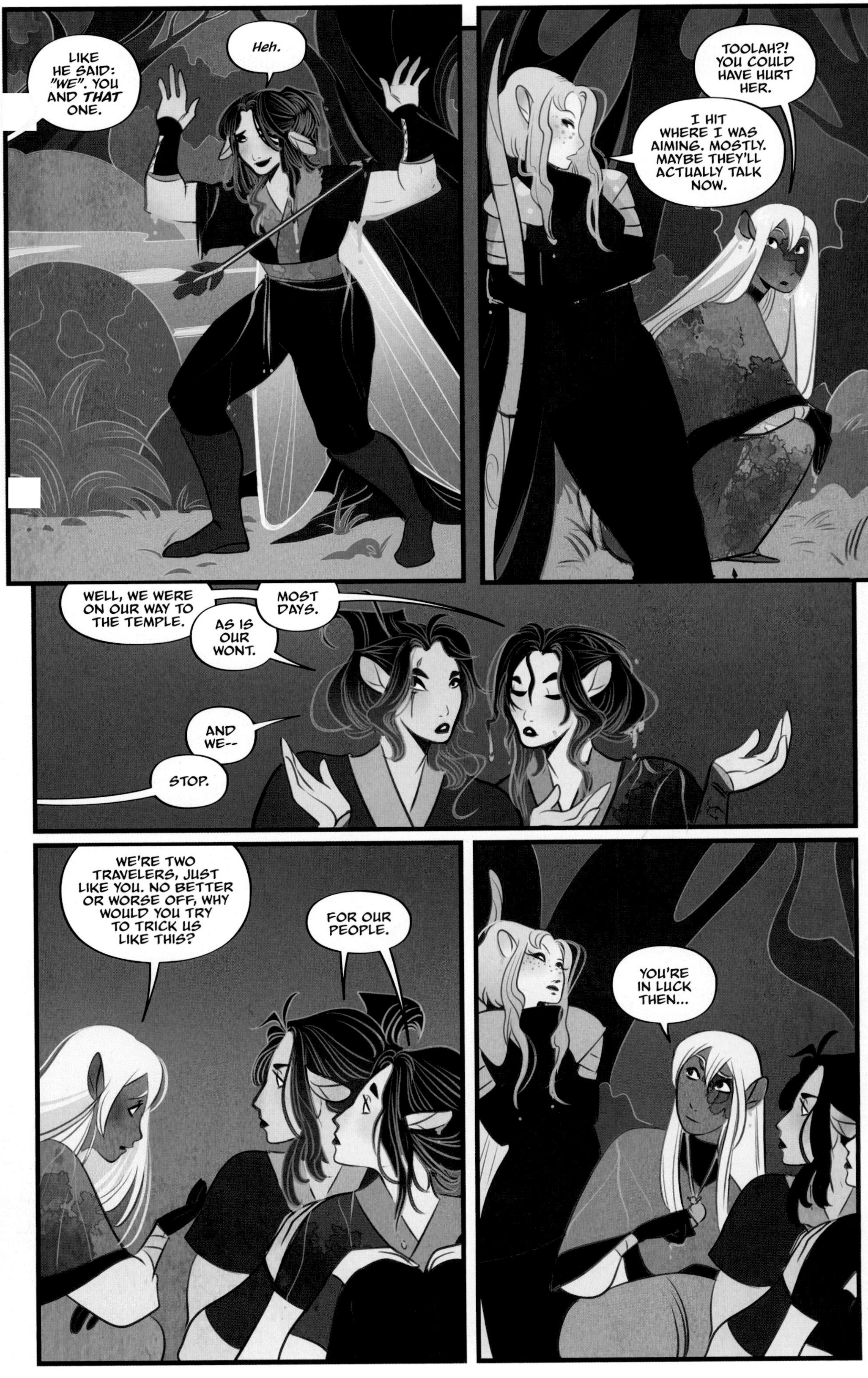
LIKE HE SAID: "WE". YOU AND *THAT* ONE.
Heh.
TOOLAH?! YOU COULD HAVE HURT HER.
I HIT WHERE I WAS AIMING. MOSTLY. MAYBE THEY'LL ACTUALLY TALK NOW.
WELL, WE WERE ON OUR WAY TO THE TEMPLE.
MOST DAYS.
AS IS OUR WONT.
AND WE--
STOP.
WE'RE TWO TRAVELERS, JUST LIKE YOU. NO BETTER OR WORSE OFF, WHY WOULD YOU TRY TO TRICK US LIKE THIS?
FOR OUR PEOPLE.
YOU'RE IN LUCK THEN...

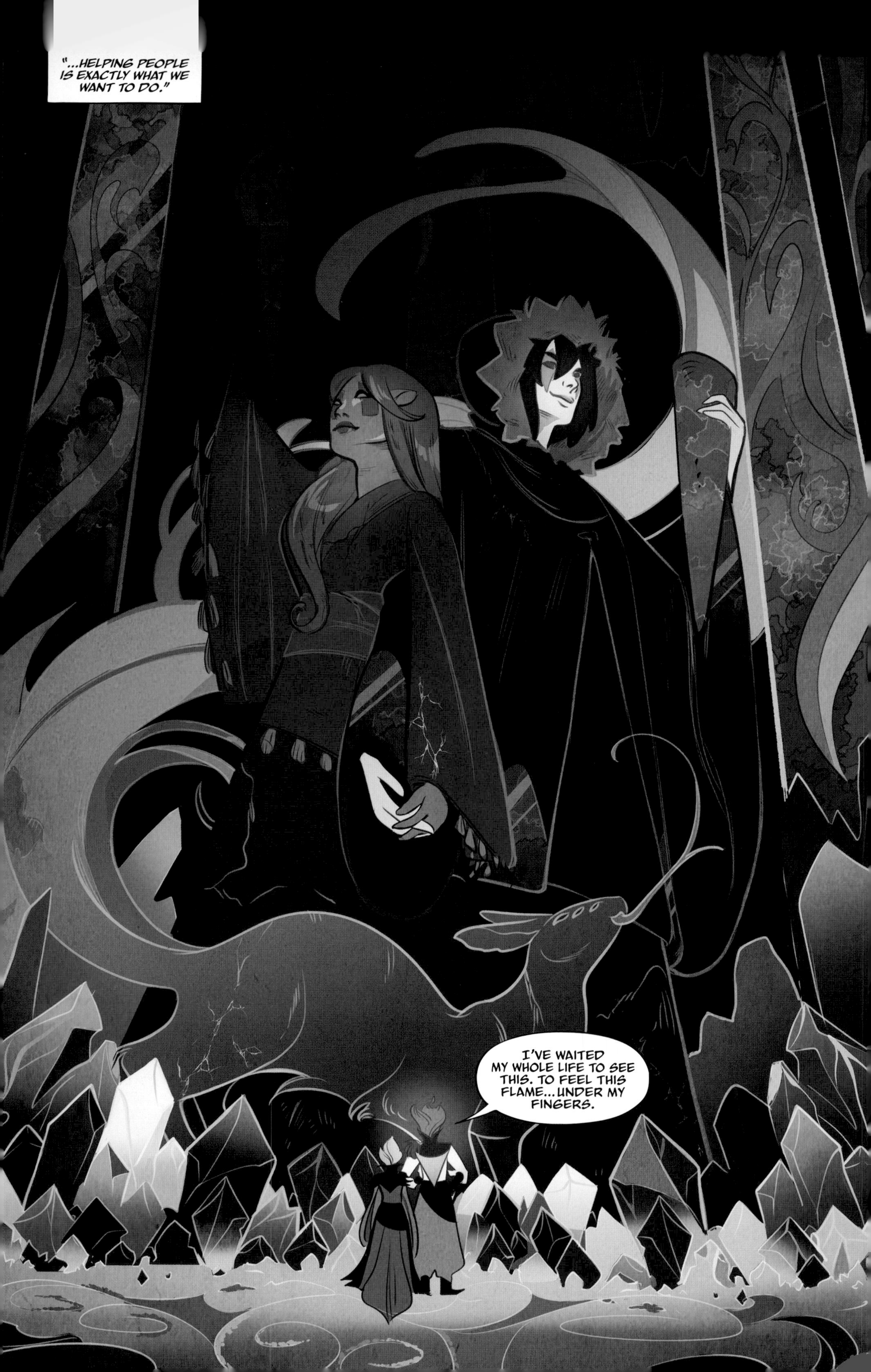
"...HELPING PEOPLE IS EXACTLY WHAT WE WANT TO DO."
I'VE WAITED MY WHOLE LIFE TO SEE THIS. TO FEEL THIS FLAME...UNDER MY FINGERS.

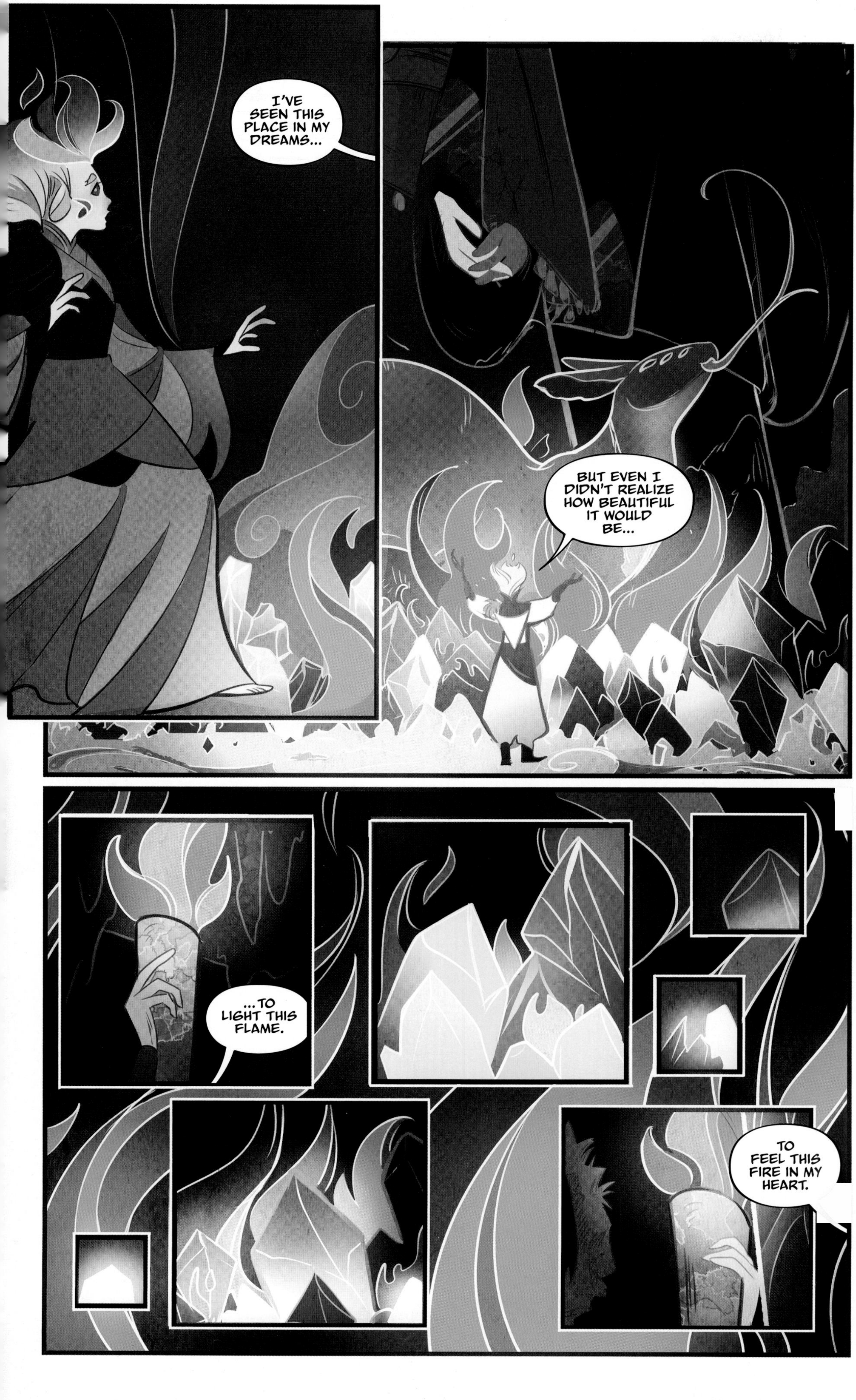
I'VE SEEN THIS PLACE IN MY DREAMS...
BUT EVEN I DIDN'T REALIZE HOW BEAUTIFUL IT WOULD BE...
...TO LIGHT THIS FLAME.
TO FEEL THIS FIRE IN MY HEART.

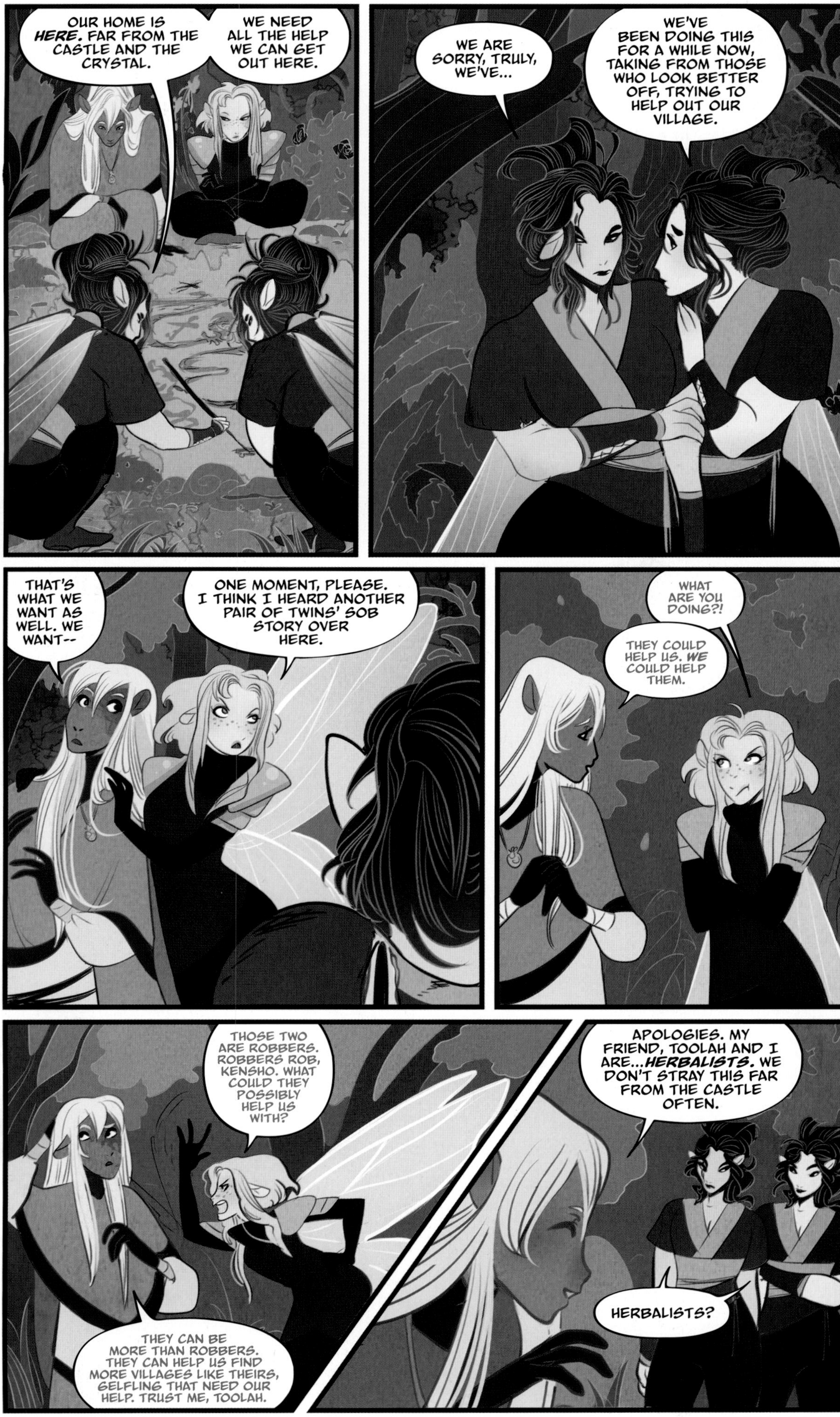
OUR HOME IS *HERE.* FAR FROM THE CASTLE AND THE CRYSTAL.
WE NEED ALL THE HELP WE CAN GET OUT HERE.
WE ARE SORRY, TRULY, WE'VE...
WE'VE BEEN DOING THIS FOR A WHILE NOW, TAKING FROM THOSE WHO LOOK BETTER OFF, TRYING TO HELP OUT OUR VILLAGE.
THAT'S WHAT WE WANT AS WELL. WE WANT--
ONE MOMENT, PLEASE. I THINK I HEARD ANOTHER PAIR OF TWINS' SOB STORY OVER HERE.
WHAT ARE YOU DOING?!
THEY COULD HELP US. *WE* COULD HELP THEM.
THOSE TWO ARE ROBBERS. ROBBERS ROB, KENSHO. WHAT COULD THEY POSSIBLY HELP US WITH?
THEY CAN BE MORE THAN ROBBERS. THEY CAN HELP US FIND MORE VILLAGES LIKE THEIRS, GELFLING THAT NEED OUR HELP. TRUST ME, TOOLAH.
APOLOGIES. MY FRIEND, TOOLAH AND I ARE...*HERBALISTS.* WE DON'T STRAY THIS FAR FROM THE CASTLE OFTEN.
HERBALISTS?

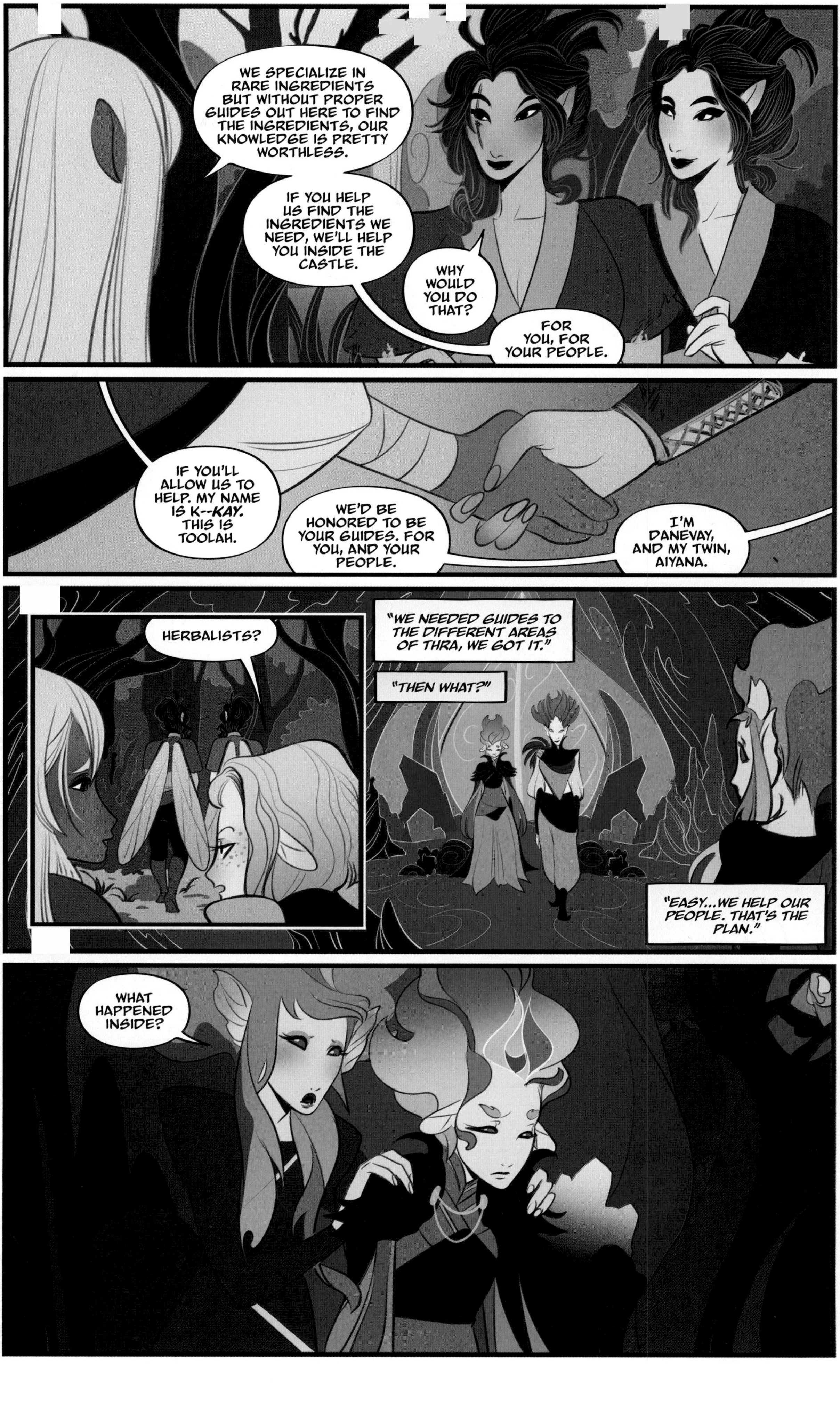

WE SPECIALIZE IN RARE INGREDIENTS BUT WITHOUT PROPER GUIDES OUT HERE TO FIND THE INGREDIENTS, OUR KNOWLEDGE IS PRETTY WORTHLESS.
IF YOU HELP US FIND THE INGREDIENTS WE NEED, WE'LL HELP YOU INSIDE THE CASTLE.
WHY WOULD YOU DO THAT?
FOR YOU, FOR YOUR PEOPLE.
IF YOU'LL ALLOW US TO HELP. MY NAME IS K--KAY. THIS IS TOOLAH.
WE'D BE HONORED TO BE YOUR GUIDES. FOR YOU, AND YOUR PEOPLE.
I'M DANEVAY, AND MY TWIN, AIYANA.
HERBALISTS?
"WE NEEDED GUIDES TO THE DIFFERENT AREAS OF THRA, WE GOT IT."
"THEN WHAT?"
"EASY...WE HELP OUR PEOPLE. THAT'S THE PLAN."
WHAT HAPPENED INSIDE?

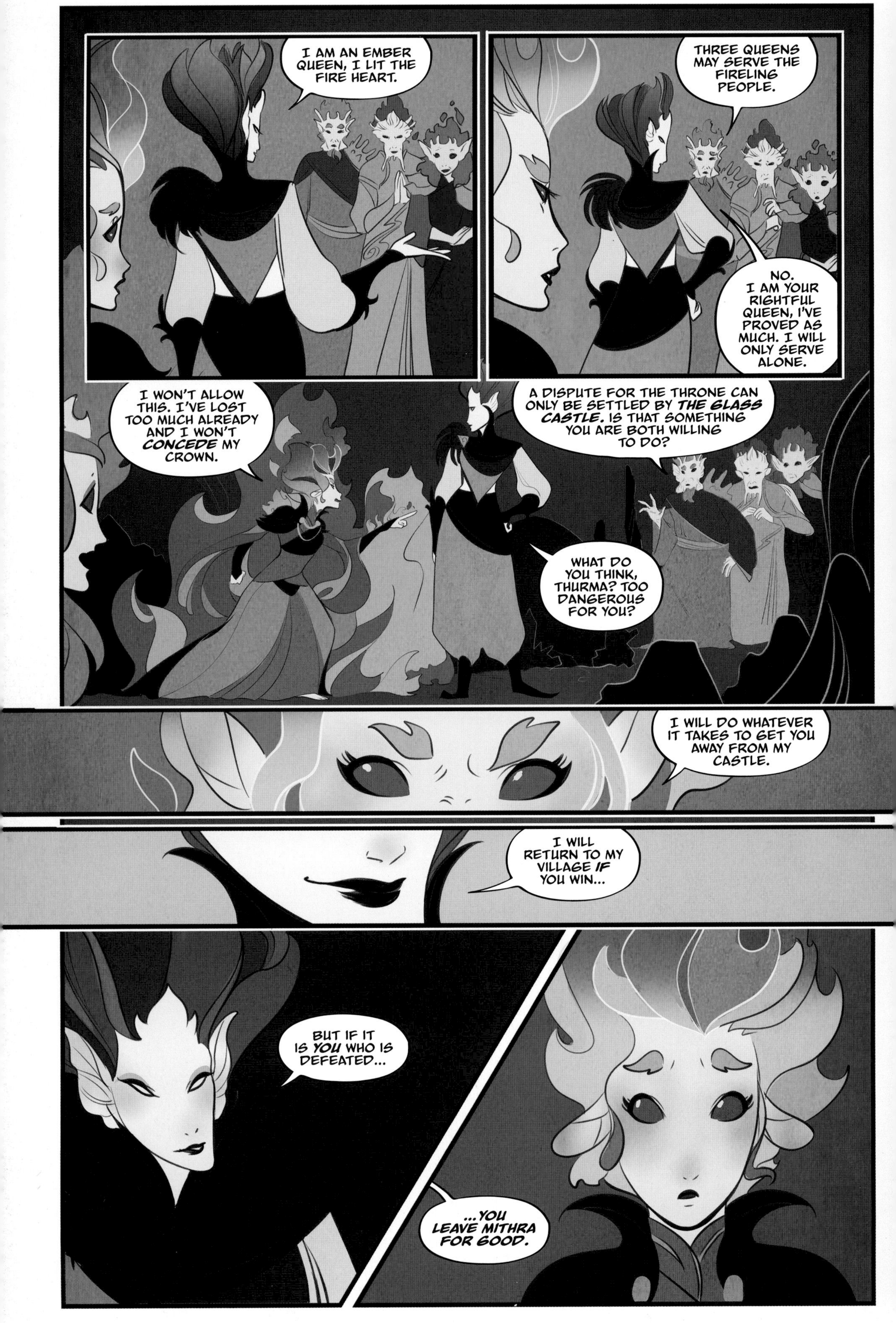
I AM AN EMBER QUEEN, I LIT THE FIRE HEART.
THREE QUEENS MAY SERVE THE FIRELING PEOPLE.
NO. I AM YOUR RIGHTFUL QUEEN, I'VE PROVED AS MUCH. I WILL ONLY SERVE ALONE.
I WON'T ALLOW THIS. I'VE LOST TOO MUCH ALREADY AND I WON'T *CONCEDE* MY CROWN.
A DISPUTE FOR THE THRONE CAN ONLY BE SETTLED BY *THE GLASS CASTLE.* IS THAT SOMETHING YOU ARE BOTH WILLING TO DO?
WHAT DO YOU THINK, THURMA? TOO DANGEROUS FOR YOU?
I WILL DO WHATEVER IT TAKES TO GET YOU AWAY FROM MY CASTLE.
I WILL RETURN TO MY VILLAGE *IF* YOU WIN...
BUT IF IT IS *YOU* WHO IS DEFEATED...
...YOU LEAVE MITHRA FOR GOOD.

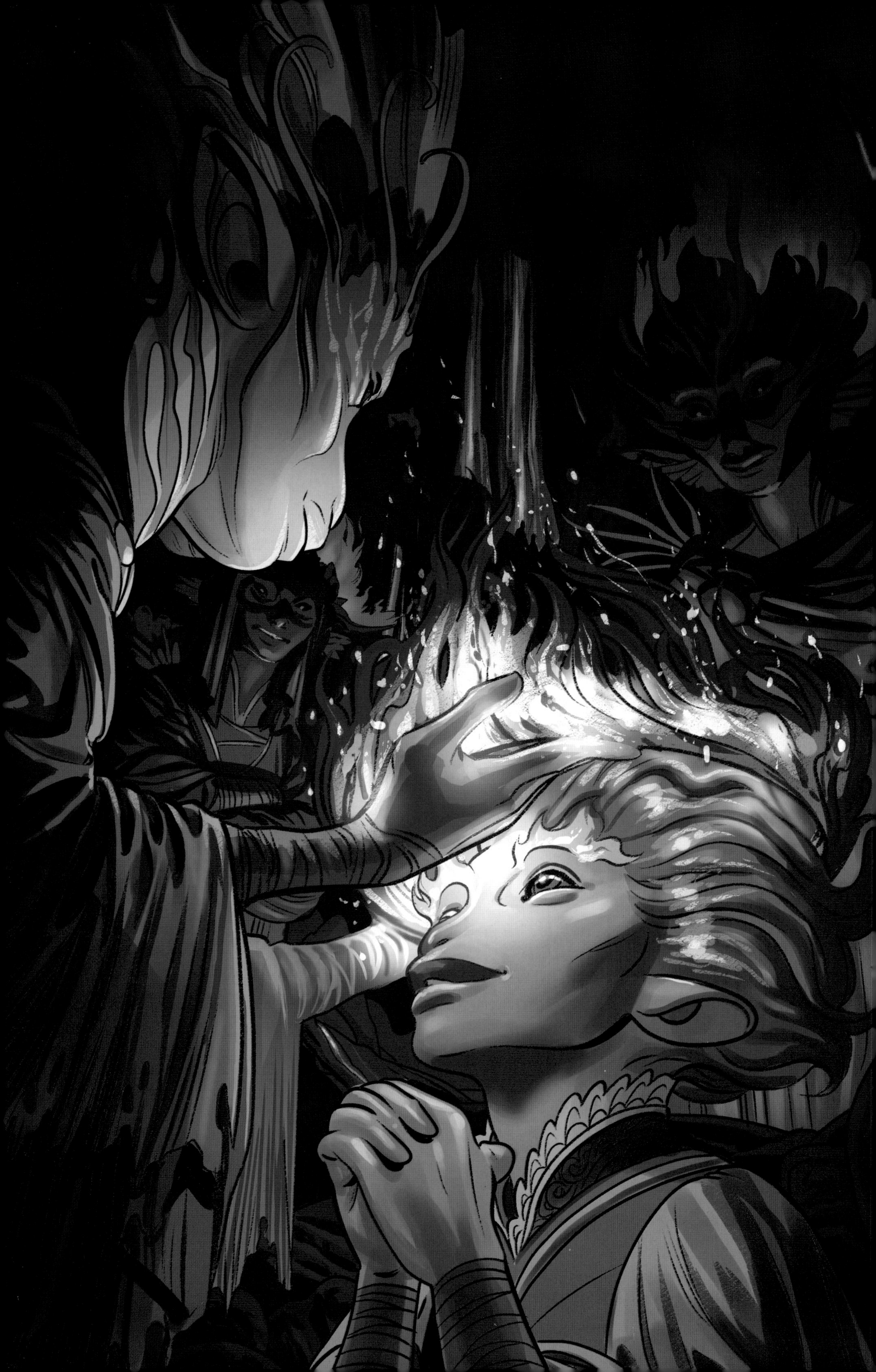

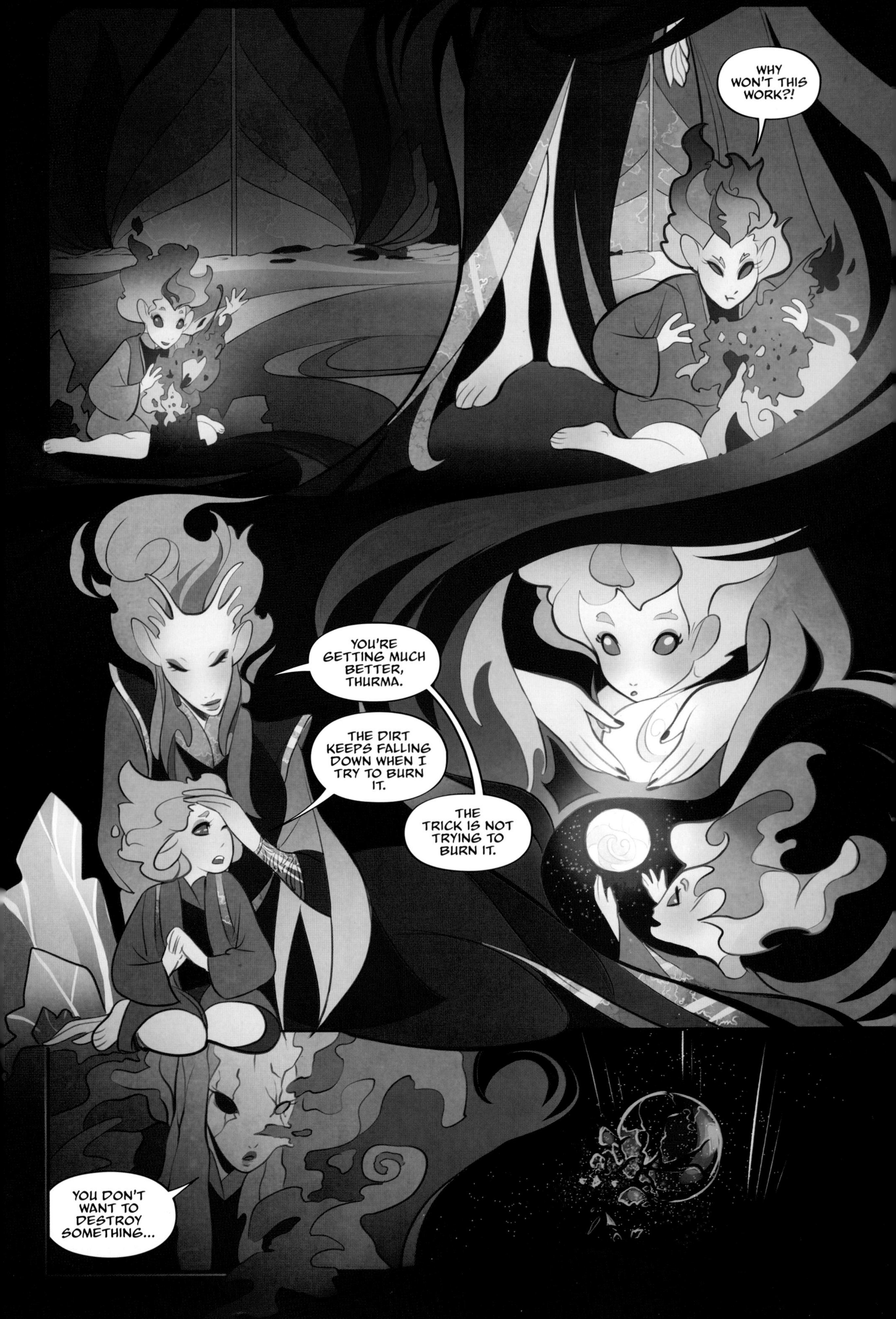
WHY WON'T THIS WORK?!
YOU'RE GETTING MUCH BETTER, THURMA.
THE DIRT KEEPS FALLING DOWN WHEN I TRY TO BURN IT.
THE TRICK IS NOT TRYING TO BURN IT.
YOU DON'T WANT TO DESTROY SOMETHING...

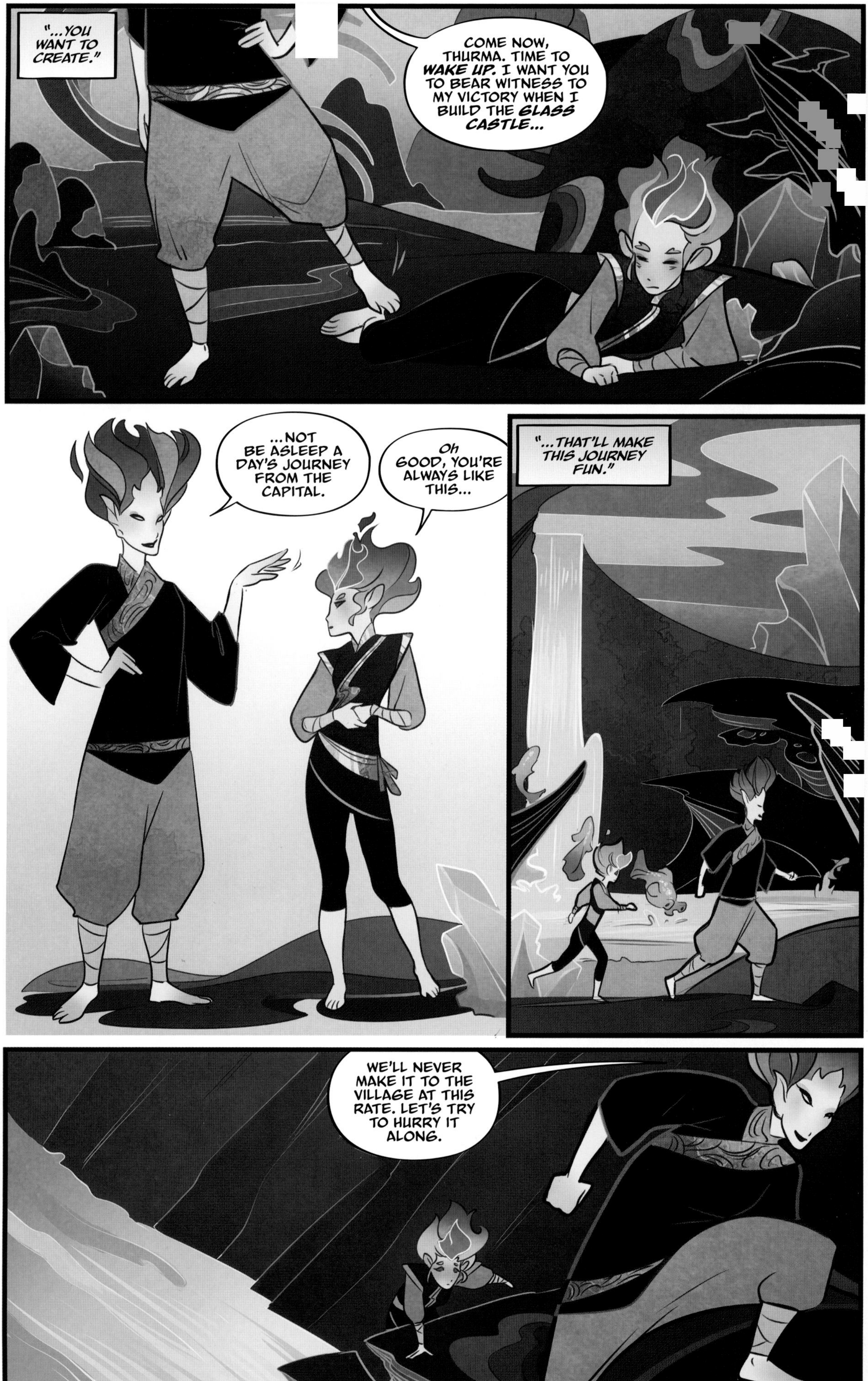
"...YOU WANT TO CREATE."
COME NOW, THURMA. TIME TO WAKE UP. I WANT YOU TO BEAR WITNESS TO MY VICTORY WHEN I BUILD THE GLASS CASTLE...
...NOT BE ASLEEP A DAY'S JOURNEY FROM THE CAPITAL.
Oh GOOD, YOU'RE ALWAYS LIKE THIS...
"...THAT'LL MAKE THIS JOURNEY FUN."
WE'LL NEVER MAKE IT TO THE VILLAGE AT THIS RATE. LET'S TRY TO HURRY IT ALONG.

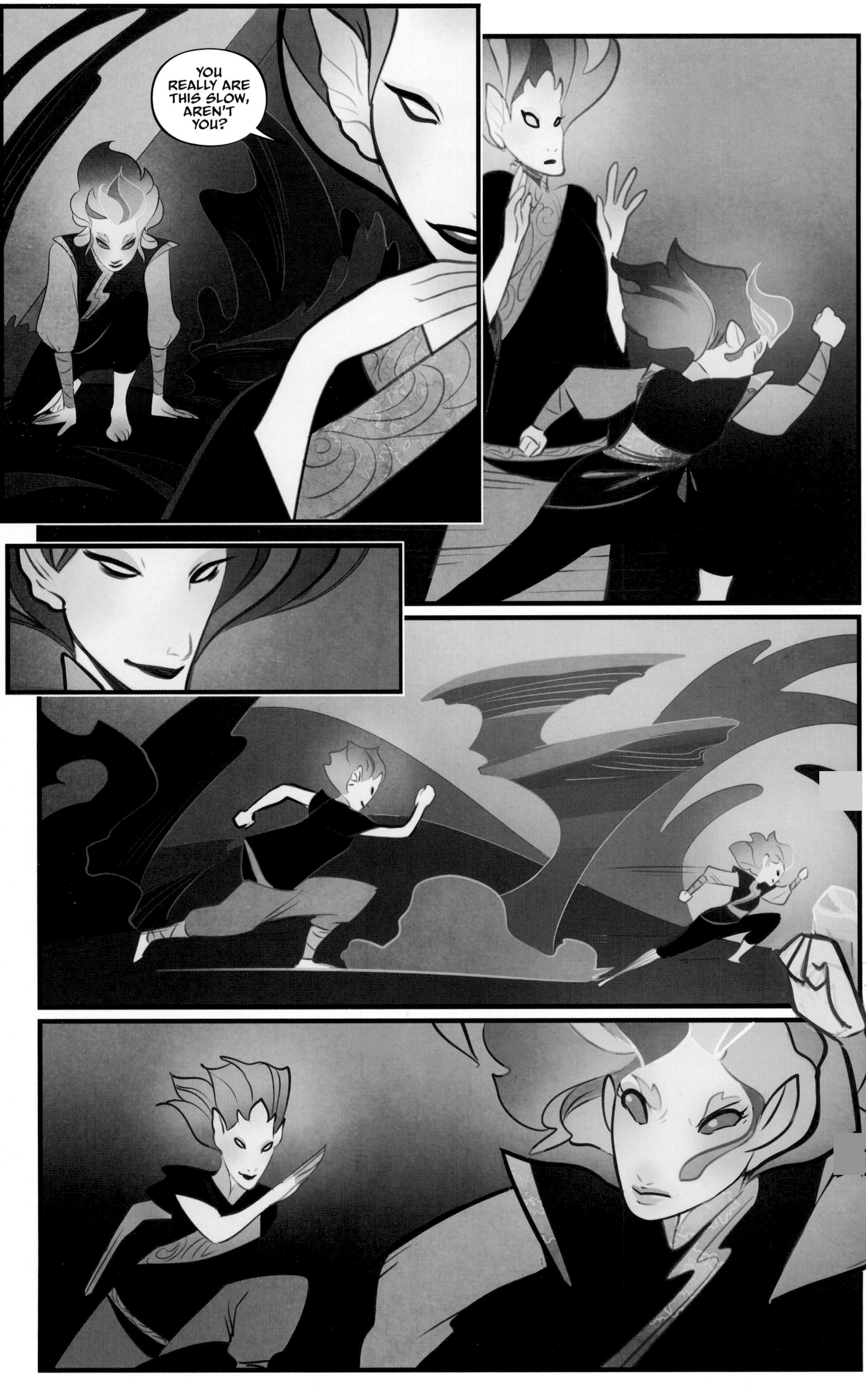
YOU REALLY ARE THIS SLOW, AREN'T YOU?

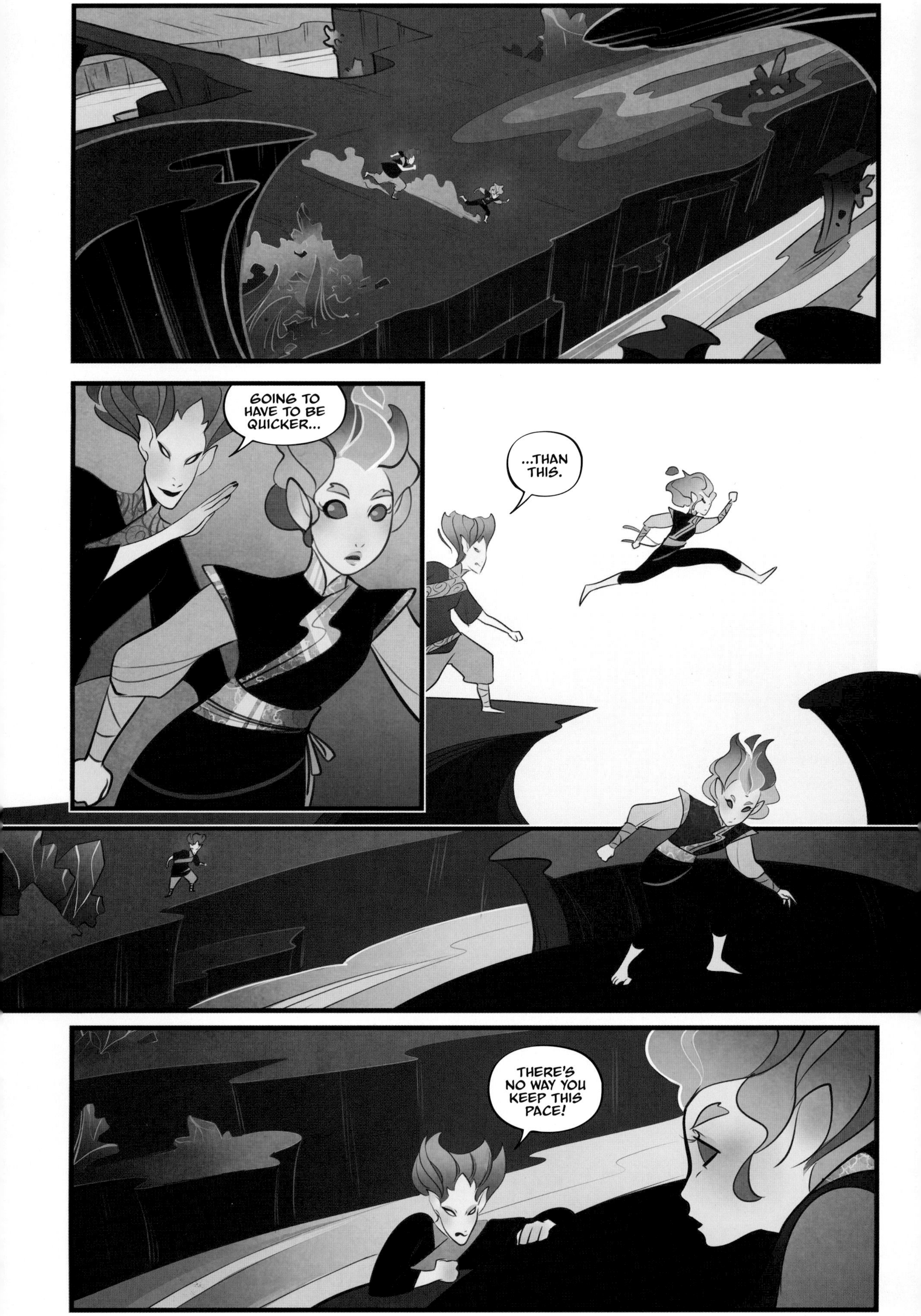
GOING TO HAVE TO BE QUICKER...
...THAN THIS.
THERE'S NO WAY YOU KEEP THIS PACE!

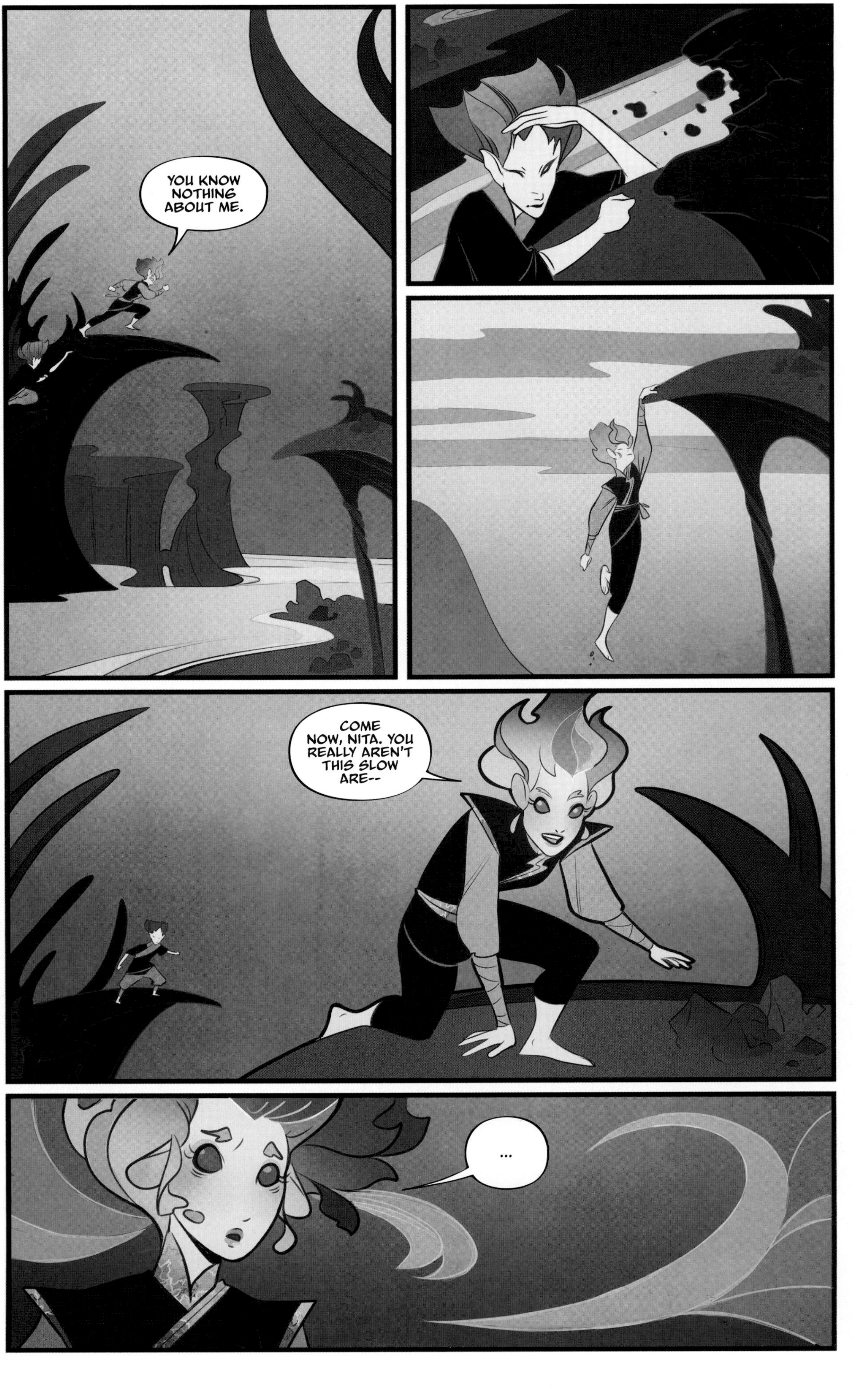
YOU KNOW NOTHING ABOUT ME.
COME NOW, NITA. YOU REALLY AREN'T THIS SLOW ARE--
...

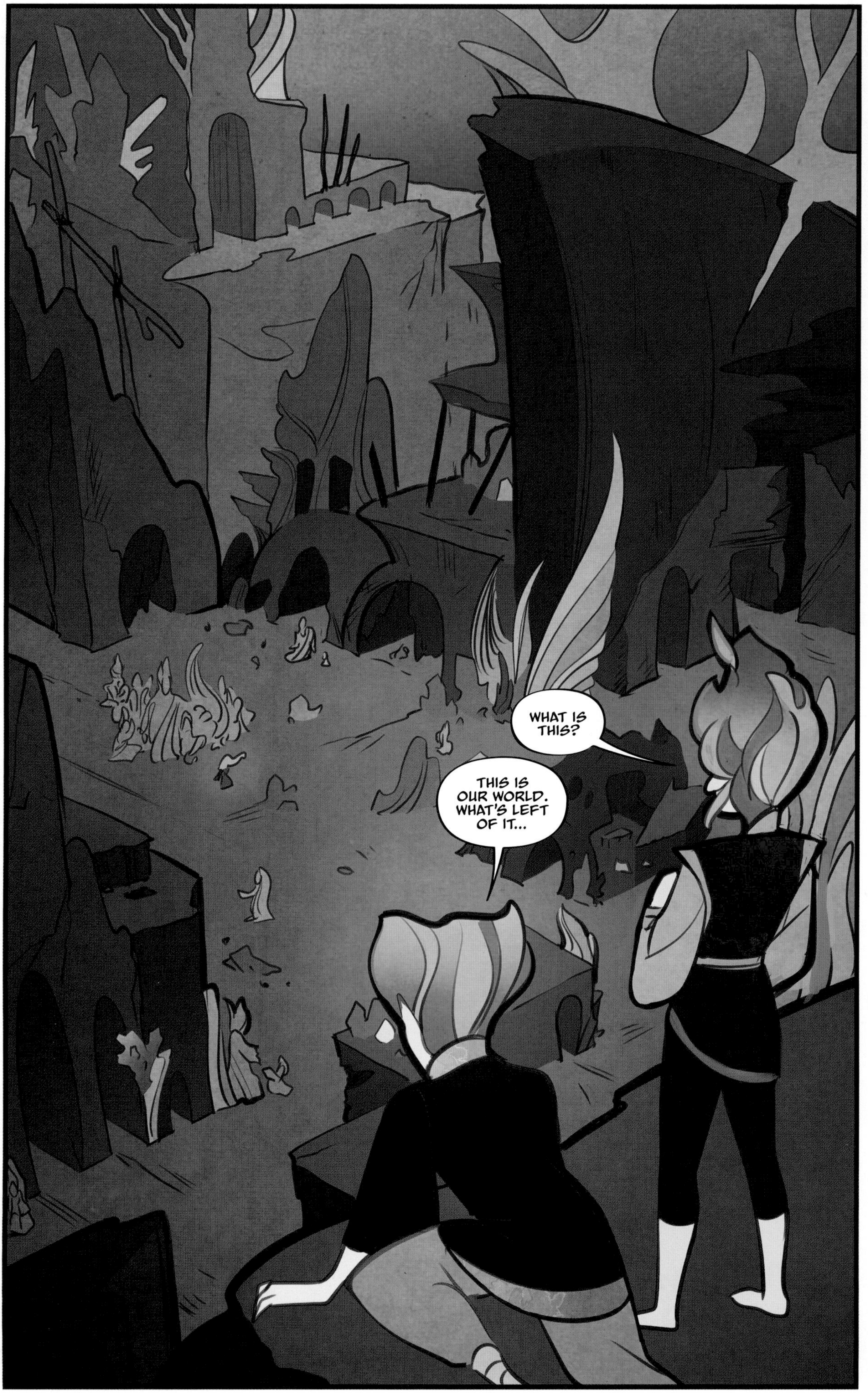
WHAT IS THIS?
THIS IS OUR WORLD. WHAT'S LEFT OF IT...

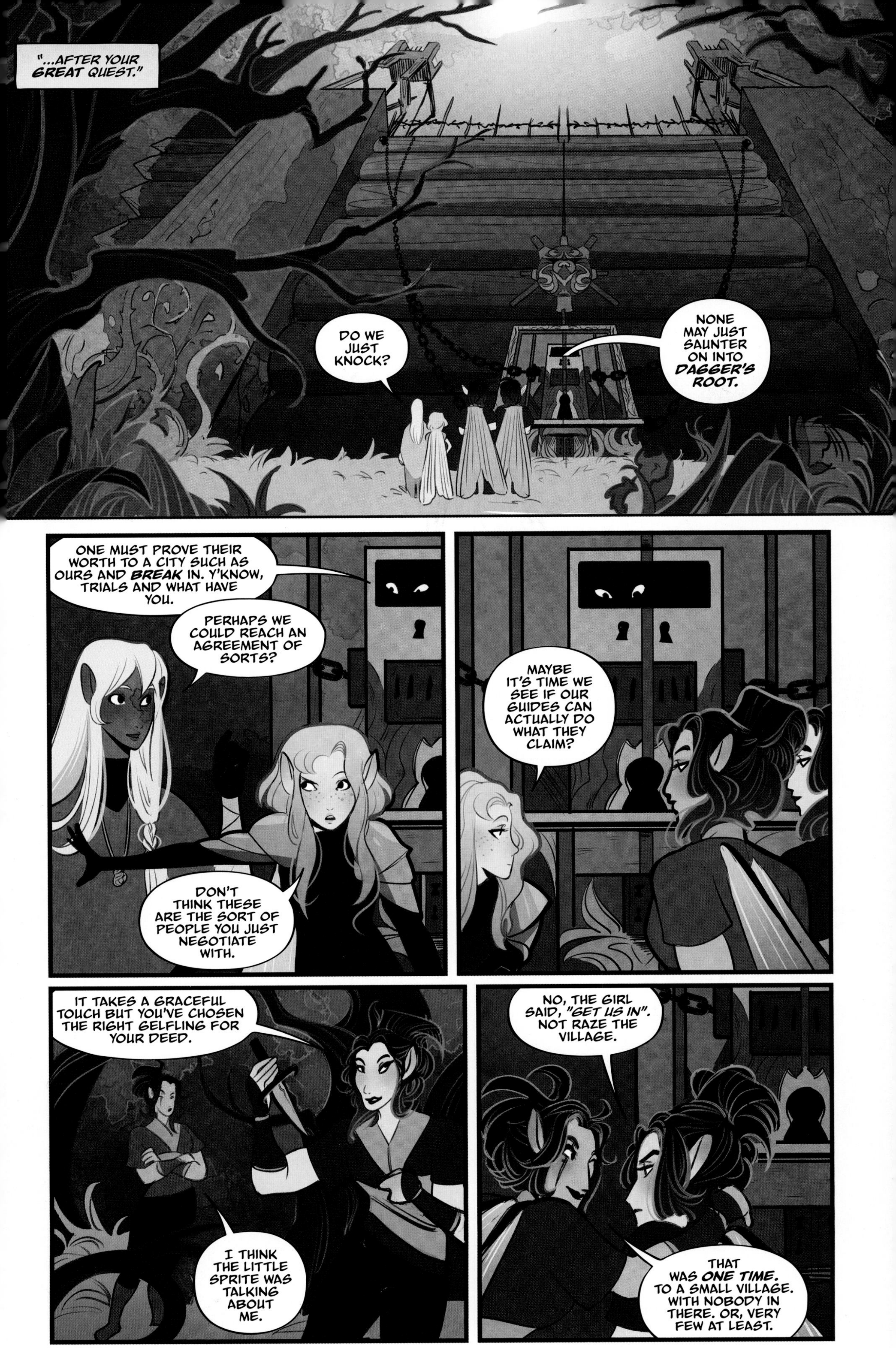
"...AFTER YOUR GREAT QUEST."
DO WE JUST KNOCK?
NONE MAY JUST SAUNTER ON INTO DAGGER'S ROOT.
ONE MUST PROVE THEIR WORTH TO A CITY SUCH AS OURS AND BREAK IN. Y'KNOW, TRIALS AND WHAT HAVE YOU.
PERHAPS WE COULD REACH AN AGREEMENT OF SORTS?
DON'T THINK THESE ARE THE SORT OF PEOPLE YOU JUST NEGOTIATE WITH.
MAYBE IT'S TIME WE SEE IF OUR GUIDES CAN ACTUALLY DO WHAT THEY CLAIM?
IT TAKES A GRACEFUL TOUCH BUT YOU'VE CHOSEN THE RIGHT GELFLING FOR YOUR DEED.
I THINK THE LITTLE SPRITE WAS TALKING ABOUT ME.
NO, THE GIRL SAID, "GET US IN". NOT RAZE THE VILLAGE.
THAT WAS ONE TIME. TO A SMALL VILLAGE. WITH NOBODY IN THERE. OR, VERY FEW AT LEAST.

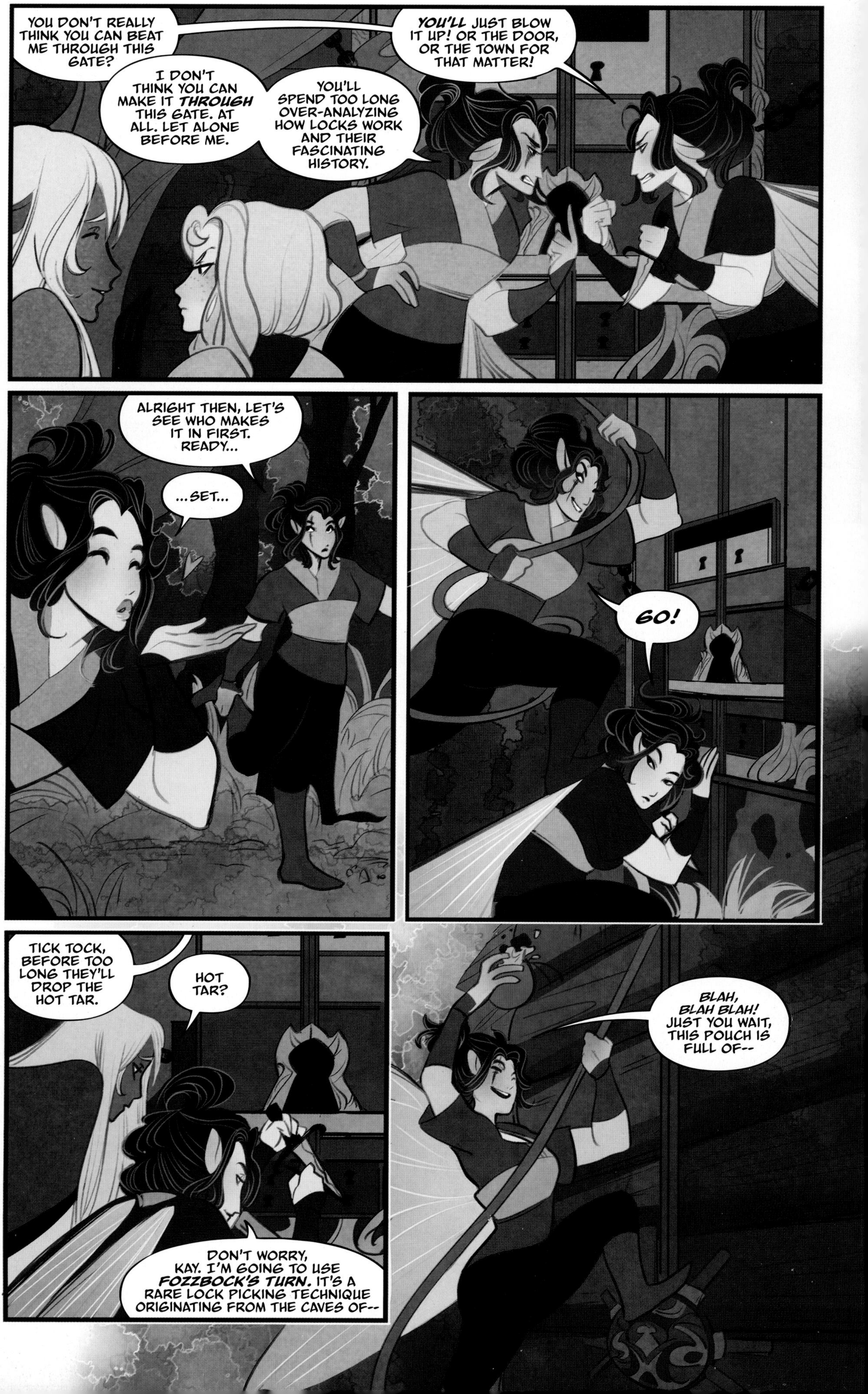
YOU DON'T REALLY THINK YOU CAN BEAT ME THROUGH THIS GATE?
I DON'T THINK YOU CAN MAKE IT THROUGH THIS GATE. AT ALL. LET ALONE BEFORE ME.
YOU'LL SPEND TOO LONG OVER-ANALYZING HOW LOCKS WORK AND THEIR FASCINATING HISTORY.
YOU'LL JUST BLOW IT UP! OR THE DOOR, OR THE TOWN FOR THAT MATTER!
ALRIGHT THEN, LET'S SEE WHO MAKES IT IN FIRST. READY...
...SET...
GO!
TICK TOCK, BEFORE TOO LONG THEY'LL DROP THE HOT TAR.
HOT TAR?
DON'T WORRY, KAY. I'M GOING TO USE FOZZBOCK'S TURN. IT'S A RARE LOCK PICKING TECHNIQUE ORIGINATING FROM THE CAVES OF--
BLAH, BLAH BLAH! JUST YOU WAIT, THIS POUCH IS FULL OF--

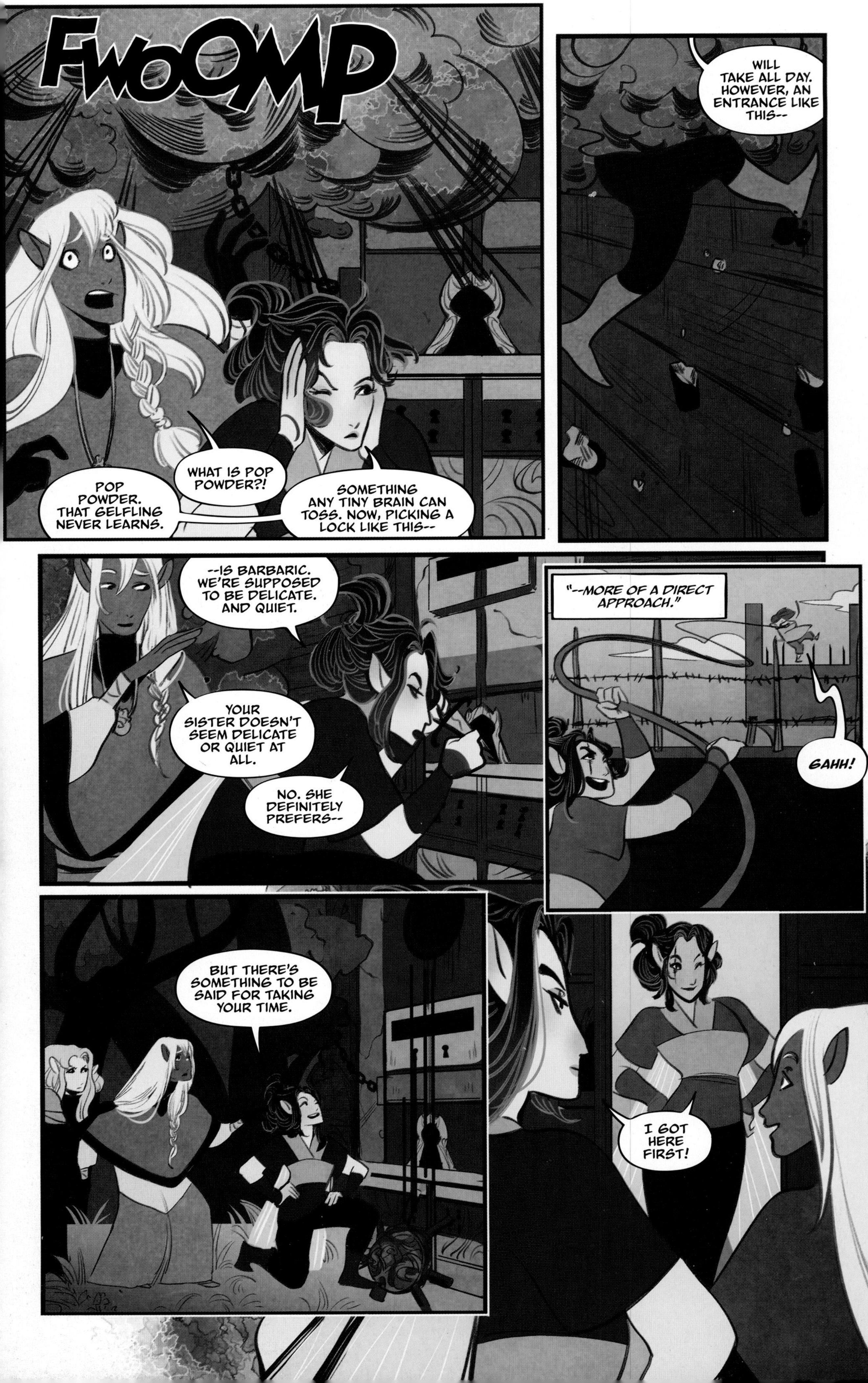
FWOOMP
WHAT IS POP POWDER?!
POP POWDER. THAT GELFLING NEVER LEARNS.
SOMETHING ANY TINY BRAIN CAN TOSS. NOW, PICKING A LOCK LIKE THIS--
WILL TAKE ALL DAY. HOWEVER, AN ENTRANCE LIKE THIS--
--IS BARBARIC. WE'RE SUPPOSED TO BE DELICATE. AND QUIET.
YOUR SISTER DOESN'T SEEM DELICATE OR QUIET AT ALL.
NO. SHE DEFINITELY PREFERS--
"--MORE OF A DIRECT APPROACH."
GAHH!
BUT THERE'S SOMETHING TO BE SAID FOR TAKING YOUR TIME.
I GOT HERE FIRST!

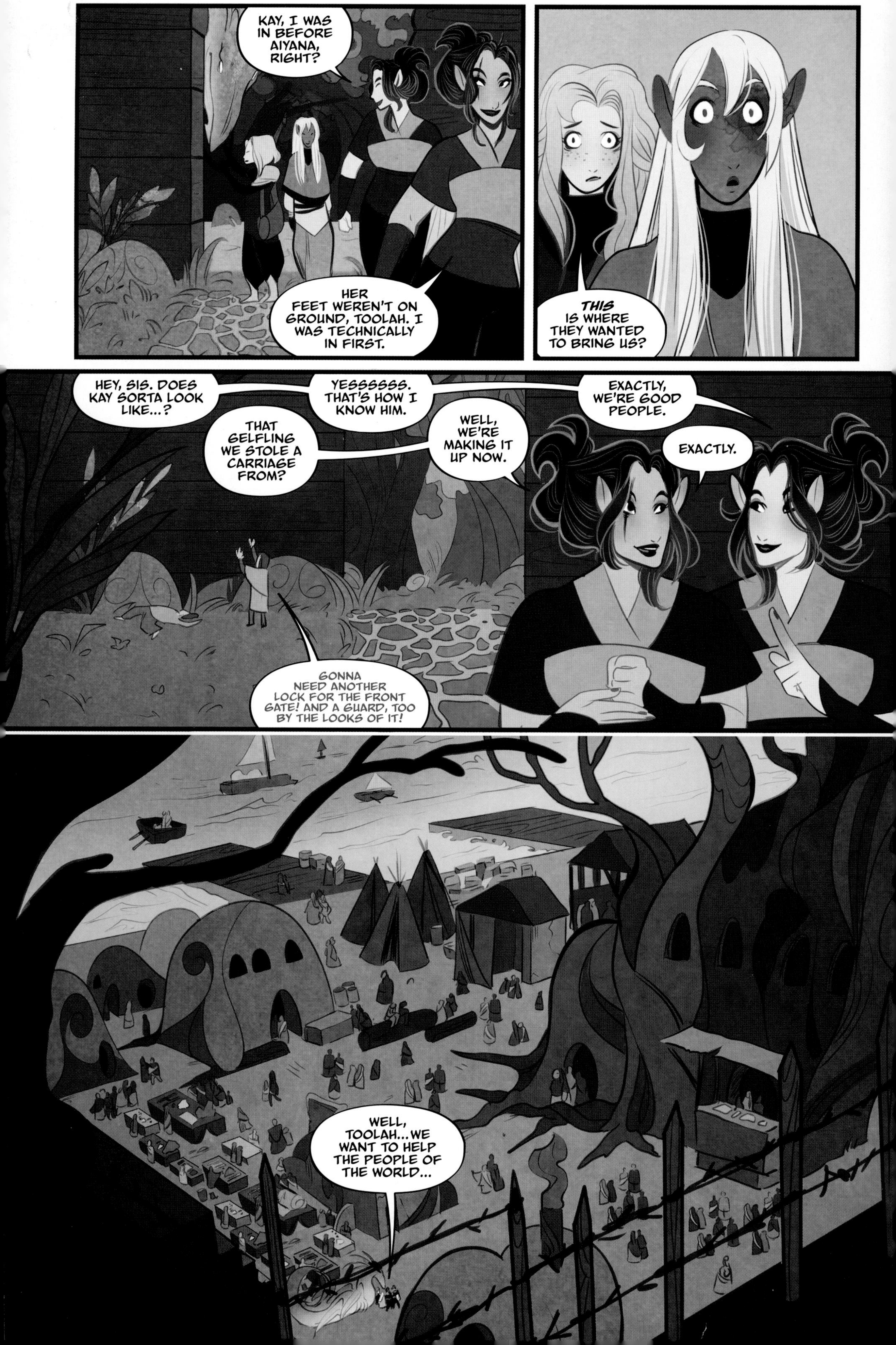
KAY, I WAS IN BEFORE AIYANA, RIGHT?
HER FEET WEREN'T ON GROUND, TOOLAH. I WAS TECHNICALLY IN FIRST.
THIS IS WHERE THEY WANTED TO BRING US?
HEY, SIS. DOES KAY SORTA LOOK LIKE...?
THAT GELFLING WE STOLE A CARRIAGE FROM?
YESSSSSS. THAT'S HOW I KNOW HIM.
WELL, WE'RE MAKING IT UP NOW.
EXACTLY, WE'RE GOOD PEOPLE.
EXACTLY.
GONNA NEED ANOTHER LOCK FOR THE FRONT GATE! AND A GUARD, TOO BY THE LOOKS OF IT!
WELL, TOOLAH...WE WANT TO HELP THE PEOPLE OF THE WORLD...

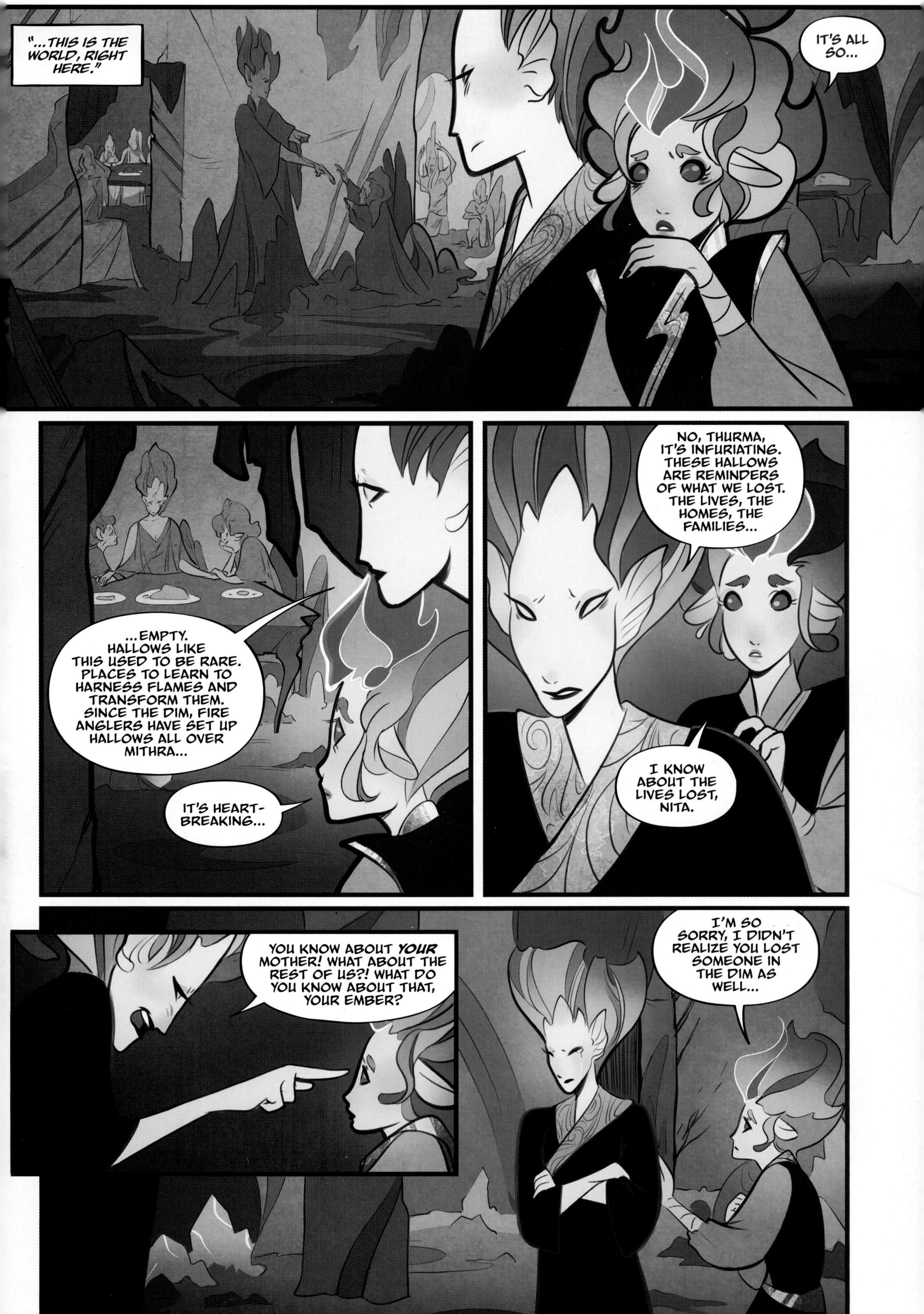
"...THIS IS THE WORLD, RIGHT HERE."
IT'S ALL SO...
...EMPTY. HALLOWS LIKE THIS USED TO BE RARE. PLACES TO LEARN TO HARNESS FLAMES AND TRANSFORM THEM. SINCE THE DIM, FIRE ANGLERS HAVE SET UP HALLOWS ALL OVER MITHRA...
IT'S HEART-BREAKING...
NO, THURMA, IT'S INFURIATING. THESE HALLOWS ARE REMINDERS OF WHAT WE LOST. THE LIVES, THE HOMES, THE FAMILIES...
I KNOW ABOUT THE LIVES LOST, NITA.
YOU KNOW ABOUT *YOUR* MOTHER! WHAT ABOUT THE REST OF US?! WHAT DO YOU KNOW ABOUT THAT, YOUR EMBER?
I'M SO SORRY, I DIDN'T REALIZE YOU LOST SOMEONE IN THE DIM AS WELL...

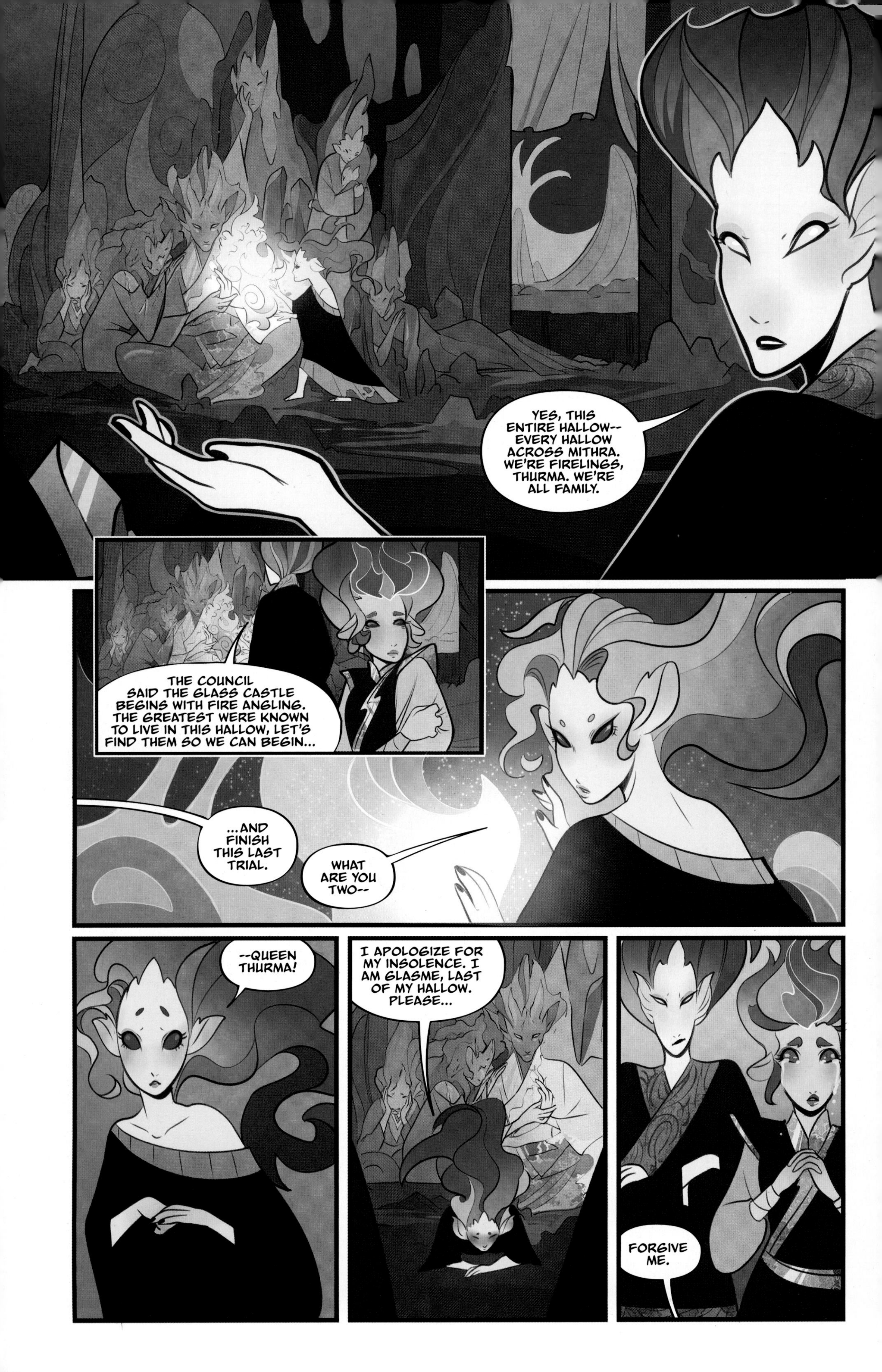
YES, THIS ENTIRE HALLOW-- EVERY HALLOW ACROSS MITHRA. WE'RE FIRELINGS, THURMA. WE'RE ALL FAMILY.
THE COUNCIL SAID THE GLASS CASTLE BEGINS WITH FIRE ANGLING. THE GREATEST WERE KNOWN TO LIVE IN THIS HALLOW, LET'S FIND THEM SO WE CAN BEGIN...
...AND FINISH THIS LAST TRIAL.
WHAT ARE YOU TWO--
--QUEEN THURMA!
I APOLOGIZE FOR MY INSOLENCE. I AM GLASME, LAST OF MY HALLOW. PLEASE...
FORGIVE ME.

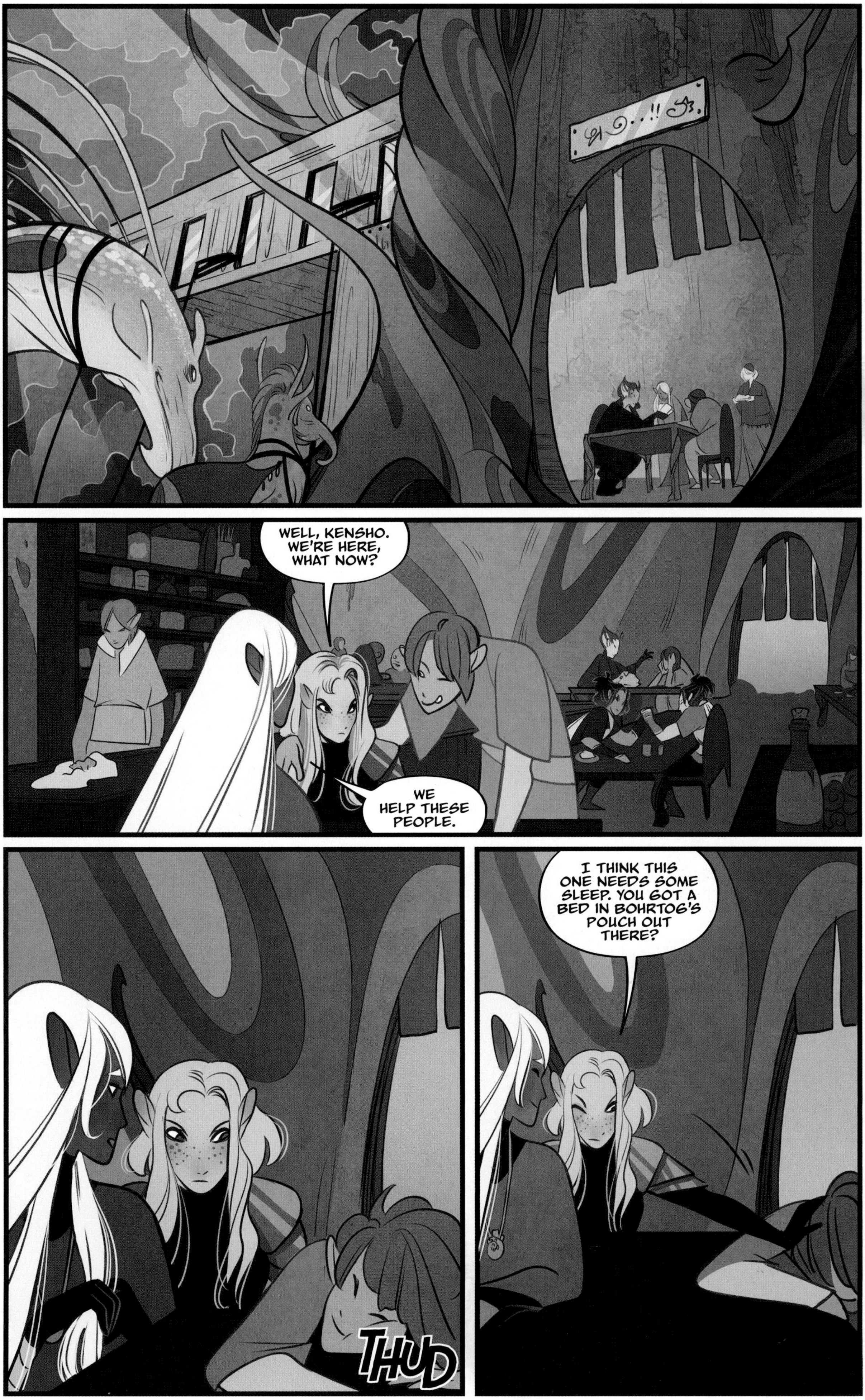
WELL, KENSHO. WE'RE HERE, WHAT NOW?
WE HELP THESE PEOPLE.
THUD
I THINK THIS ONE NEEDS SOME SLEEP. YOU GOT A BED IN BOHRTOG'S POUCH OUT THERE?

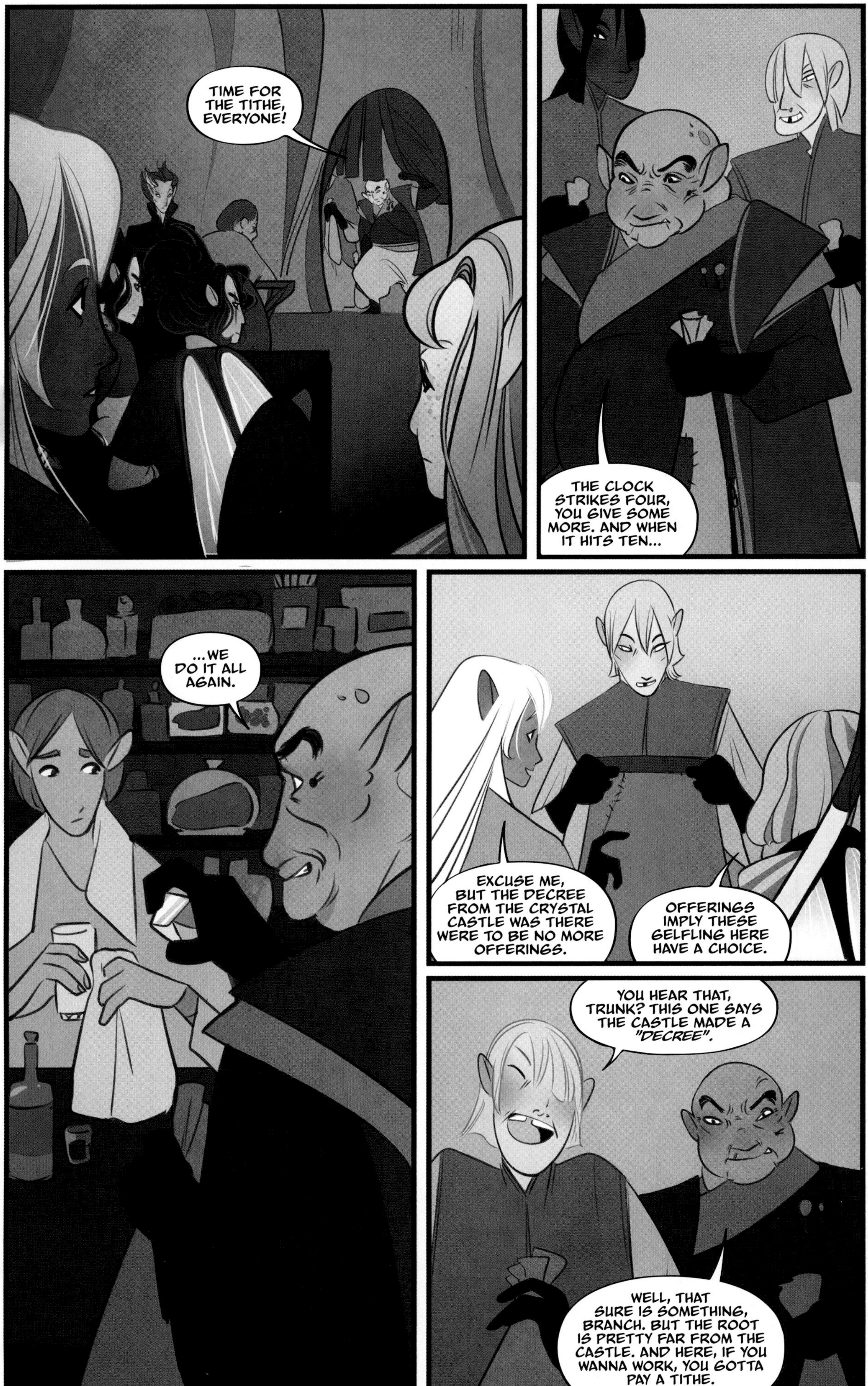
TIME FOR THE TITHE, EVERYONE!
THE CLOCK STRIKES FOUR, YOU GIVE SOME MORE. AND WHEN IT HITS TEN...
...WE DO IT ALL AGAIN.
EXCUSE ME, BUT THE DECREE FROM THE CRYSTAL CASTLE WAS THERE WERE TO BE NO MORE OFFERINGS.
OFFERINGS IMPLY THESE GELFLING HERE HAVE A CHOICE.
YOU HEAR THAT, TRUNK? THIS ONE SAYS THE CASTLE MADE A "DECREE".
WELL, THAT SURE IS SOMETHING, BRANCH. BUT THE ROOT IS PRETTY FAR FROM THE CASTLE. AND HERE, IF YOU WANNA WORK, YOU GOTTA PAY A TITHE.

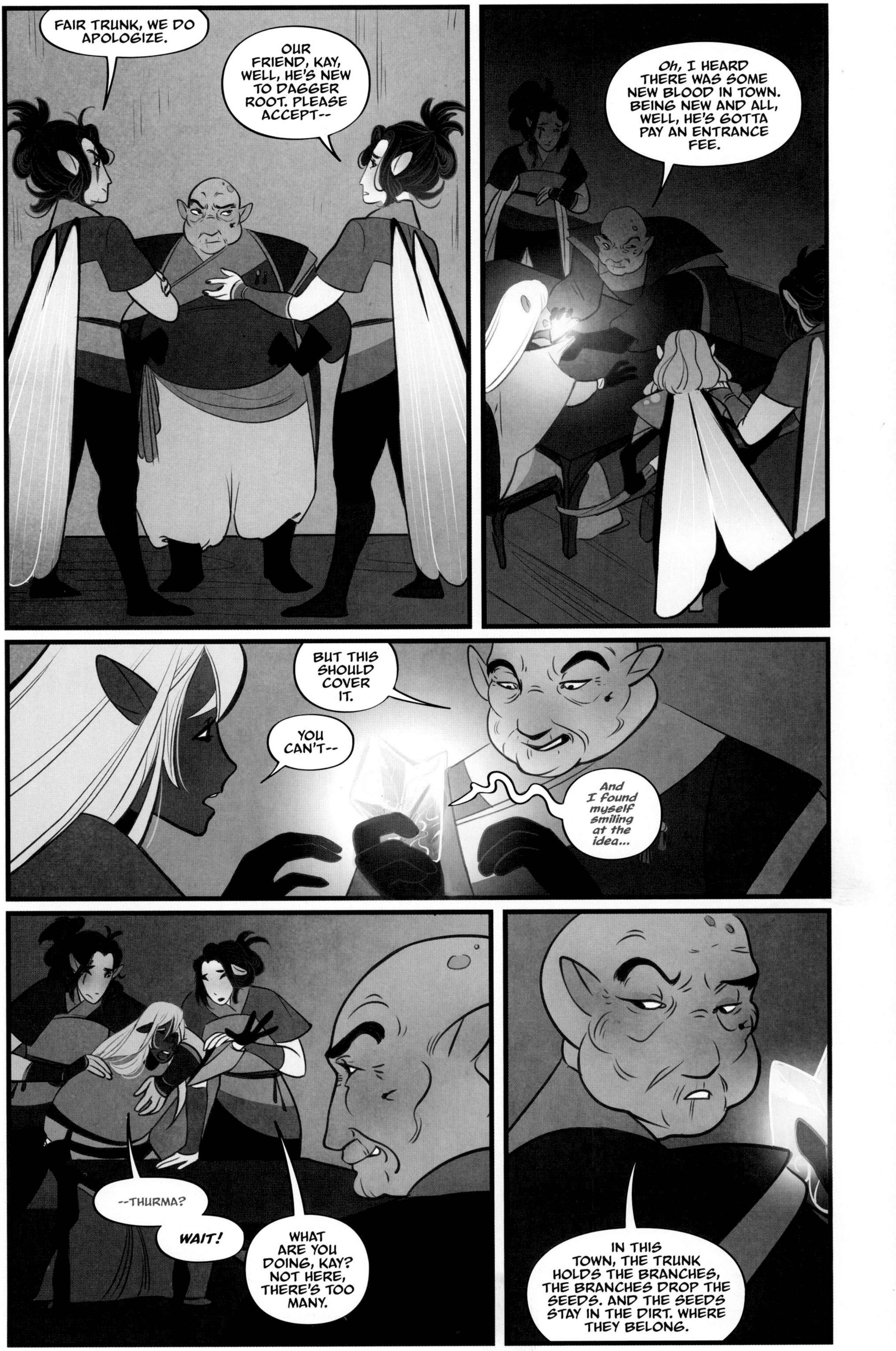
FAIR TRUNK, WE DO APOLOGIZE.
OUR FRIEND, KAY, WELL, HE'S NEW TO DAGGER ROOT. PLEASE ACCEPT--
Oh, I HEARD THERE WAS SOME NEW BLOOD IN TOWN. BEING NEW AND ALL, WELL, HE'S GOTTA PAY AN ENTRANCE FEE.
BUT THIS SHOULD COVER IT.
YOU CAN'T--
And I found myself smiling at the idea...
--THURMA?
WAIT!
WHAT ARE YOU DOING, KAY? NOT HERE, THERE'S TOO MANY.
IN THIS TOWN, THE TRUNK HOLDS THE BRANCHES, THE BRANCHES DROP THE SEEDS. AND THE SEEDS STAY IN THE DIRT. WHERE THEY BELONG.

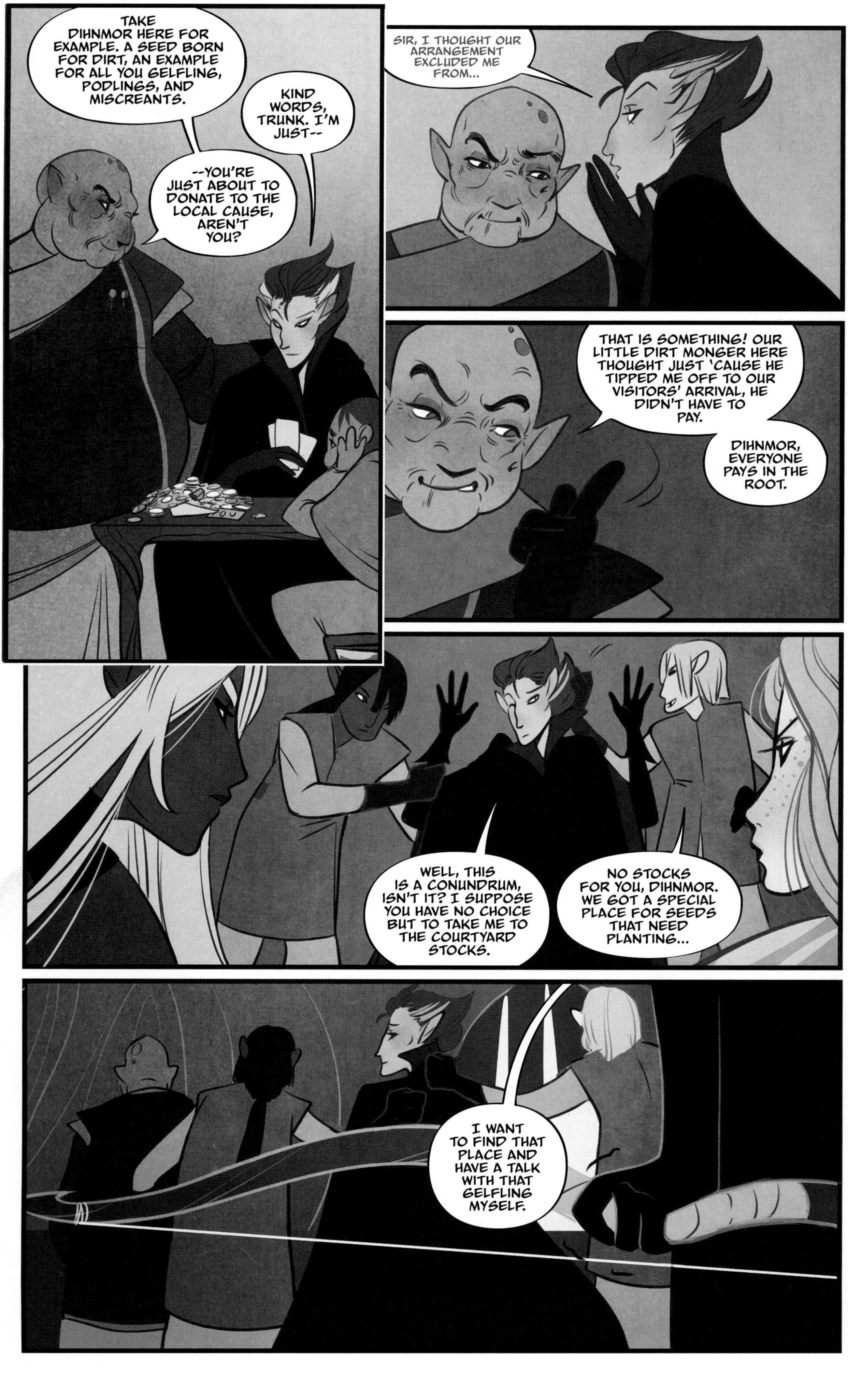
TAKE DIHNMOR HERE FOR EXAMPLE. A SEED BORN FOR DIRT, AN EXAMPLE FOR ALL YOU GELFLING, PODLINGS, AND MISCREANTS.
KIND WORDS, TRUNK. I'M JUST--
--YOU'RE JUST ABOUT TO DONATE TO THE LOCAL CAUSE, AREN'T YOU?
SIR, I THOUGHT OUR ARRANGEMENT EXCLUDED ME FROM...
THAT IS SOMETHING! OUR LITTLE DIRT MONGER HERE THOUGHT JUST 'CAUSE HE TIPPED ME OFF TO OUR VISITORS' ARRIVAL, HE DIDN'T HAVE TO PAY.
DIHNMOR, EVERYONE PAYS IN THE ROOT.
WELL, THIS IS A CONUNDRUM, ISN'T IT? I SUPPOSE YOU HAVE NO CHOICE BUT TO TAKE ME TO THE COURTYARD STOCKS.
NO STOCKS FOR YOU, DIHNMOR. WE GOT A SPECIAL PLACE FOR SEEDS THAT NEED PLANTING...
I WANT TO FIND THAT PLACE AND HAVE A TALK WITH THAT GELFLING MYSELF.

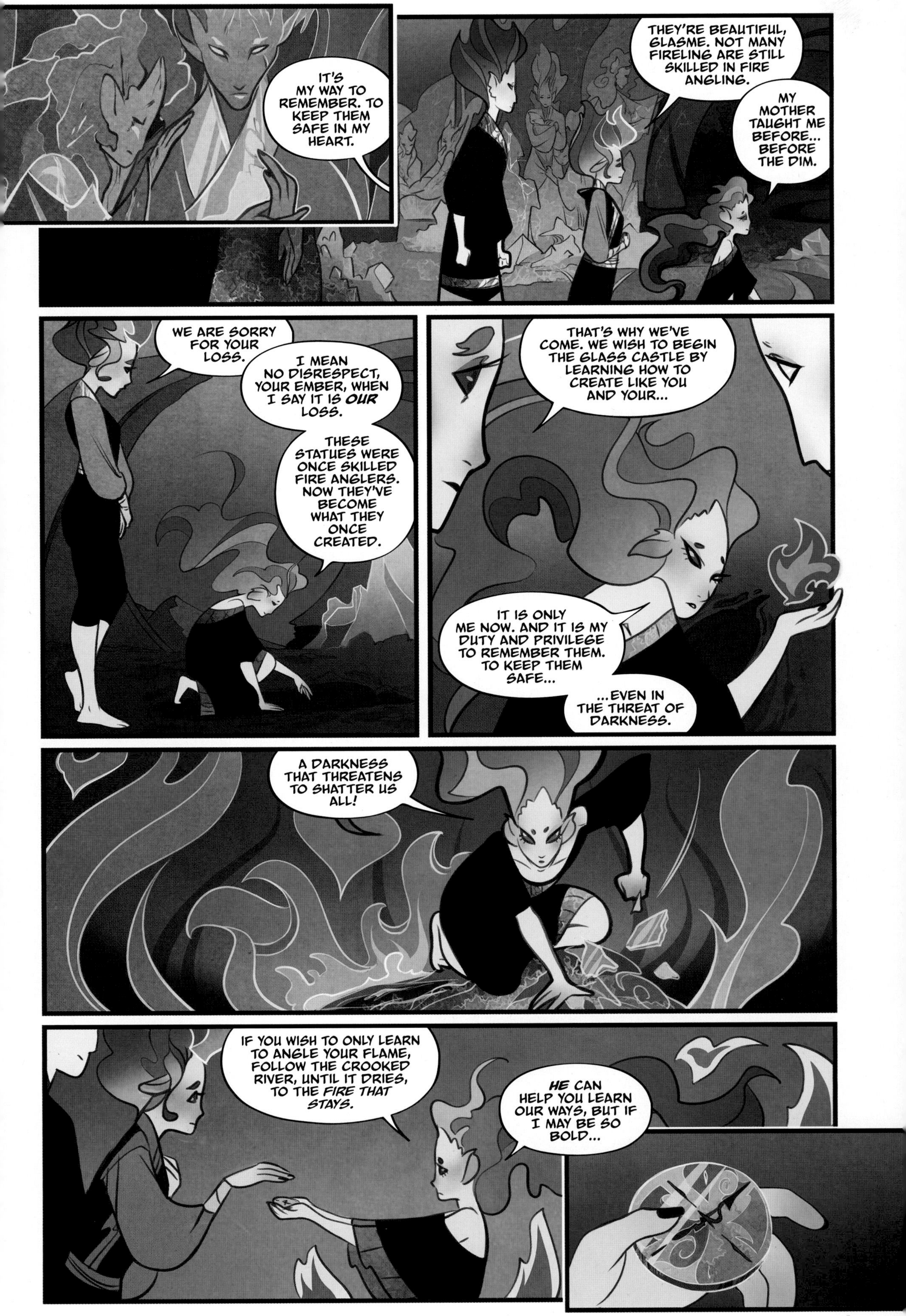
IT'S MY WAY TO REMEMBER. TO KEEP THEM SAFE IN MY HEART.
THEY'RE BEAUTIFUL, GLASME. NOT MANY FIRELING ARE STILL SKILLED IN FIRE ANGLING.
MY MOTHER TAUGHT ME BEFORE... BEFORE THE DIM.
WE ARE SORRY FOR YOUR LOSS.
I MEAN NO DISRESPECT, YOUR EMBER, WHEN I SAY IT IS *OUR* LOSS.
THESE STATUES WERE ONCE SKILLED FIRE ANGLERS. NOW THEY'VE BECOME WHAT THEY ONCE CREATED.
THAT'S WHY WE'VE COME. WE WISH TO BEGIN THE GLASS CASTLE BY LEARNING HOW TO CREATE LIKE YOU AND YOUR...
IT IS ONLY ME NOW. AND IT IS MY DUTY AND PRIVILEGE TO REMEMBER THEM. TO KEEP THEM SAFE...
...EVEN IN THE THREAT OF DARKNESS.
A DARKNESS THAT THREATENS TO SHATTER US ALL!
IF YOU WISH TO ONLY LEARN TO ANGLE YOUR FLAME, FOLLOW THE CROOKED RIVER, UNTIL IT DRIES, TO THE *FIRE THAT STAYS.*
HE CAN HELP YOU LEARN OUR WAYS, BUT IF I MAY BE SO BOLD...

"I NEED YOUR HELP...
BOTH OF YOU."

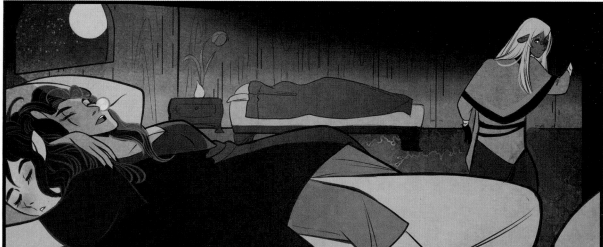

GAH!

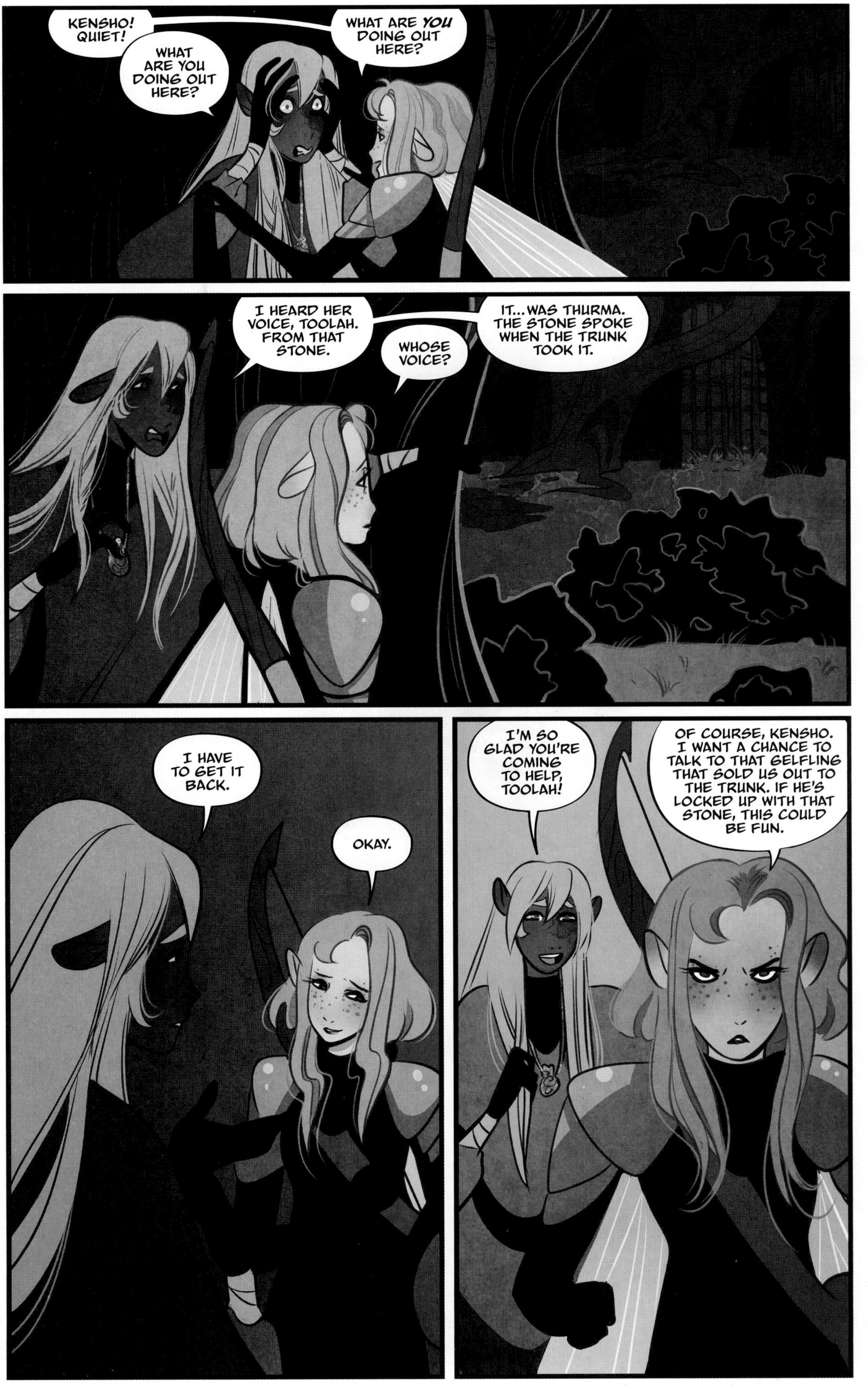
KENSHO! QUIET!
WHAT ARE YOU DOING OUT HERE?
WHAT ARE *YOU* DOING OUT HERE?
I HEARD HER VOICE, TOOLAH. FROM THAT STONE.
WHOSE VOICE?
IT...WAS THURMA. THE STONE SPOKE WHEN THE TRUNK TOOK IT.
I HAVE TO GET IT BACK.
OKAY.
I'M SO GLAD YOU'RE COMING TO HELP, TOOLAH!
OF COURSE, KENSHO. I WANT A CHANCE TO TALK TO THAT GELFLING THAT SOLD US OUT TO THE TRUNK. IF HE'S LOCKED UP WITH THAT STONE, THIS COULD BE FUN.

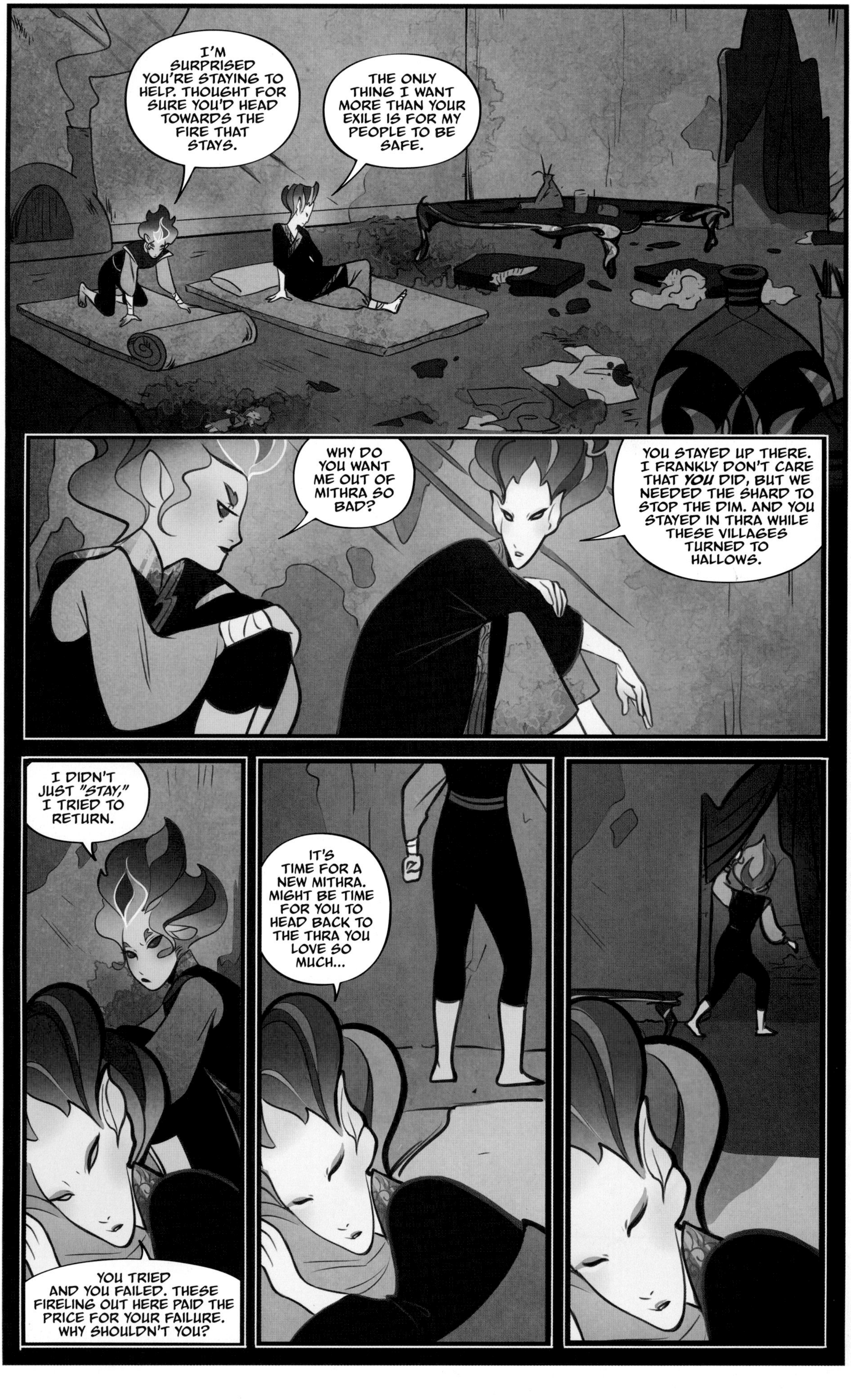
I'M SURPRISED YOU'RE STAYING TO HELP. THOUGHT FOR SURE YOU'D HEAD TOWARDS THE FIRE THAT STAYS.
THE ONLY THING I WANT MORE THAN YOUR EXILE IS FOR MY PEOPLE TO BE SAFE.
WHY DO YOU WANT ME OUT OF MITHRA SO BAD?
YOU STAYED UP THERE. I FRANKLY DON'T CARE THAT *YOU* DID, BUT WE NEEDED THE SHARD TO STOP THE DIM. AND YOU STAYED IN THRA WHILE THESE VILLAGES TURNED TO HALLOWS.
I DIDN'T JUST "STAY," I TRIED TO RETURN.
YOU TRIED AND YOU FAILED. THESE FIRELING OUT HERE PAID THE PRICE FOR YOUR FAILURE. WHY SHOULDN'T YOU?
IT'S TIME FOR A NEW MITHRA. MIGHT BE TIME FOR YOU TO HEAD BACK TO THE THRA YOU LOVE SO MUCH...

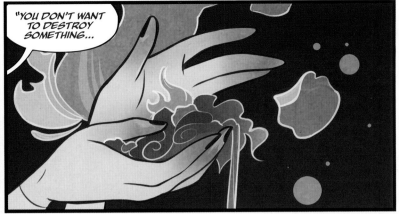

"YOU DON'T WANT TO DESTROY SOMETHING...

"YOU WANT TO CREATE."

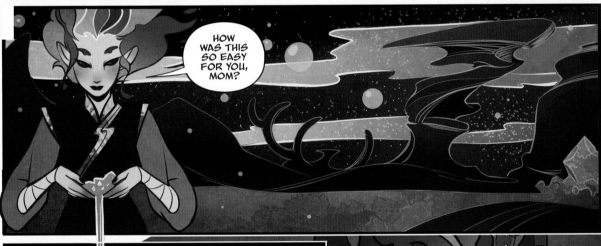

HOW WAS THIS SO EASY FOR YOU, MOM?

UGGHHARRGGHTT

WHAT WAS THAT?!

MUST BE THE DARKNESS THE CHILD CHIEF SPOKE OF.

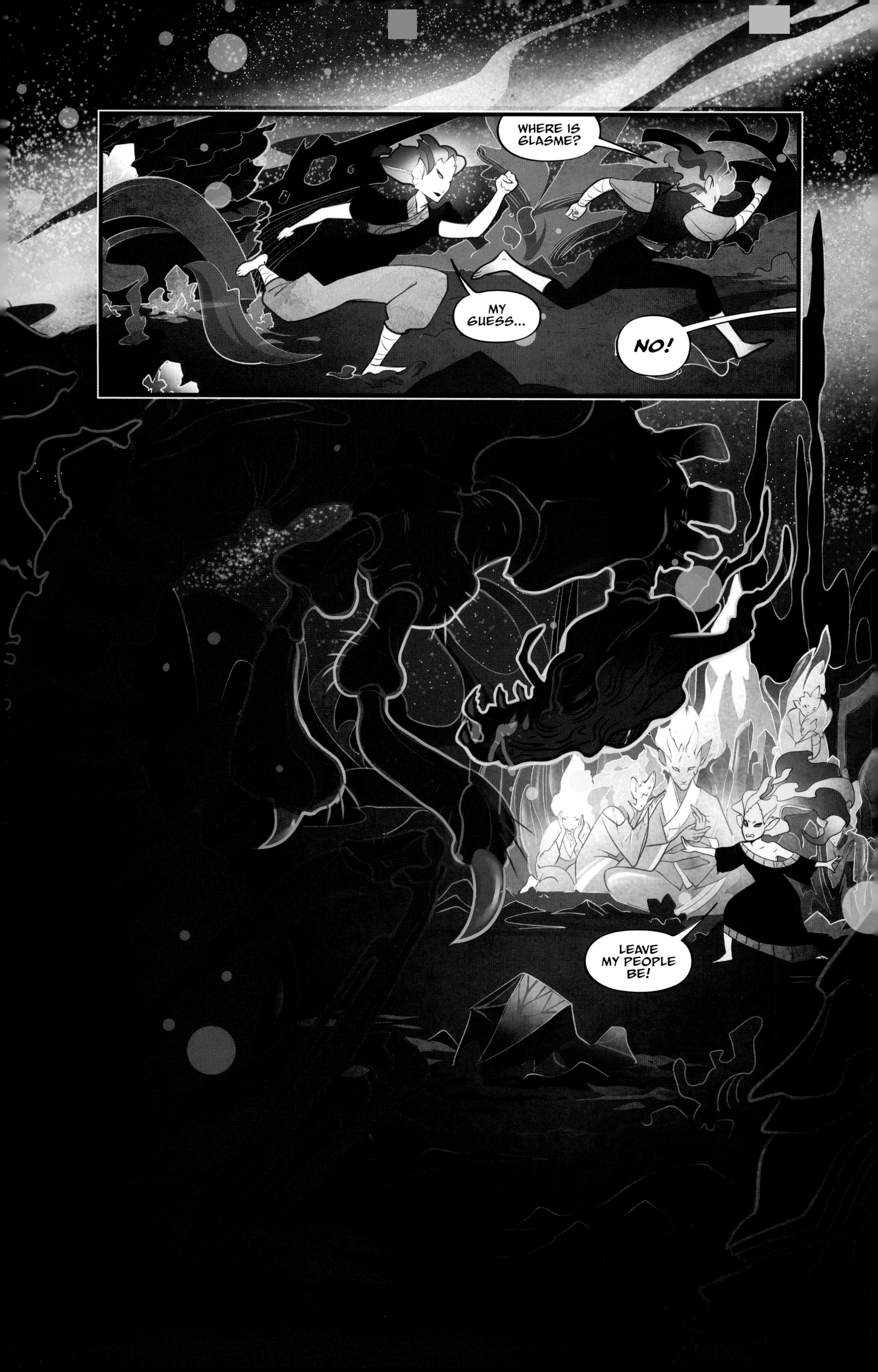
WHERE IS GLASME?
MY GUESS...
NO!
LEAVE MY PEOPLE BE!

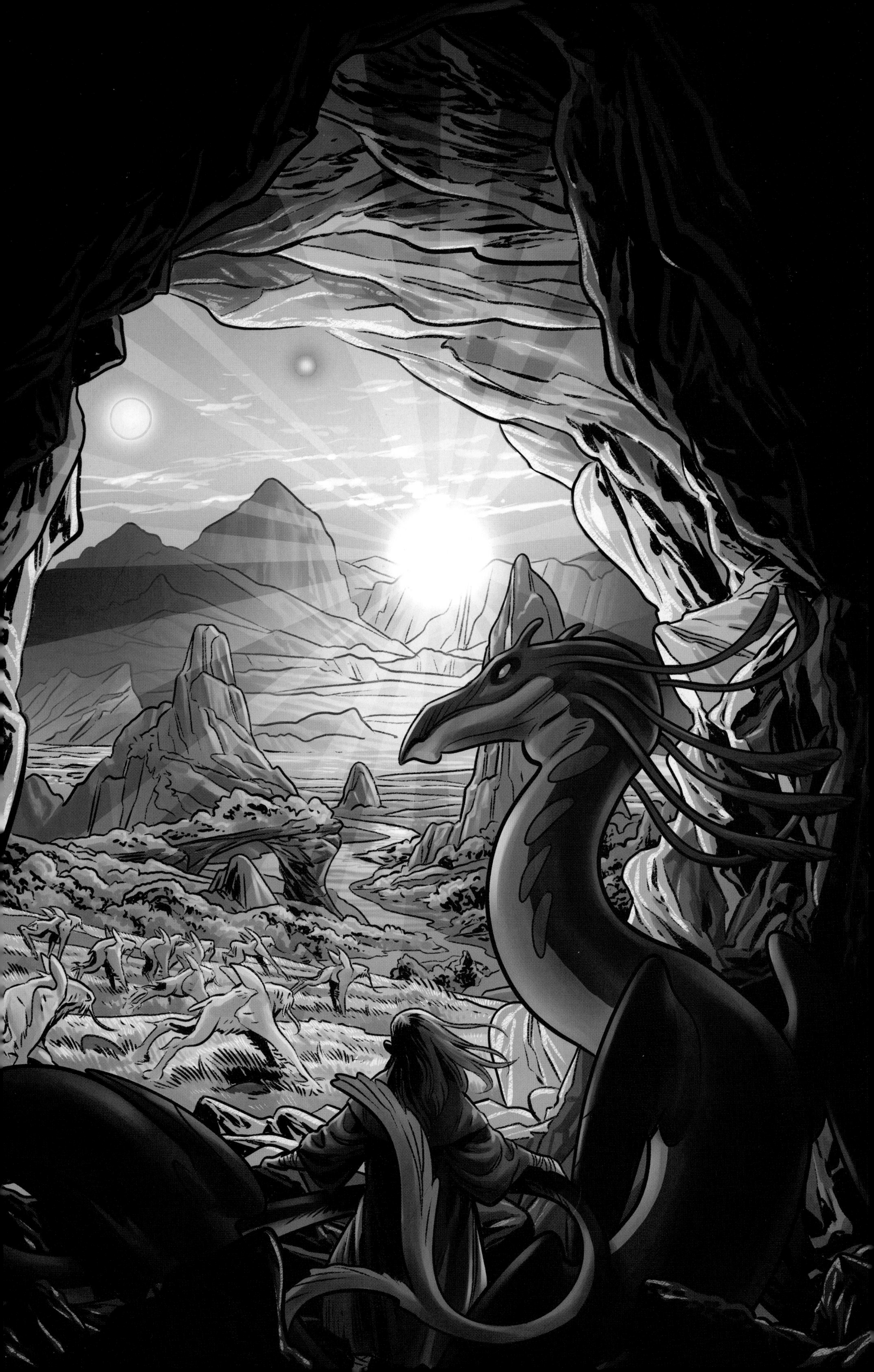

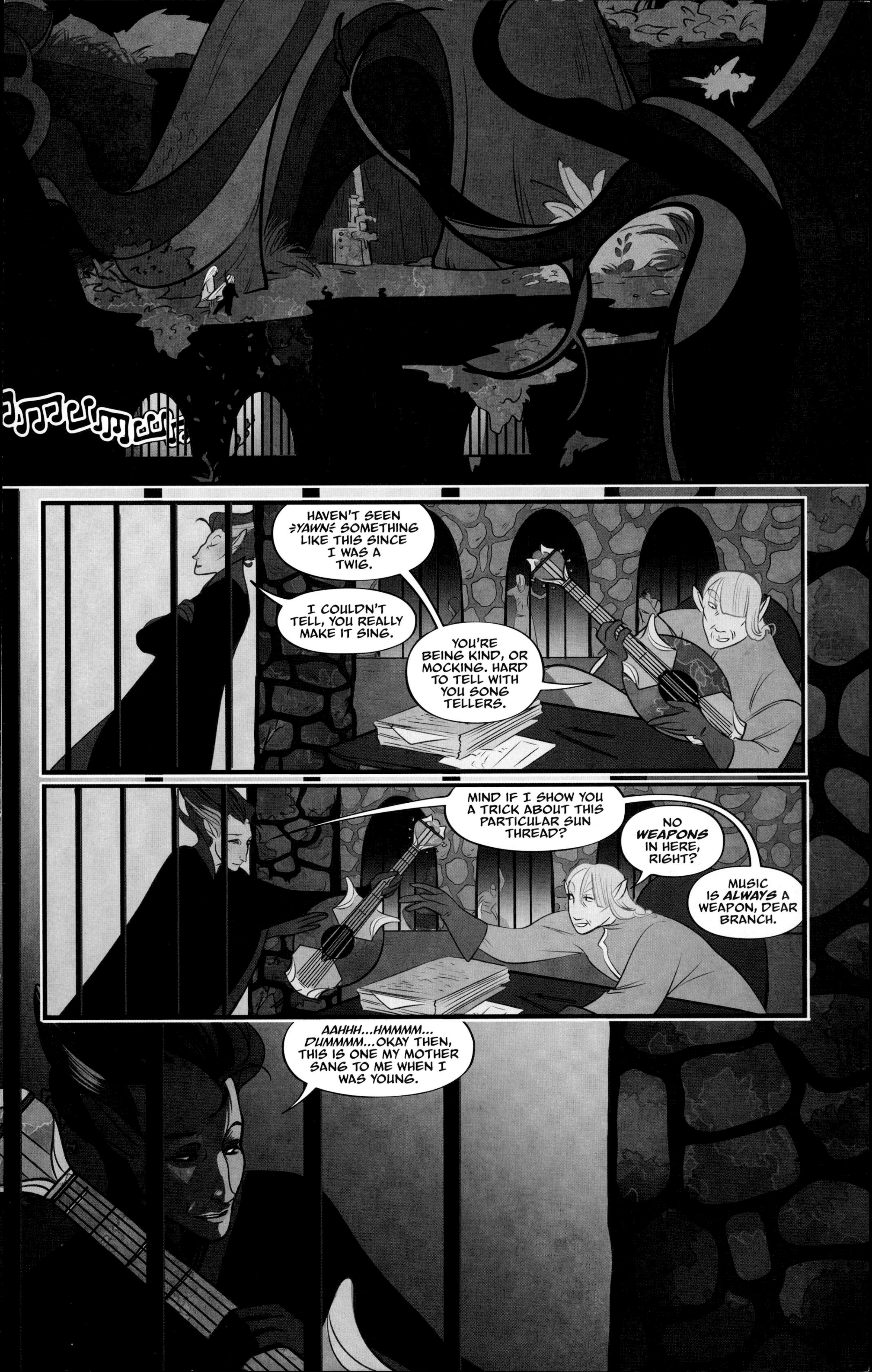
HAVEN'T SEEN *YAWN* SOMETHING LIKE THIS SINCE I WAS A TWIG.
I COULDN'T TELL, YOU REALLY MAKE IT SING.
YOU'RE BEING KIND, OR MOCKING. HARD TO TELL WITH YOU SONG TELLERS.
MIND IF I SHOW YOU A TRICK ABOUT THIS PARTICULAR SUN THREAD?
NO WEAPONS IN HERE, RIGHT?
MUSIC IS ALWAYS A WEAPON, DEAR BRANCH.
AAHHH...HMMMM... DUMMMM...OKAY THEN, THIS IS ONE MY MOTHER SANG TO ME WHEN I WAS YOUNG.

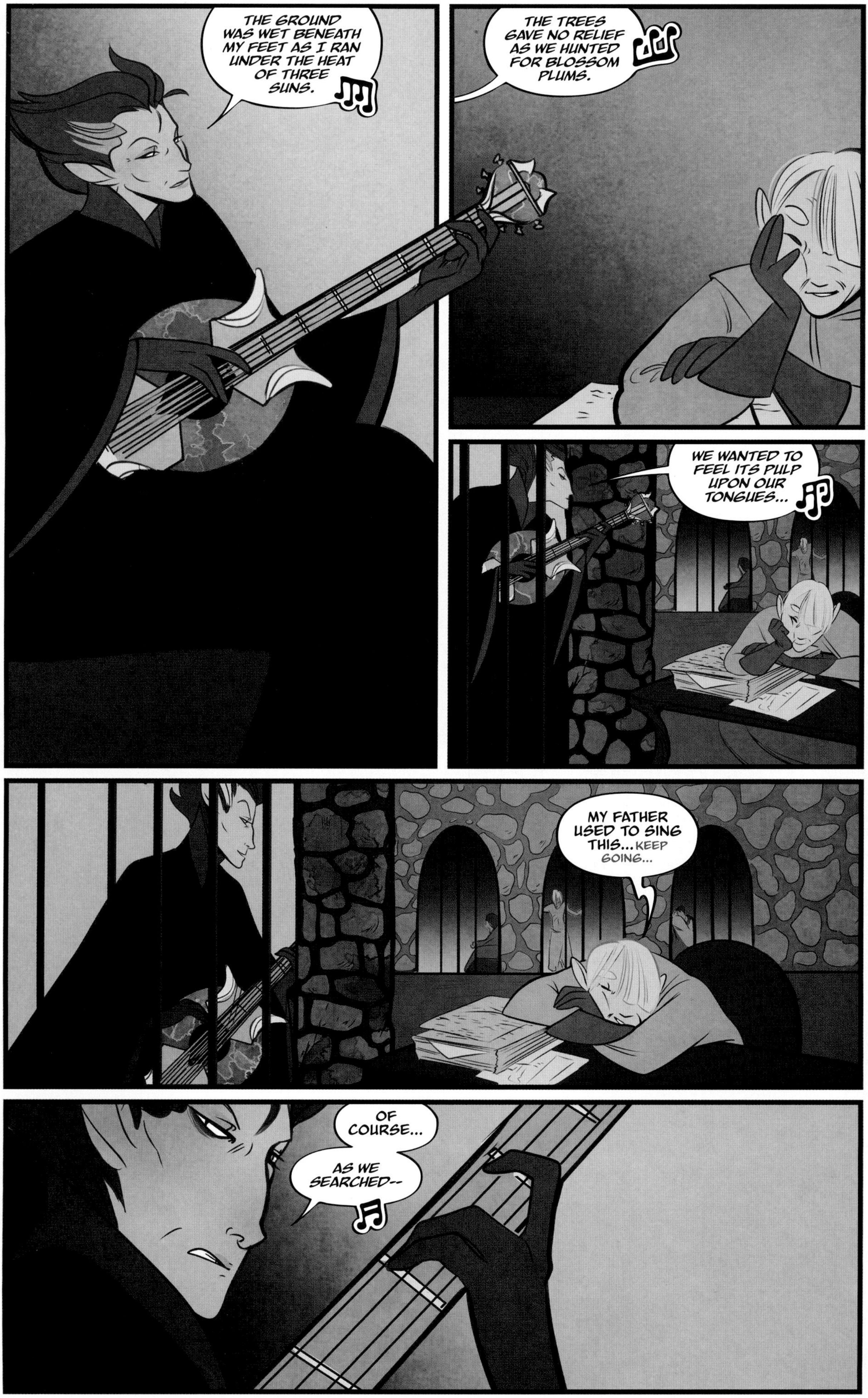
THE GROUND WAS WET BENEATH MY FEET AS I RAN UNDER THE HEAT OF THREE SUNS.
THE TREES GAVE NO RELIEF AS WE HUNTED FOR BLOSSOM PLUMS.
WE WANTED TO FEEL ITS PULP UPON OUR TONGUES...
MY FATHER USED TO SING THIS... KEEP GOING...
OF COURSE...
AS WE SEARCHED--

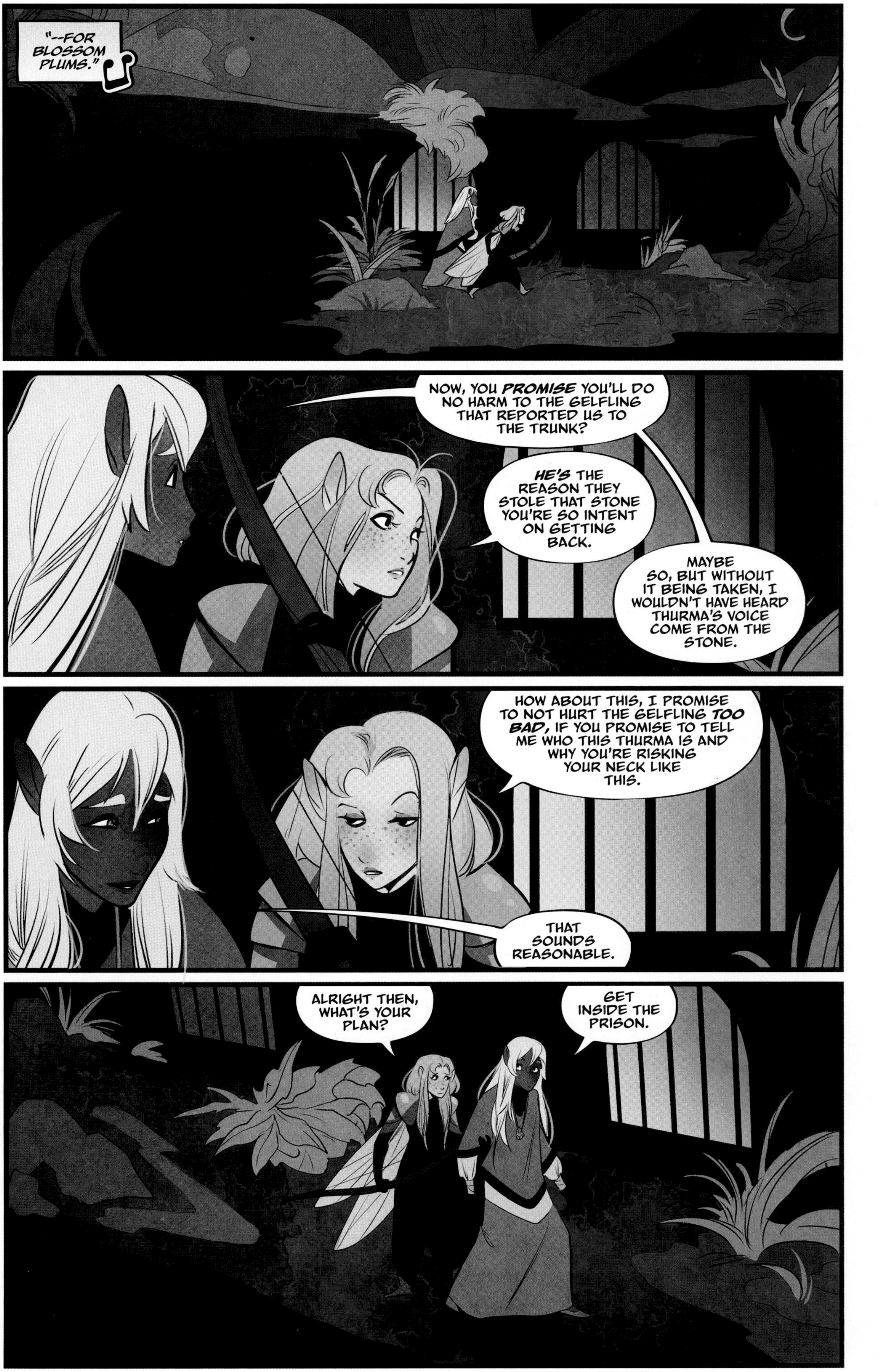
"--FOR BLOSSOM PLUMS."
NOW, YOU PROMISE YOU'LL DO NO HARM TO THE GELFLING THAT REPORTED US TO THE TRUNK?
HE'S THE REASON THEY STOLE THAT STONE YOU'RE SO INTENT ON GETTING BACK.
MAYBE SO, BUT WITHOUT IT BEING TAKEN, I WOULDN'T HAVE HEARD THURMA'S VOICE COME FROM THE STONE.
HOW ABOUT THIS, I PROMISE TO NOT HURT THE GELFLING TOO BAD, IF YOU PROMISE TO TELL ME WHO THIS THURMA IS AND WHY YOU'RE RISKING YOUR NECK LIKE THIS.
THAT SOUNDS REASONABLE.
ALRIGHT THEN, WHAT'S YOUR PLAN?
GET INSIDE THE PRISON.

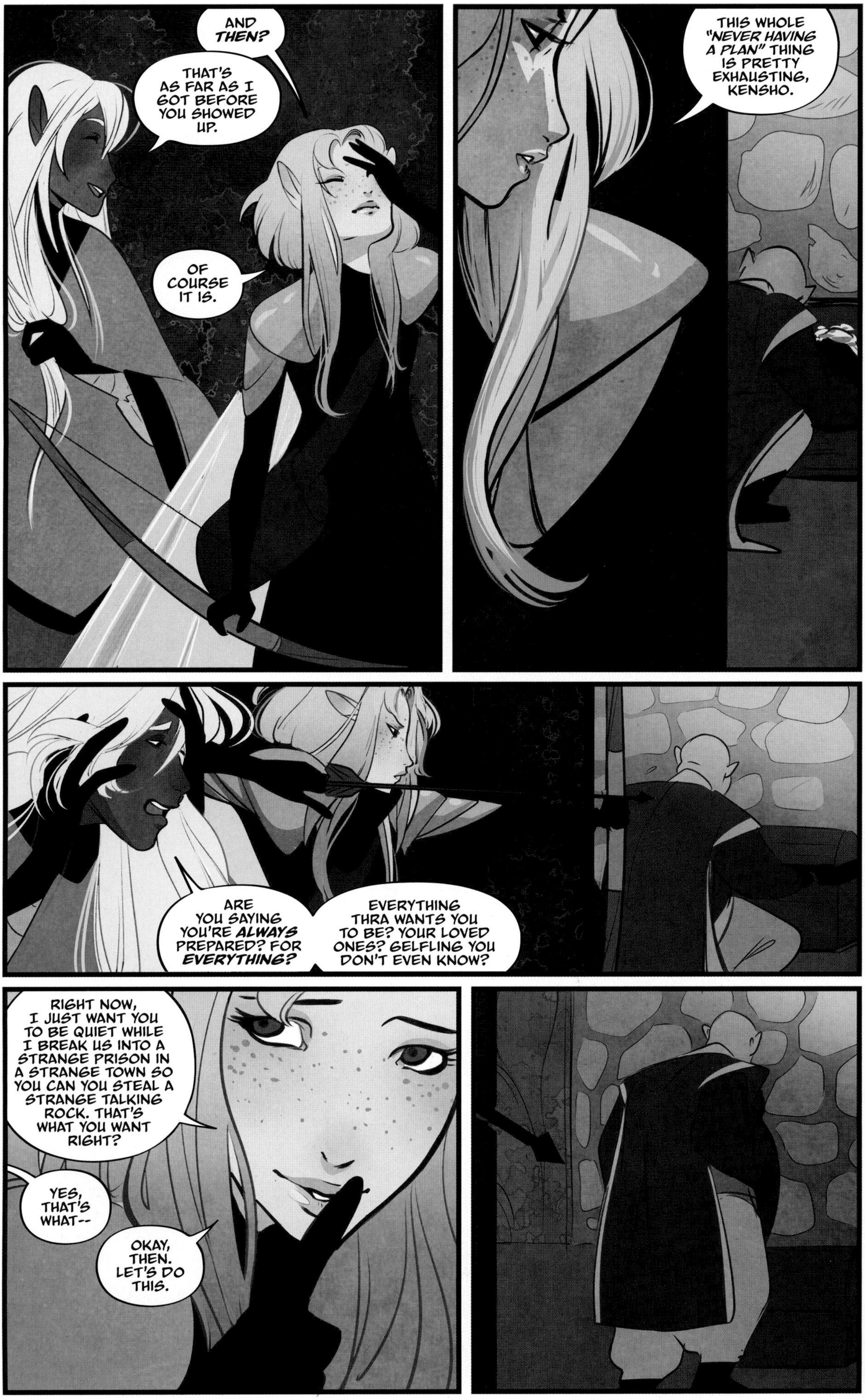
AND *THEN?*
THAT'S AS FAR AS I GOT BEFORE YOU SHOWED UP.
OF COURSE IT IS.
THIS WHOLE *"NEVER HAVING A PLAN"* THING IS PRETTY EXHAUSTING, KENSHO.
ARE YOU SAYING YOU'RE *ALWAYS* PREPARED? FOR *EVERYTHING?*
EVERYTHING THRA WANTS YOU TO BE? YOUR LOVED ONES? GELFLING YOU DON'T EVEN KNOW?
RIGHT NOW, I JUST WANT YOU TO BE QUIET WHILE I BREAK US INTO A STRANGE PRISON IN A STRANGE TOWN SO YOU CAN YOU STEAL A STRANGE TALKING ROCK. THAT'S WHAT YOU WANT RIGHT?
YES, THAT'S WHAT--
OKAY, THEN. LET'S DO THIS.

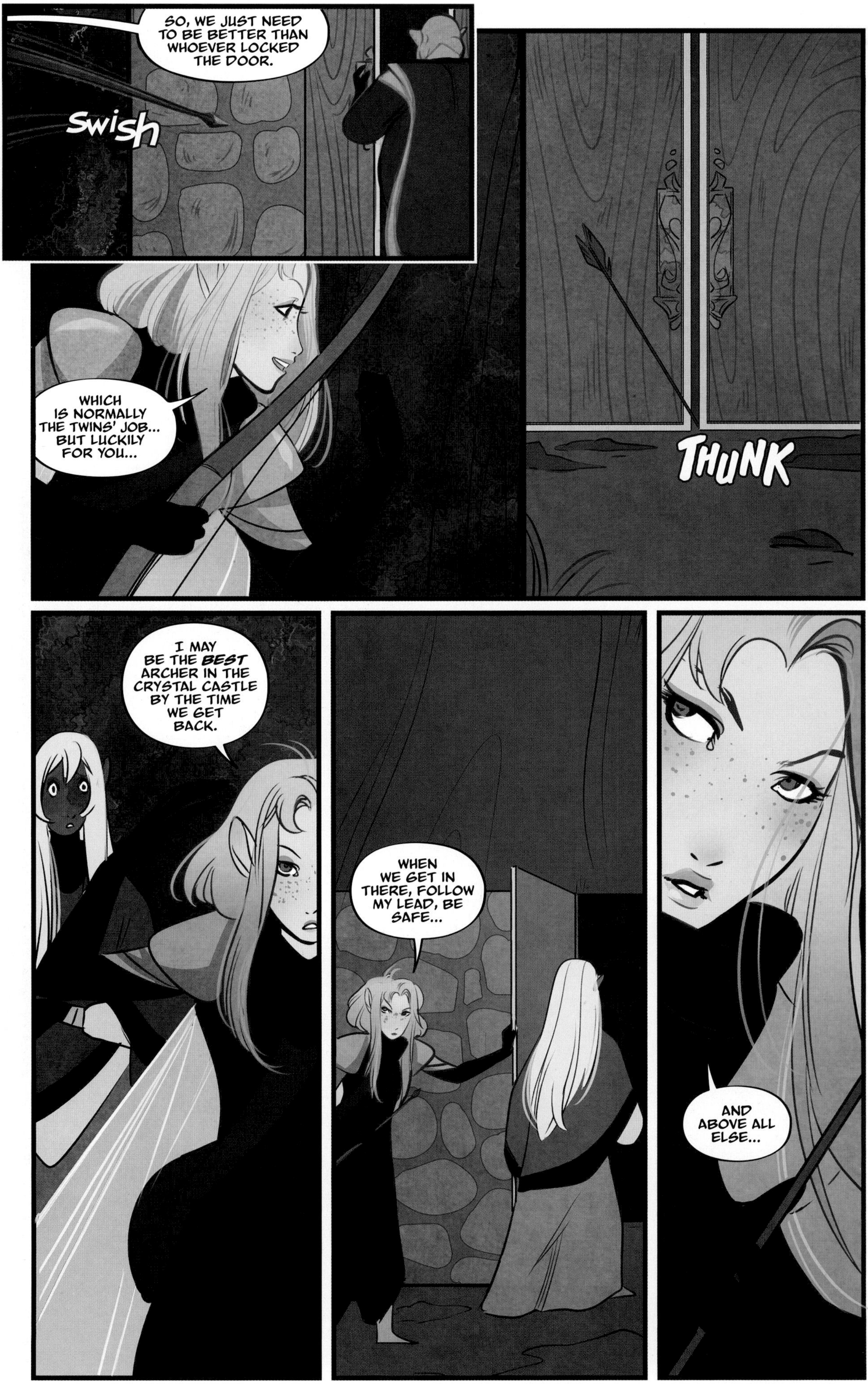
SO, WE JUST NEED TO BE BETTER THAN WHOEVER LOCKED THE DOOR.
SWISH
WHICH IS NORMALLY THE TWINS' JOB... BUT LUCKILY FOR YOU...
THUNK
I MAY BE THE BEST ARCHER IN THE CRYSTAL CASTLE BY THE TIME WE GET BACK.
WHEN WE GET IN THERE, FOLLOW MY LEAD, BE SAFE...
AND ABOVE ALL ELSE...

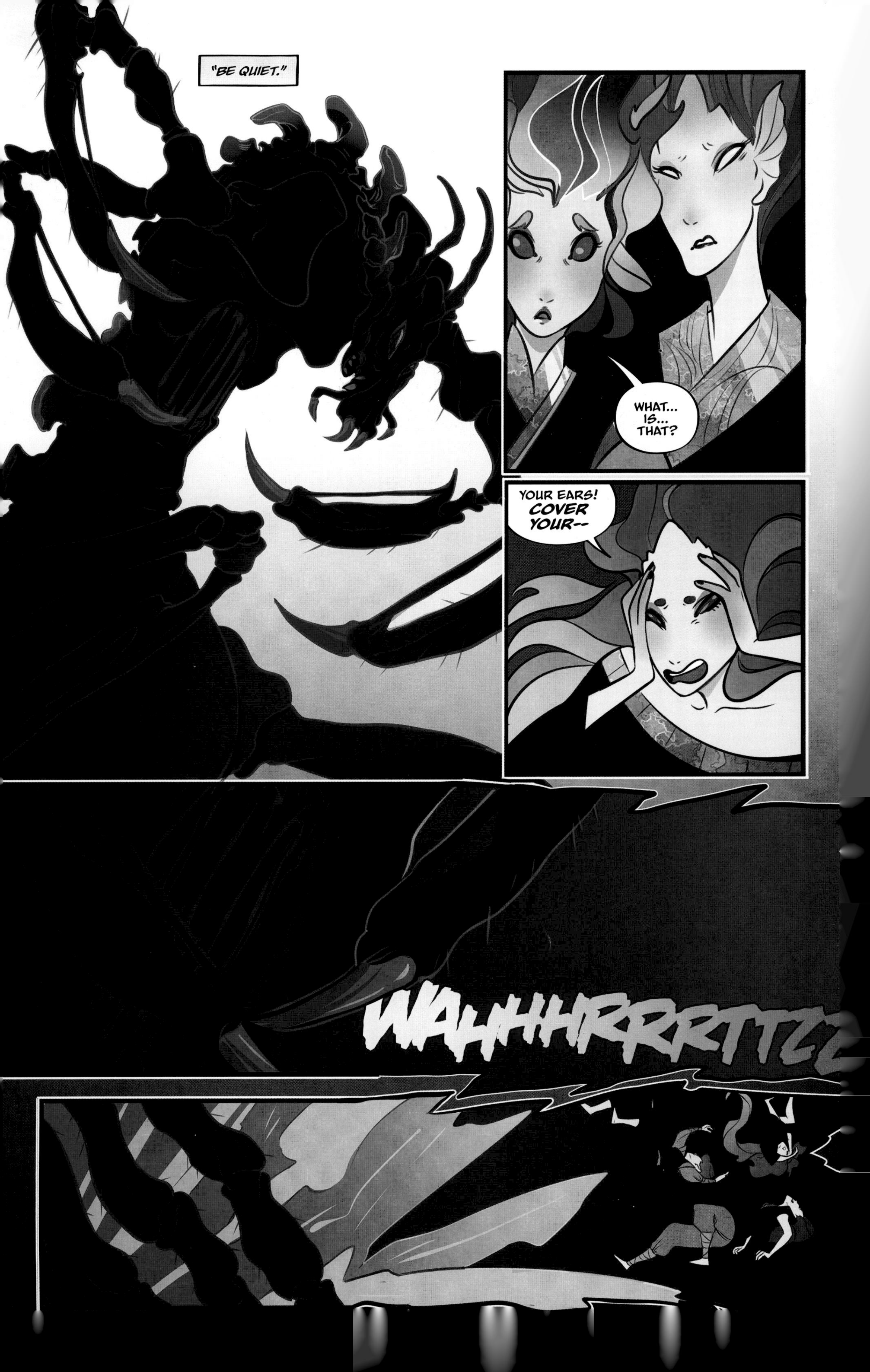
"BE QUIET."
WHAT... IS... THAT?
YOUR EARS! COVER YOUR--
WAHHHRRRTTLE

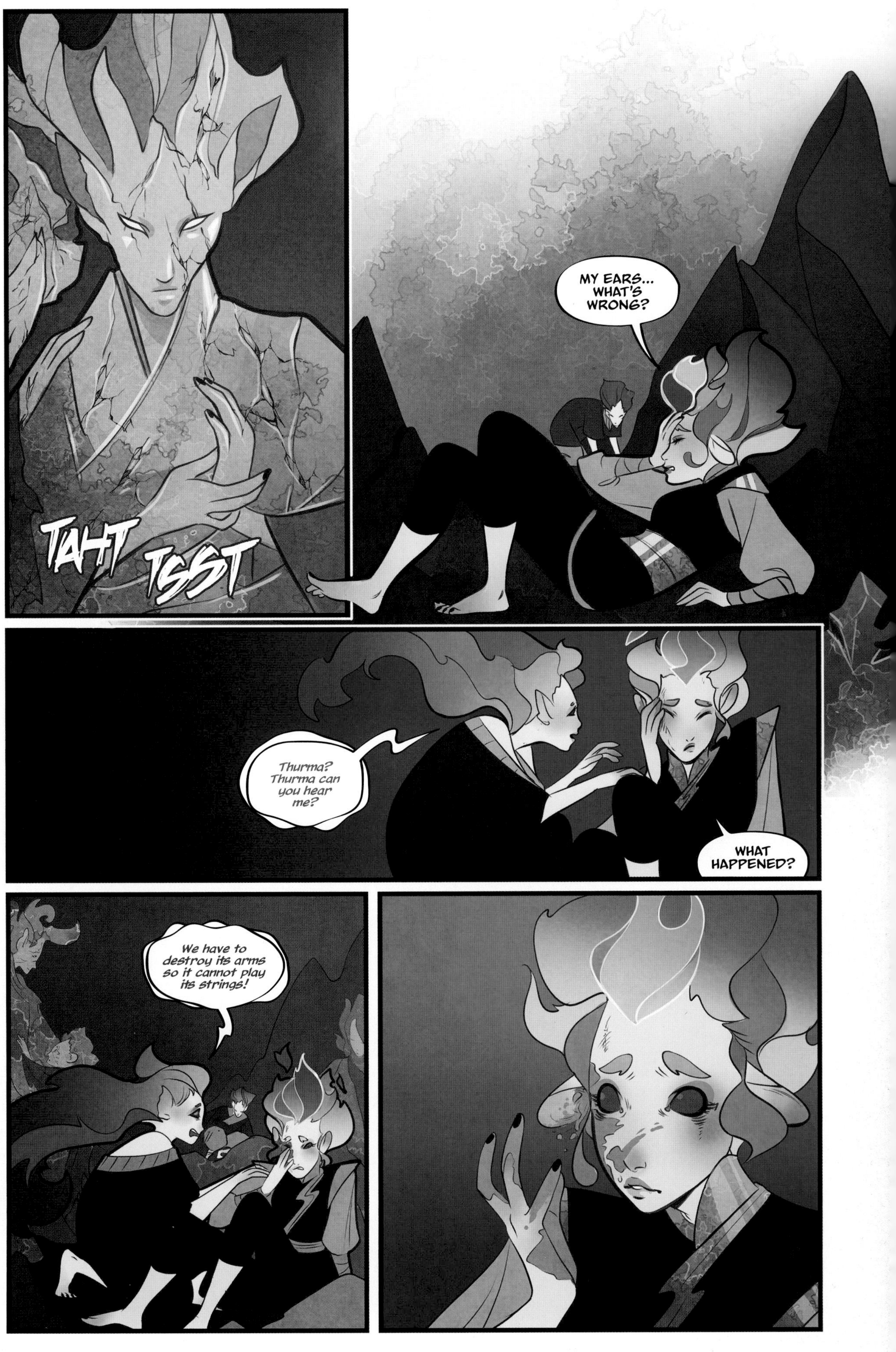
TAHT
TSST
MY EARS... WHAT'S WRONG?
Thurma? Thurma can you hear me?
WHAT HAPPENED?
We have to destroy its arms so it cannot play its strings!

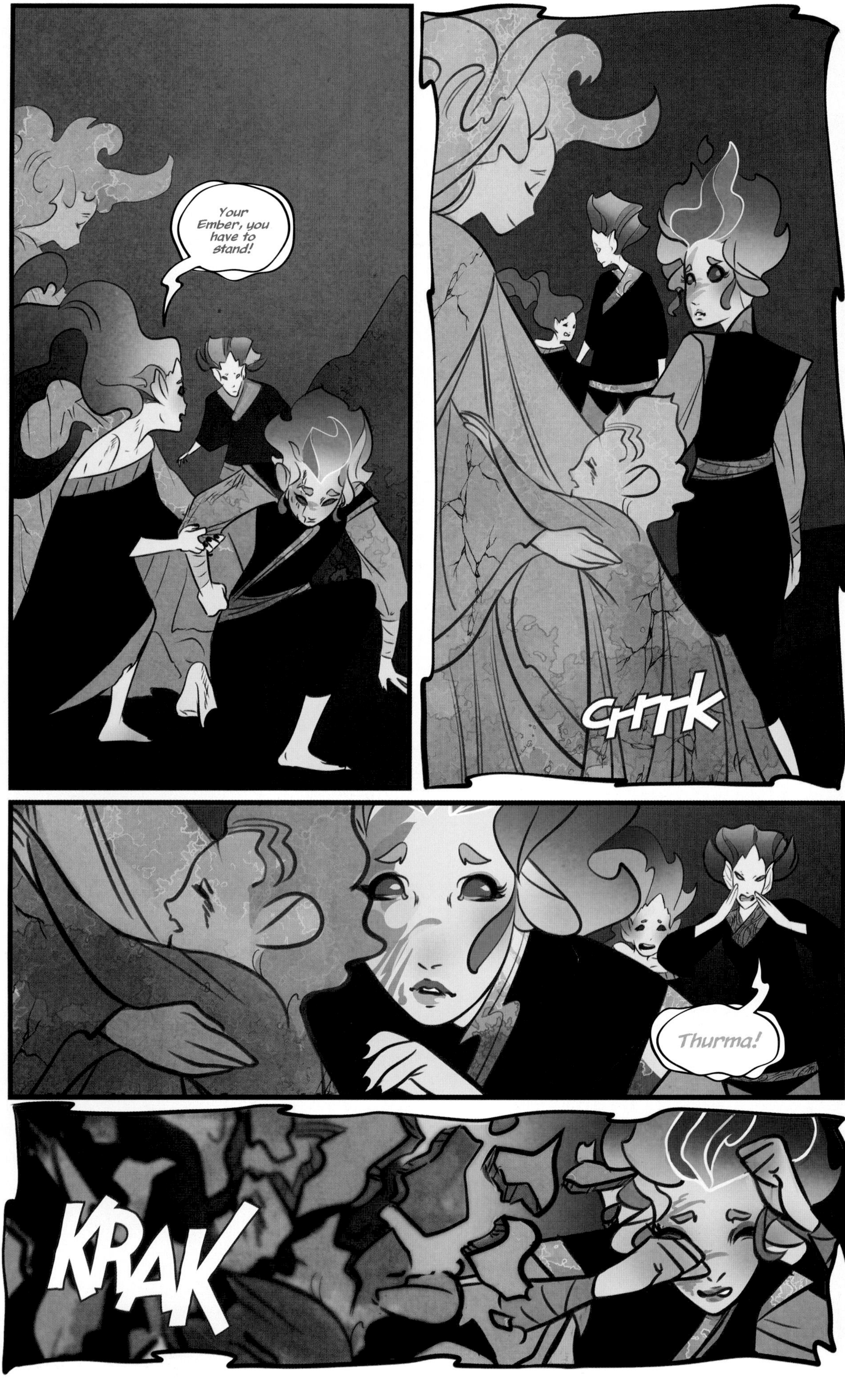
Your Ember, you have to stand!
CHHK
Thurma!
KRAK

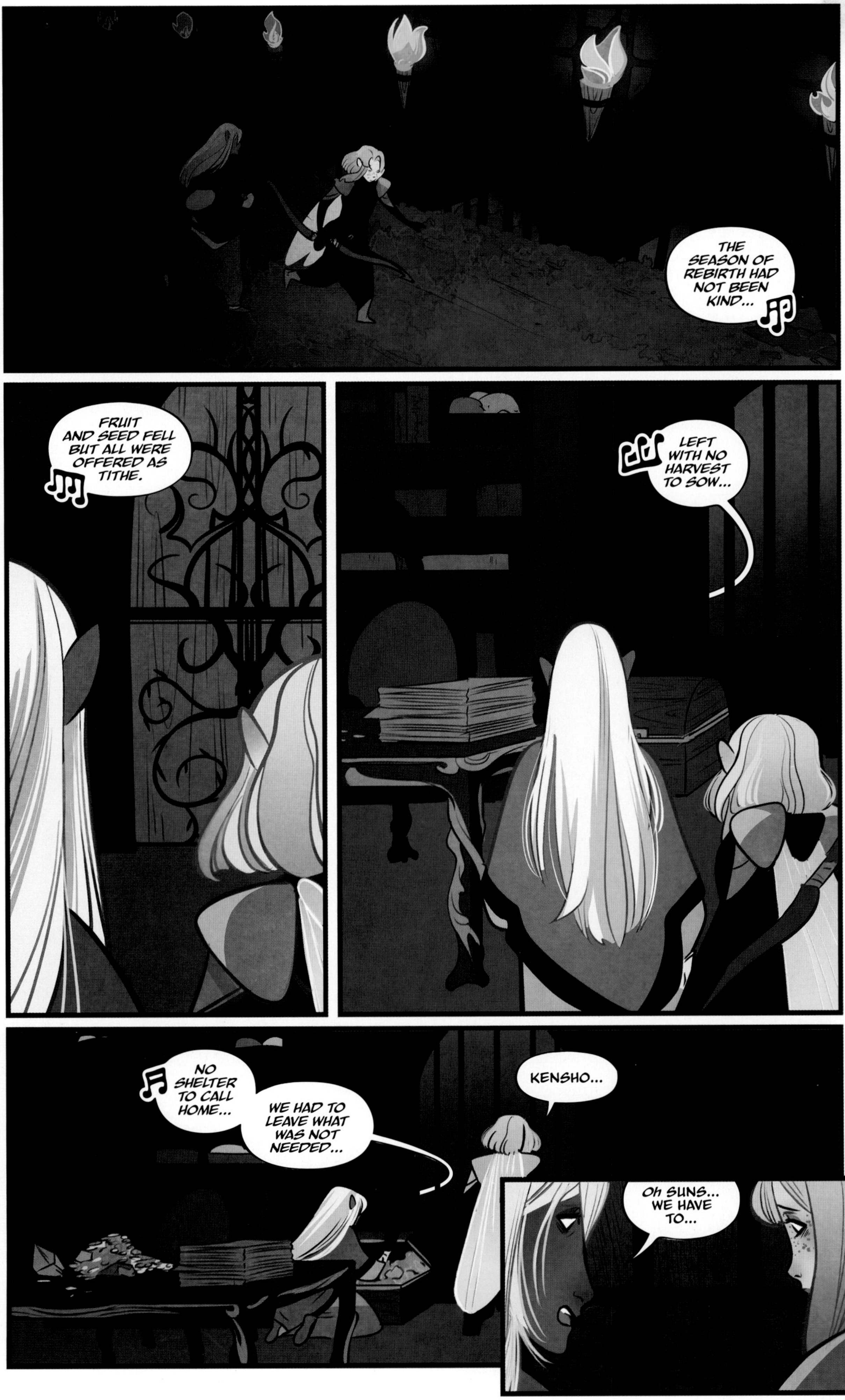
THE SEASON OF REBIRTH HAD NOT BEEN KIND...
FRUIT AND SEED FELL BUT ALL WERE OFFERED AS TITHE.
LEFT WITH NO HARVEST TO SOW...
NO SHELTER TO CALL HOME...
WE HAD TO LEAVE WHAT WAS NOT NEEDED...
KENSHO...
Oh SUNS... WE HAVE TO...

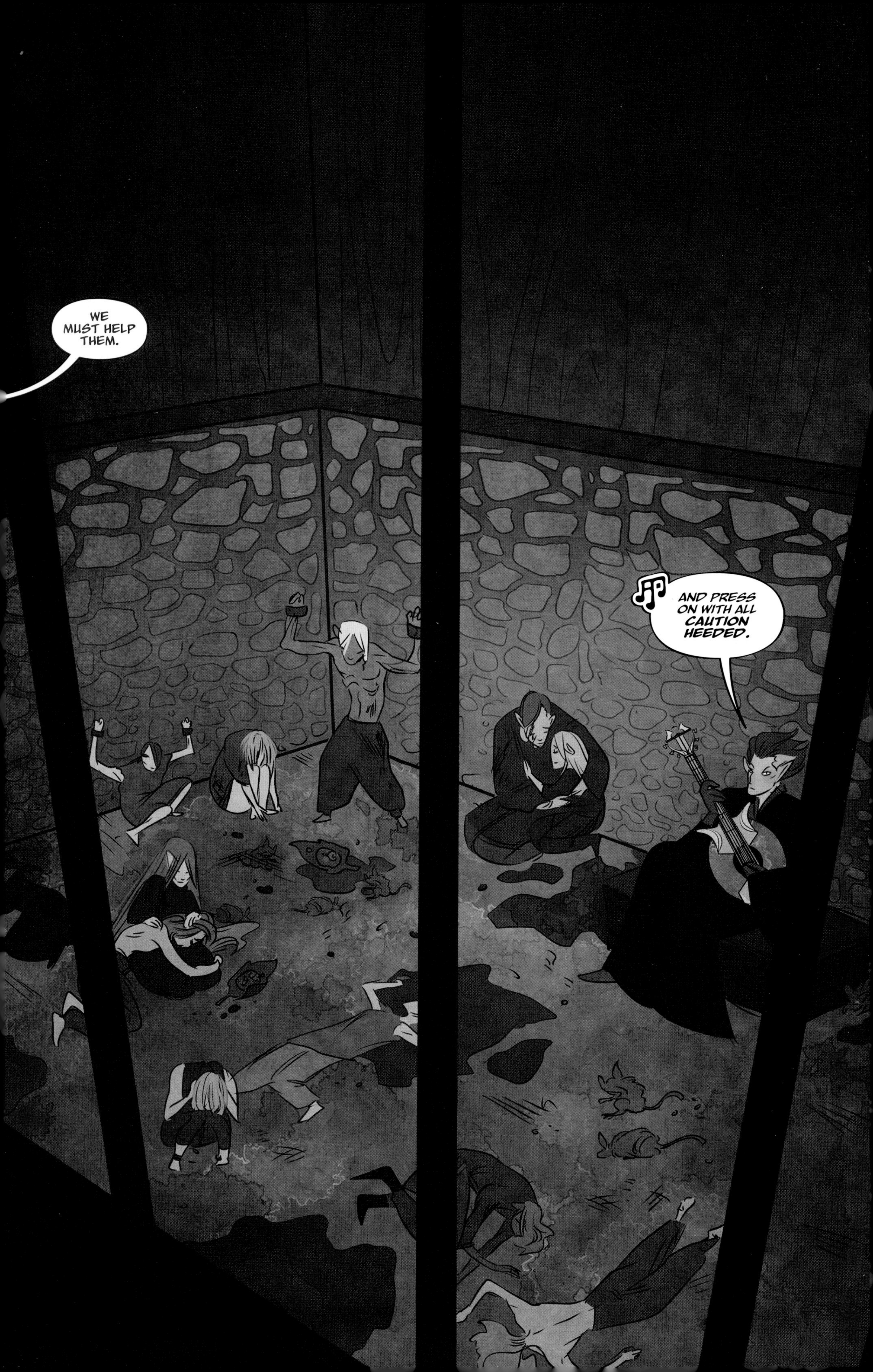
WE MUST HELP THEM.
AND PRESS ON WITH ALL CAUTION HEEDED.

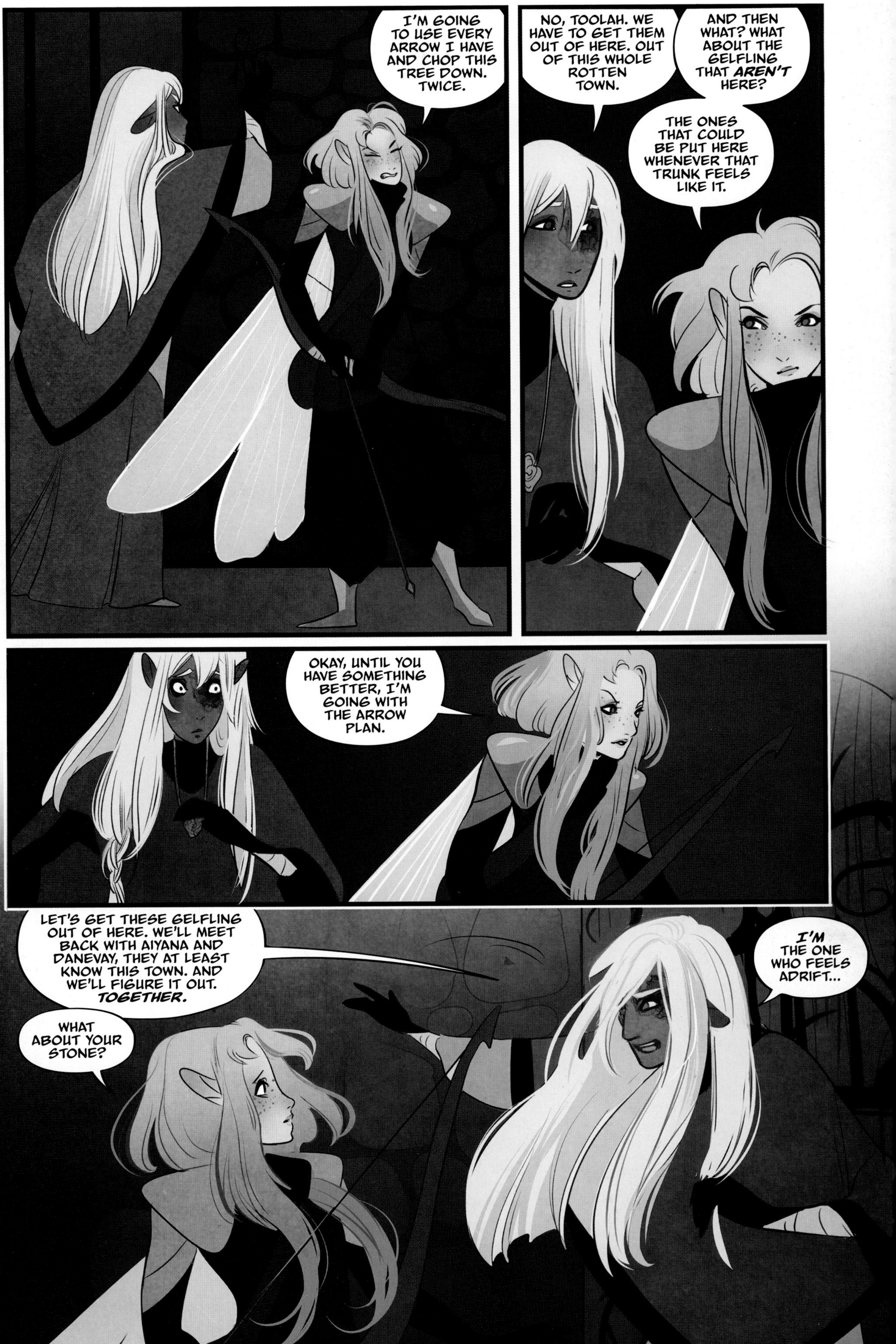

I'M GOING TO USE EVERY ARROW I HAVE AND CHOP THIS TREE DOWN. TWICE.
NO, TOOLAH. WE HAVE TO GET THEM OUT OF HERE. OUT OF THIS WHOLE ROTTEN TOWN.
AND THEN WHAT? WHAT ABOUT THE GELFLING THAT *AREN'T* HERE?
THE ONES THAT COULD BE PUT HERE WHENEVER THAT TRUNK FEELS LIKE IT.
OKAY, UNTIL YOU HAVE SOMETHING BETTER, I'M GOING WITH THE ARROW PLAN.
LET'S GET THESE GELFLING OUT OF HERE. WE'LL MEET BACK WITH AIYANA AND DANEVAY, THEY AT LEAST KNOW THIS TOWN. AND WE'LL FIGURE IT OUT. ***TOGETHER.***
WHAT ABOUT YOUR STONE?
I'M THE ONE WHO FEELS ADRIFT...

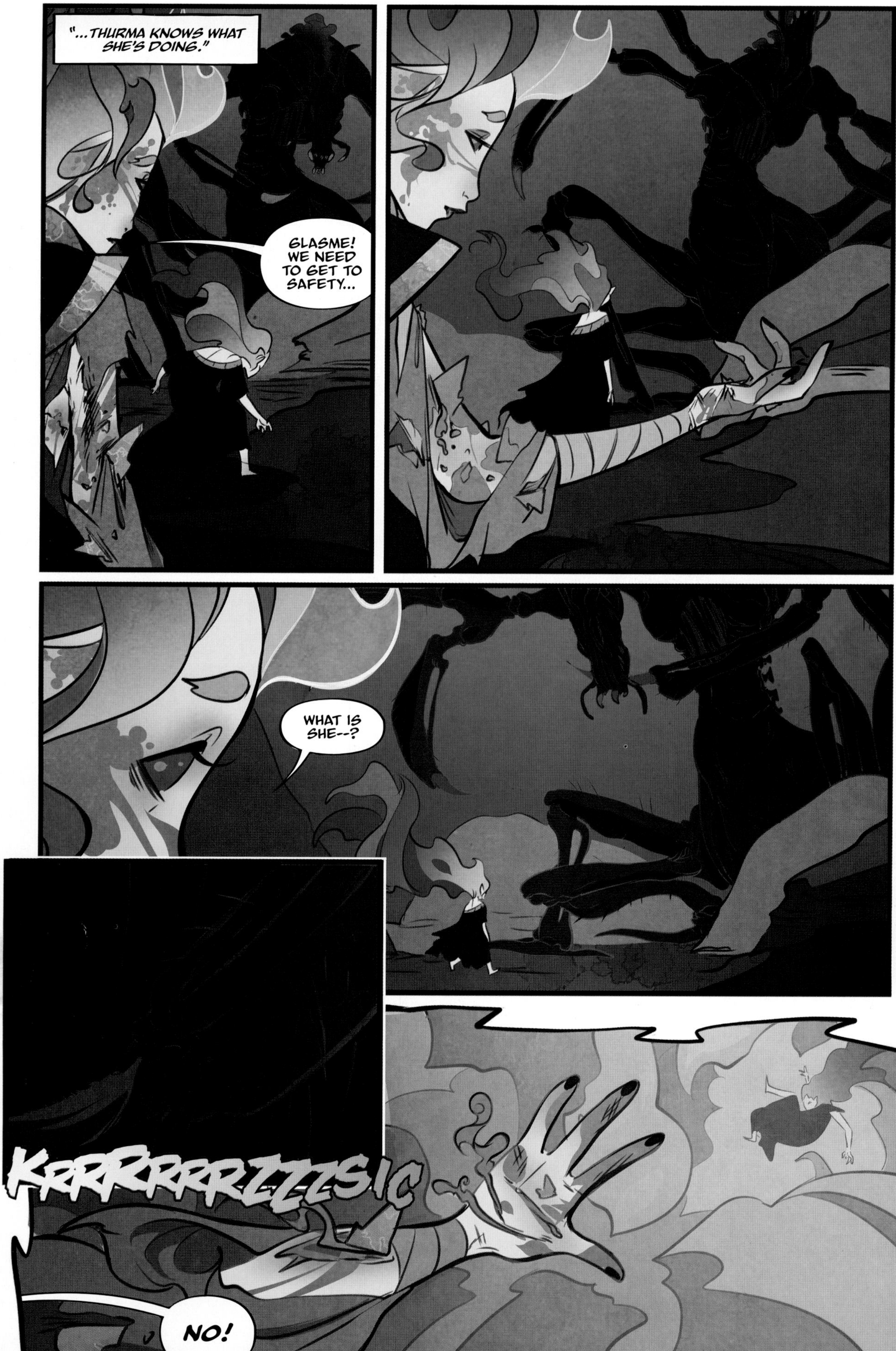
"...THURMA KNOWS WHAT SHE'S DOING."
GLASME! WE NEED TO GET TO SAFETY...
WHAT IS SHE--?
KRRRRRRRZZZSIC
NO!

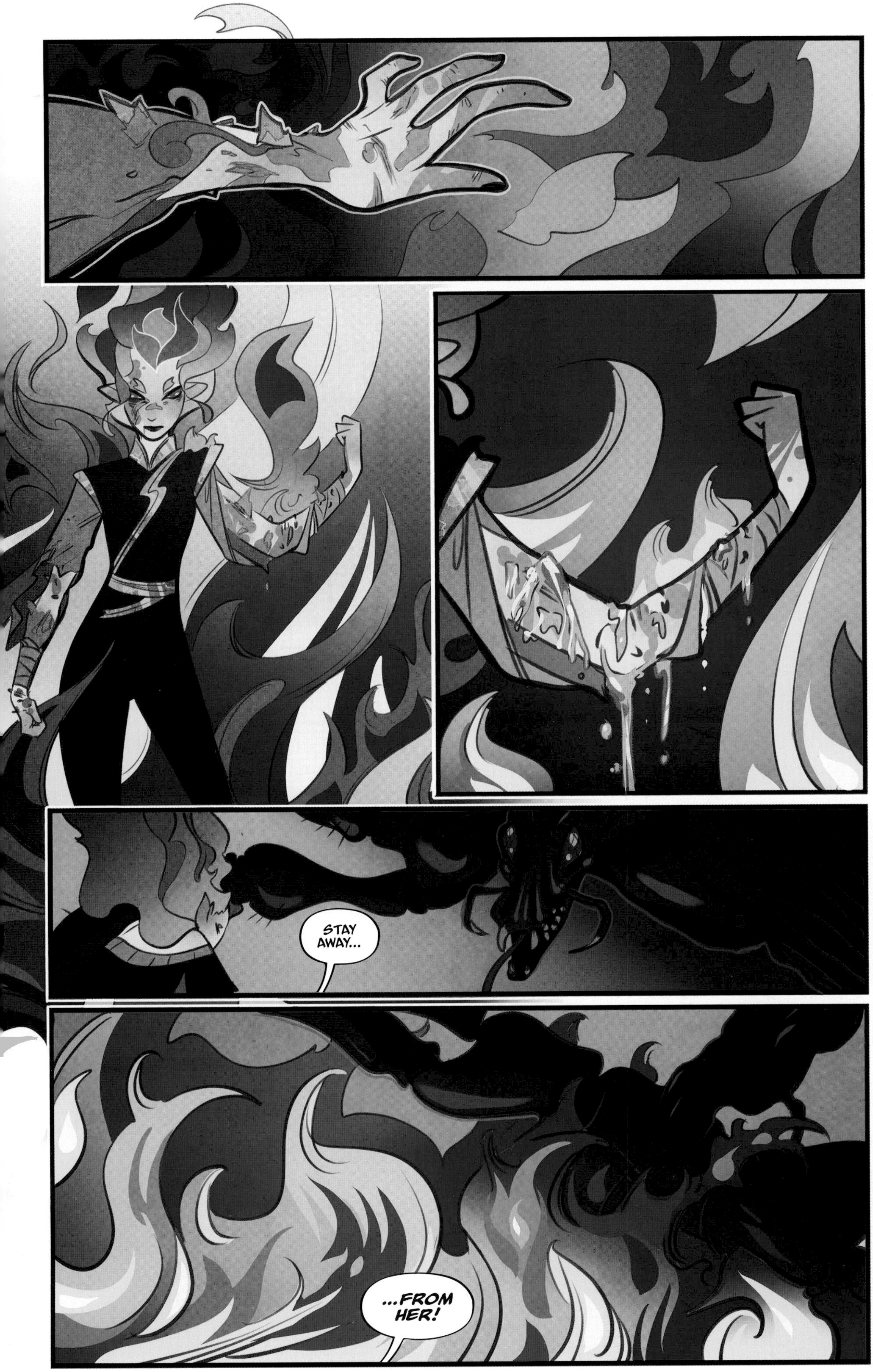
STAY AWAY...
...FROM HER!

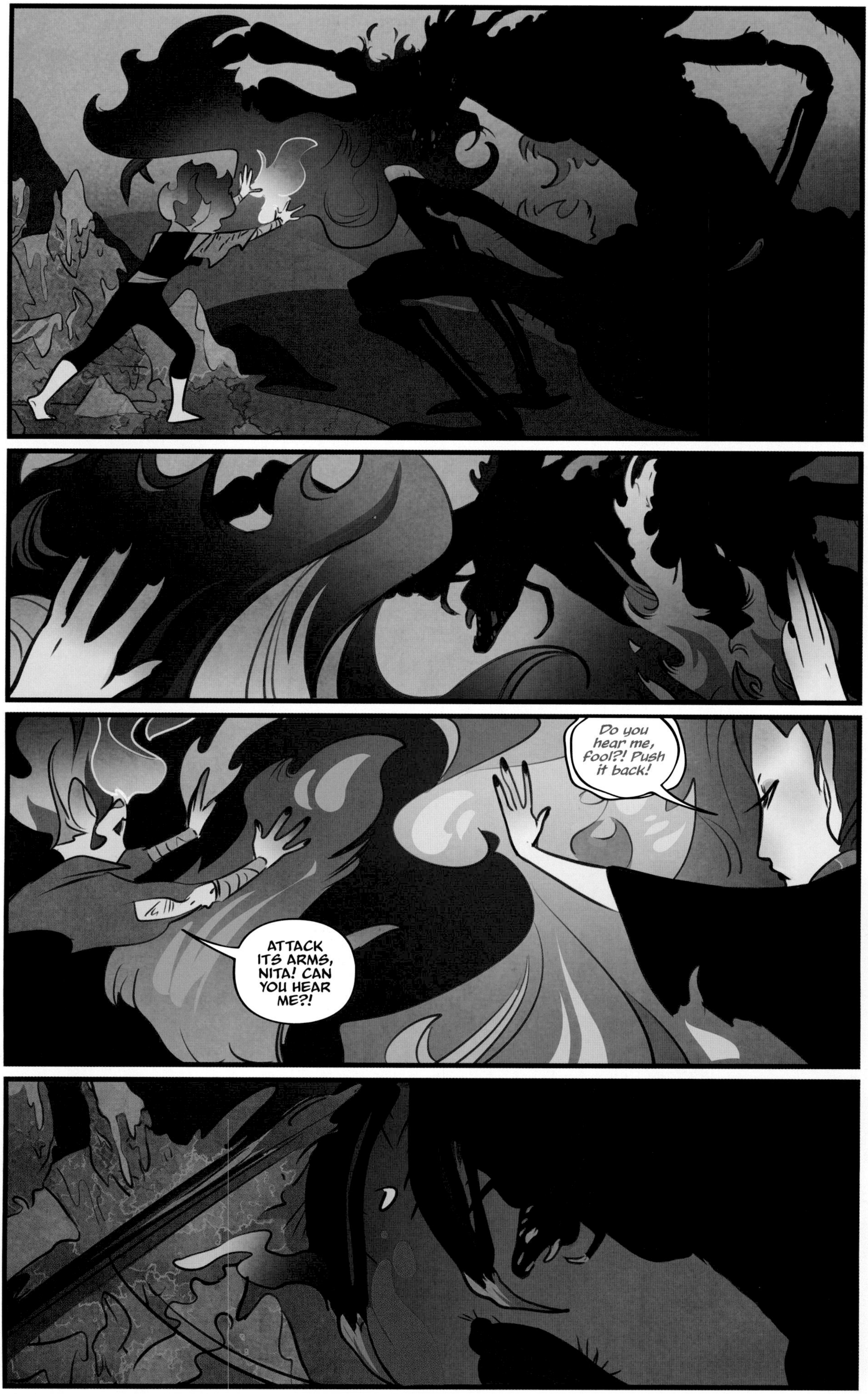
Do you hear me, fool?! Push it back!
ATTACK ITS ARMS, NITA! CAN YOU HEAR ME?!

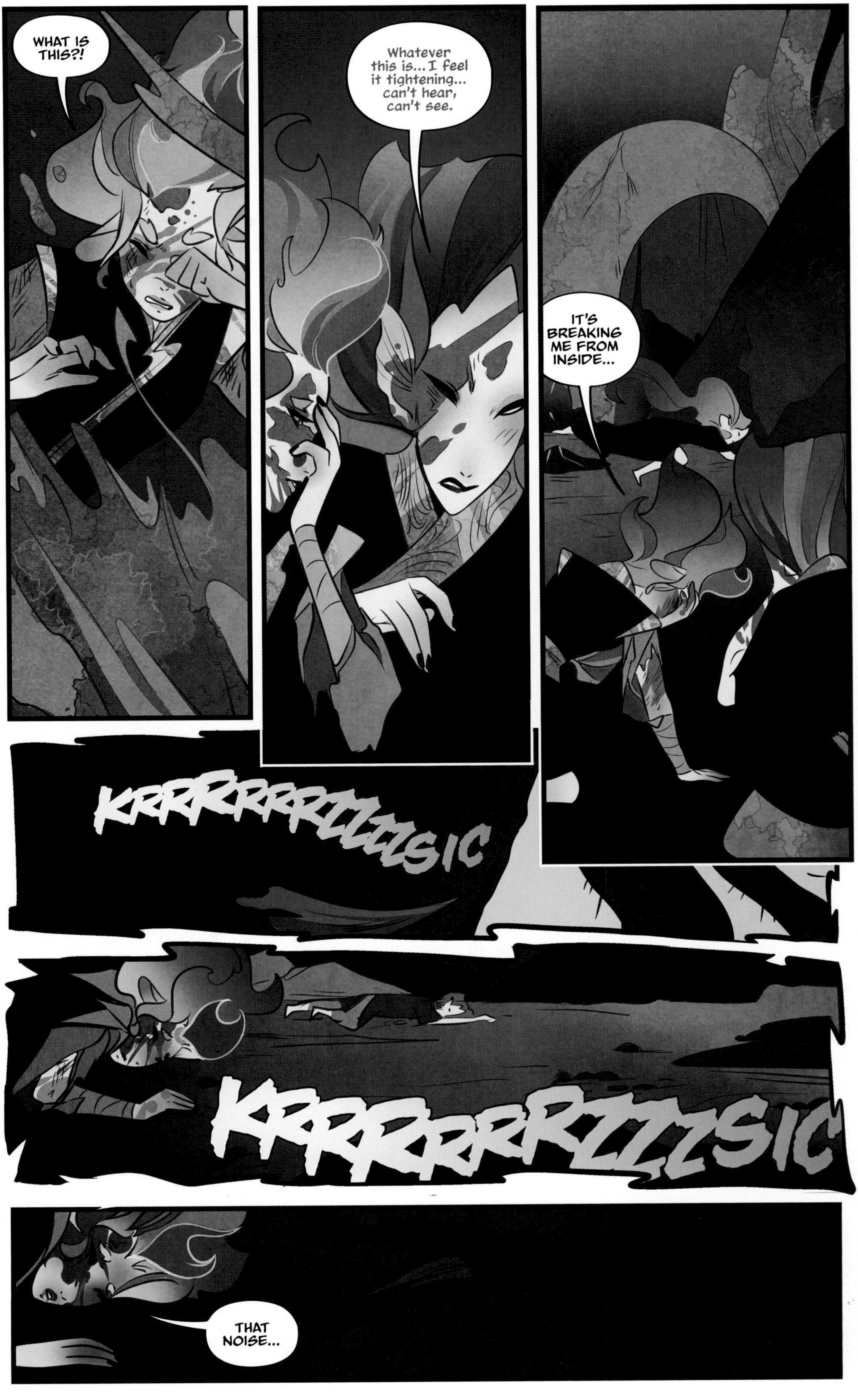
WHAT IS THIS?!
Whatever this is... I feel it tightening... can't hear, can't see.
IT'S BREAKING ME FROM INSIDE...
KRRRRRRZZZSIC
KRRRRRRZZZSIC
THAT NOISE...

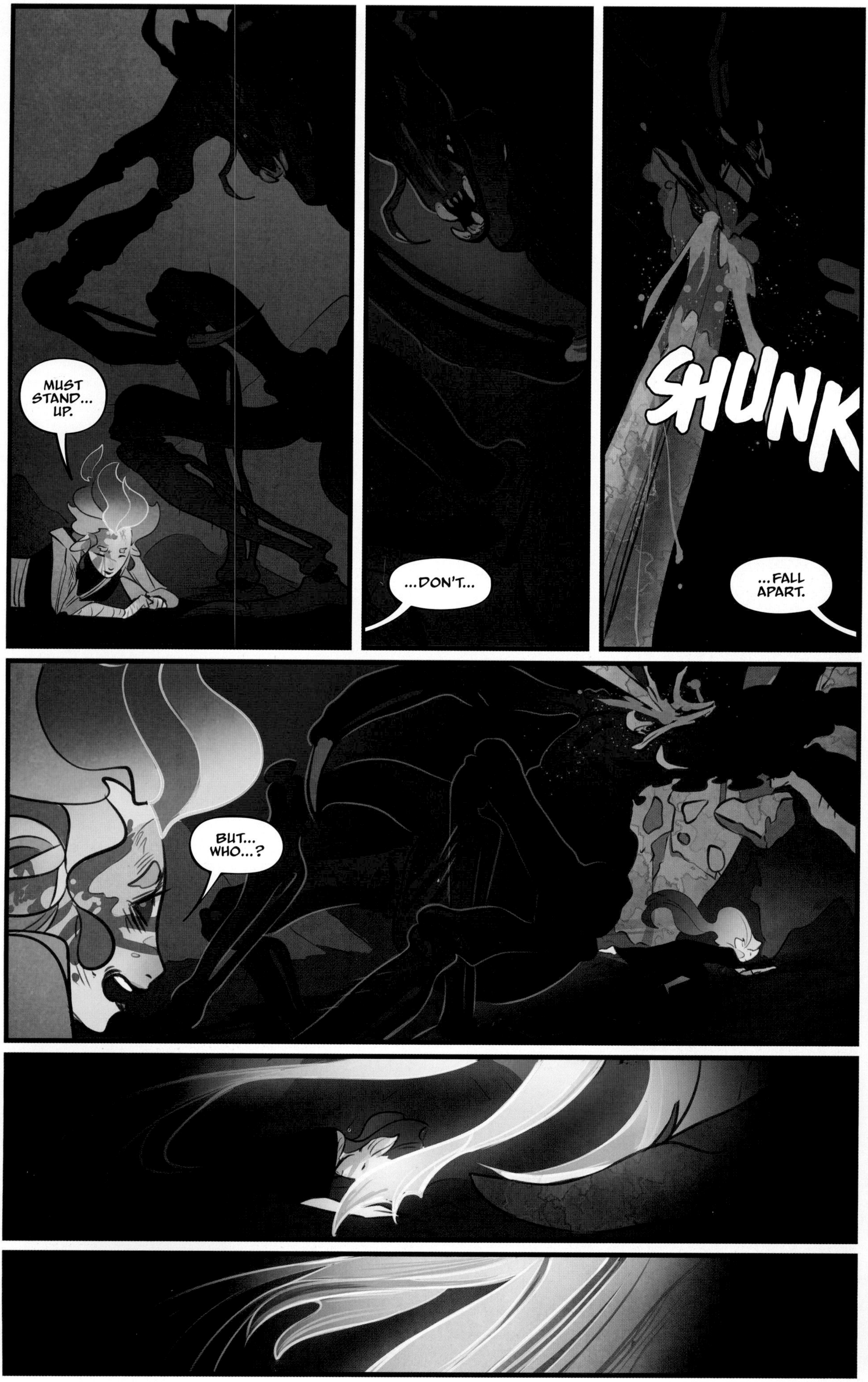
MUST STAND... UP.
...DON'T...
SHUNK
...FALL APART.
BUT... WHO...?

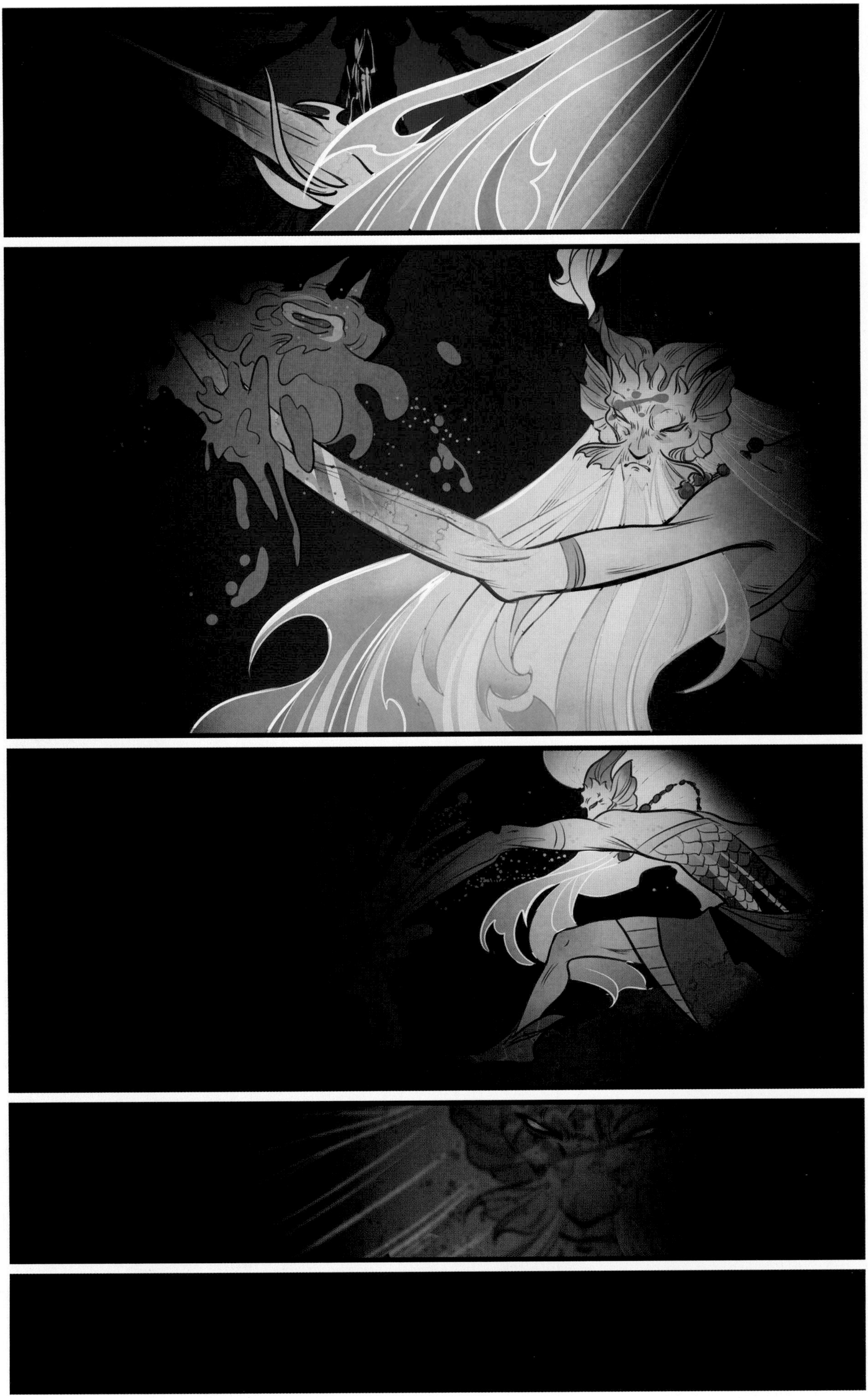

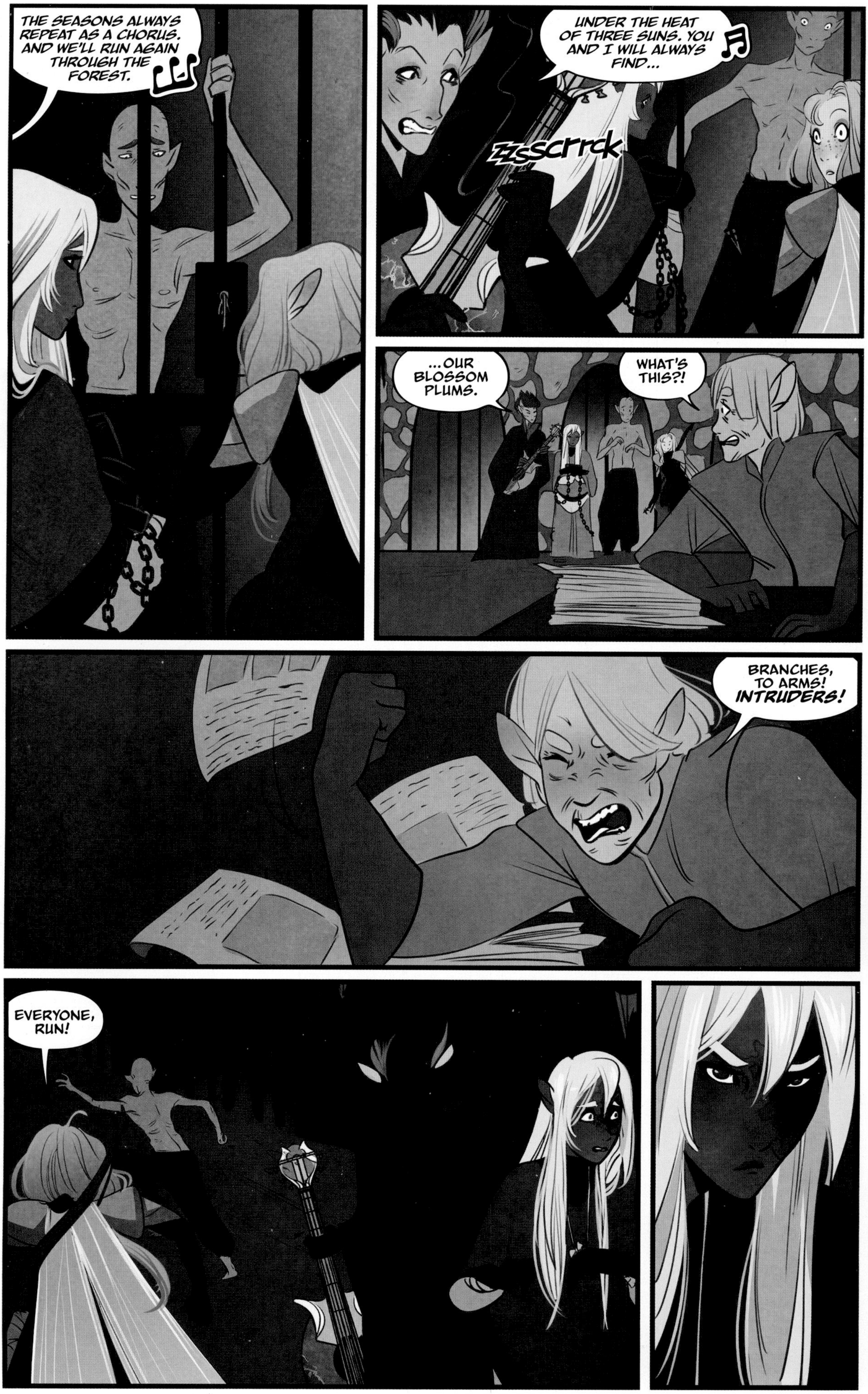
THE SEASONS ALWAYS REPEAT AS A CHORUS. AND WE'LL RUN AGAIN THROUGH THE FOREST.
UNDER THE HEAT OF THREE SUNS. YOU AND I WILL ALWAYS FIND...
ZZSSCRRCK
...OUR BLOSSOM PLUMS.
WHAT'S THIS?!
BRANCHES, TO ARMS! INTRUDERS!
EVERYONE, RUN!

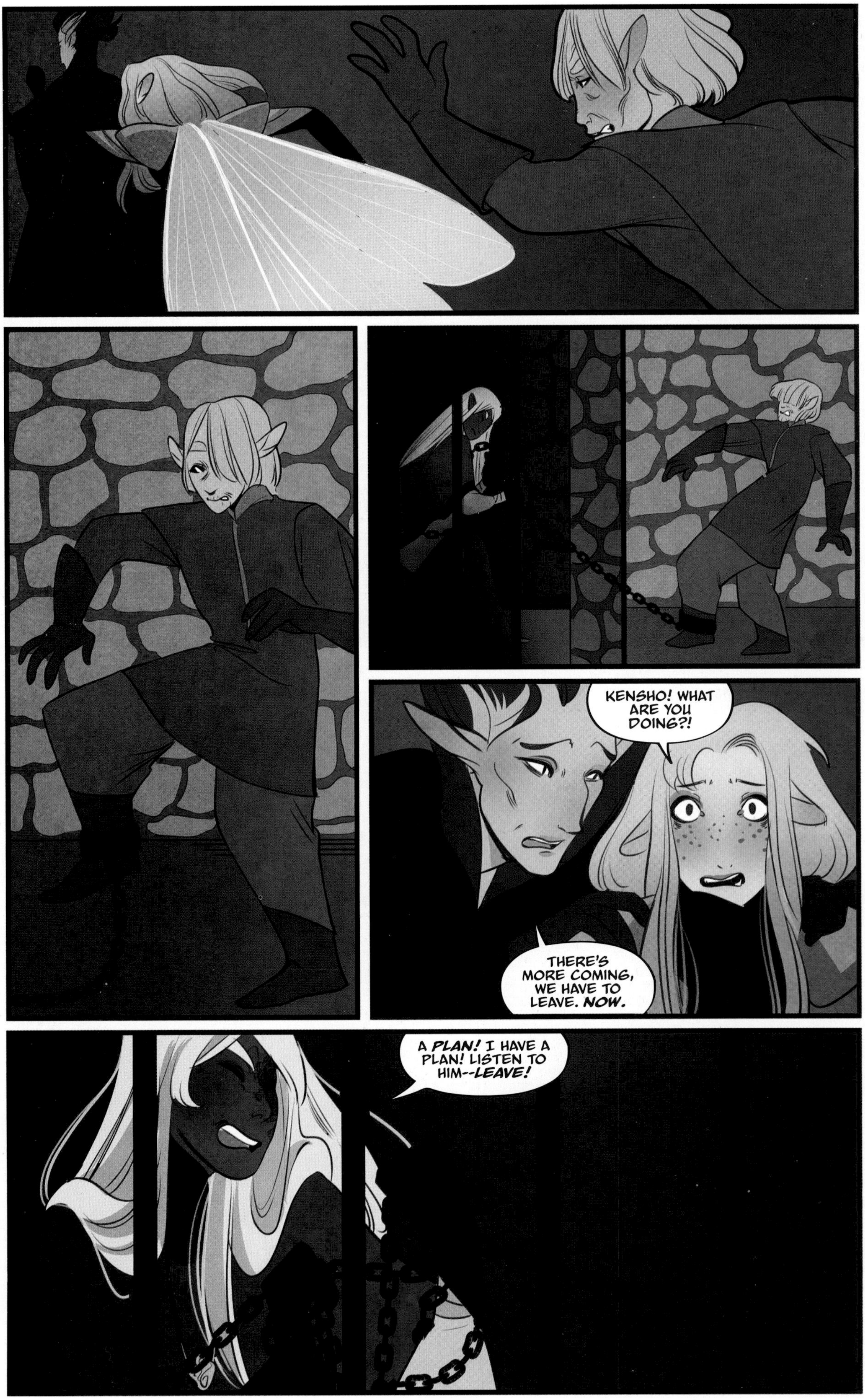
KENSHO! WHAT ARE YOU DOING?!
THERE'S MORE COMING, WE HAVE TO LEAVE. **NOW.**
A ***PLAN!*** I HAVE A PLAN! LISTEN TO HIM--***LEAVE!***

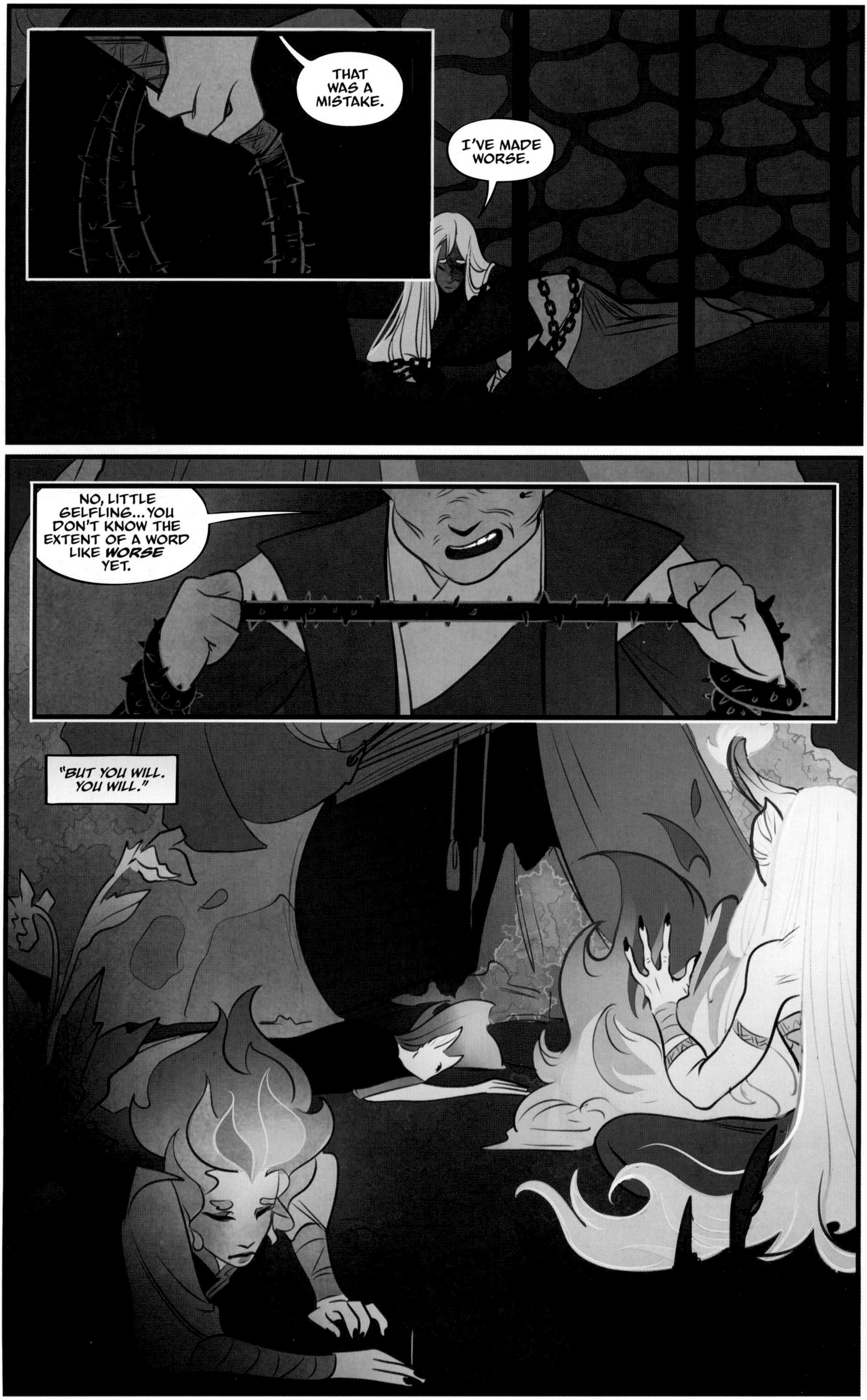
THAT WAS A MISTAKE.
I'VE MADE WORSE.
NO, LITTLE GELFLING... YOU DON'T KNOW THE EXTENT OF A WORD LIKE *WORSE* YET.
"BUT YOU WILL. YOU WILL."

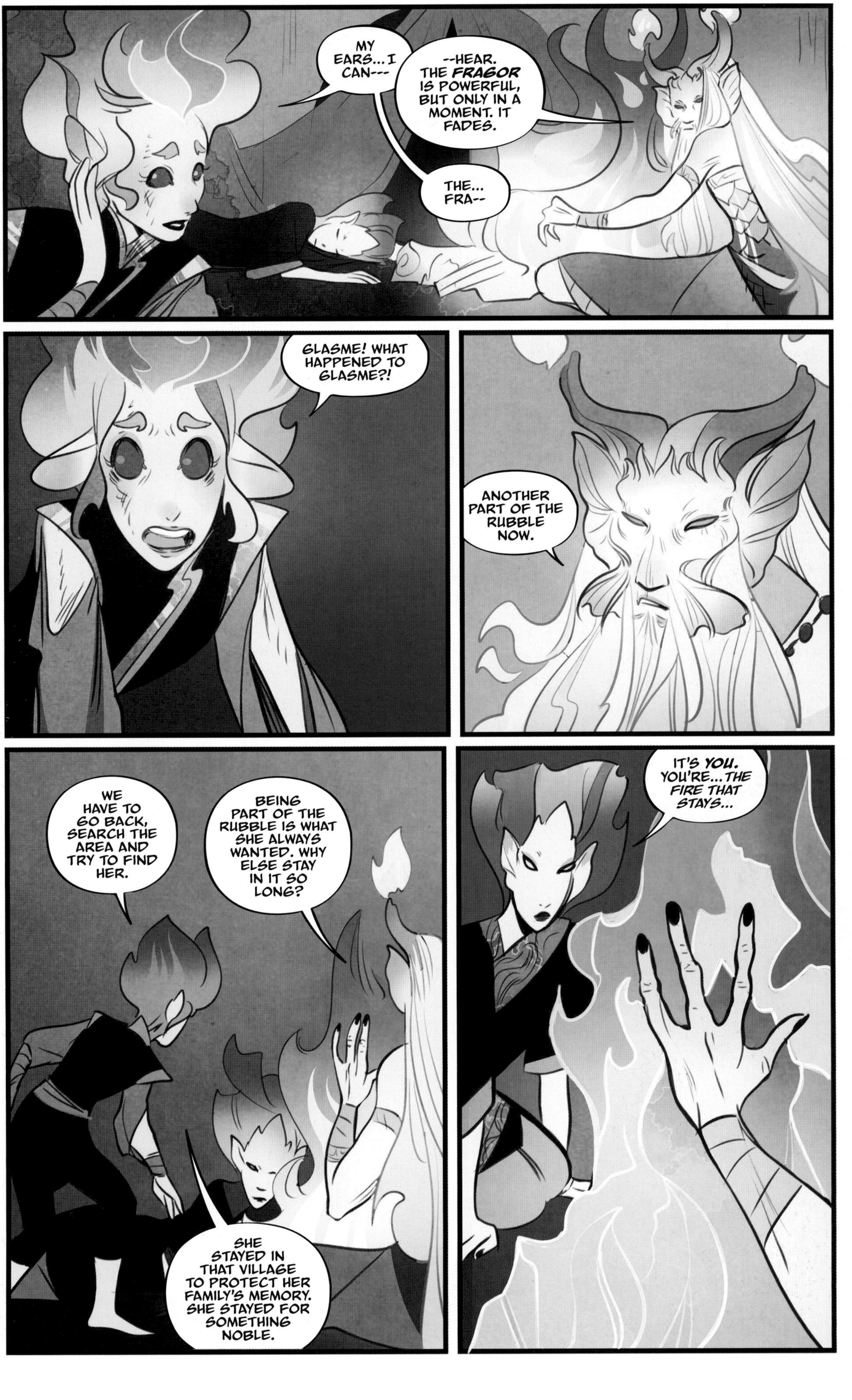
MY EARS... I CAN---
--HEAR. THE FRAGOR IS POWERFUL, BUT ONLY IN A MOMENT. IT FADES.
THE... FRA--
GLASME! WHAT HAPPENED TO GLASME?!
ANOTHER PART OF THE RUBBLE NOW.
WE HAVE TO GO BACK, SEARCH THE AREA AND TRY TO FIND HER.
BEING PART OF THE RUBBLE IS WHAT SHE ALWAYS WANTED. WHY ELSE STAY IN IT SO LONG?
SHE STAYED IN THAT VILLAGE TO PROTECT HER FAMILY'S MEMORY. SHE STAYED FOR SOMETHING NOBLE.
IT'S YOU. YOU'RE... THE FIRE THAT STAYS...

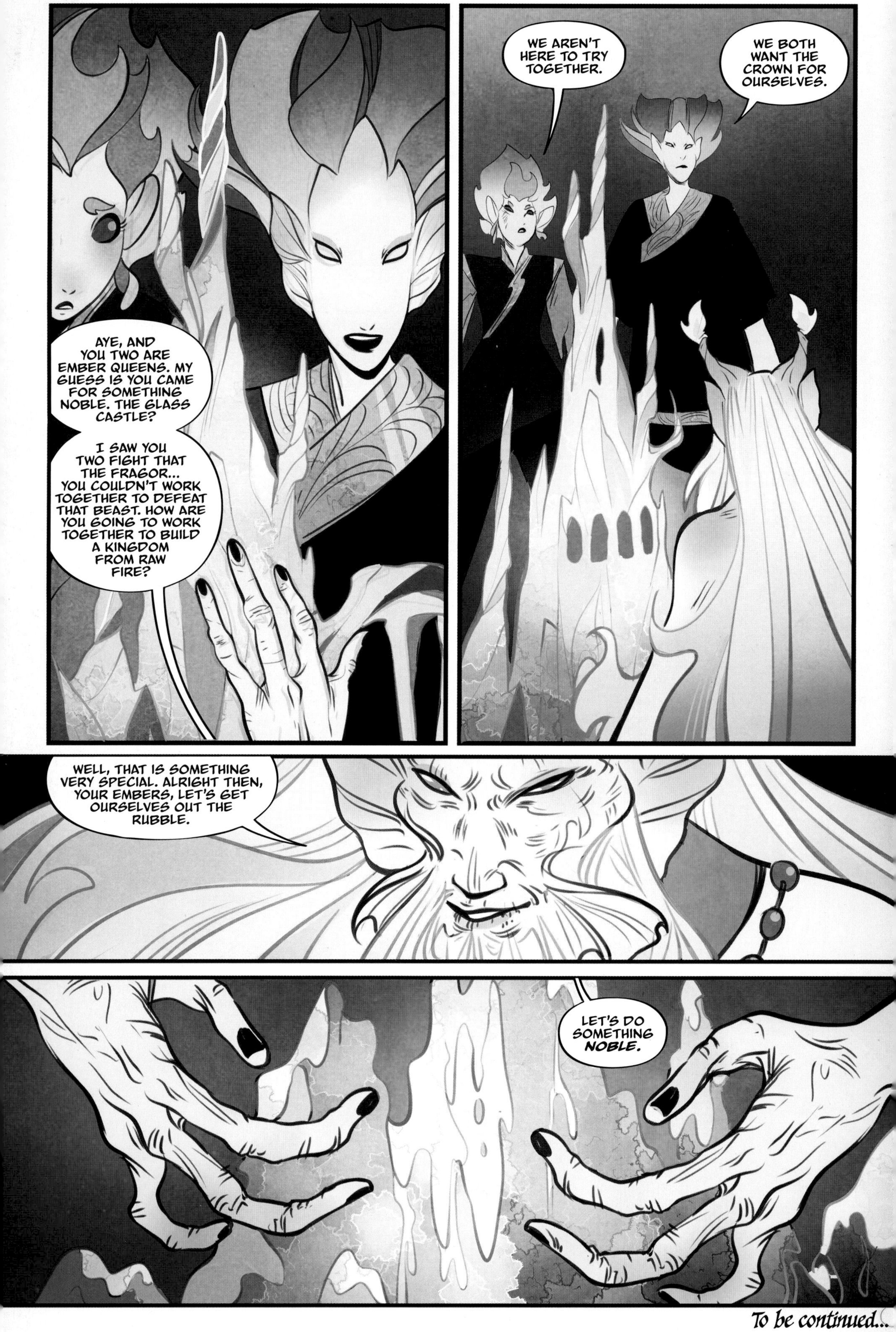
AYE, AND YOU TWO ARE EMBER QUEENS. MY GUESS IS YOU CAME FOR SOMETHING NOBLE. THE GLASS CASTLE?
I SAW YOU TWO FIGHT THAT THE FRAGOR... YOU COULDN'T WORK TOGETHER TO DEFEAT THAT BEAST. HOW ARE YOU GOING TO WORK TOGETHER TO BUILD A KINGDOM FROM RAW FIRE?
WE AREN'T HERE TO TRY TOGETHER.
WE BOTH WANT THE CROWN FOR OURSELVES.
WELL, THAT IS SOMETHING VERY SPECIAL. ALRIGHT THEN, YOUR EMBERS, LET'S GET OURSELVES OUT THE RUBBLE.
LET'S DO SOMETHING *NOBLE*.

To be continued...

COVER
GALLERY

Facing Page: Issue #1 Subscription Cover by David Petersen.
Following Pages: Issue #2-4 Subscription Covers by David Petersen.
Page 107: Issue #1 Variant Cover by Ramón K. Pérez.
Page 108: Issue #1 Variant Cover by Dave McKean.

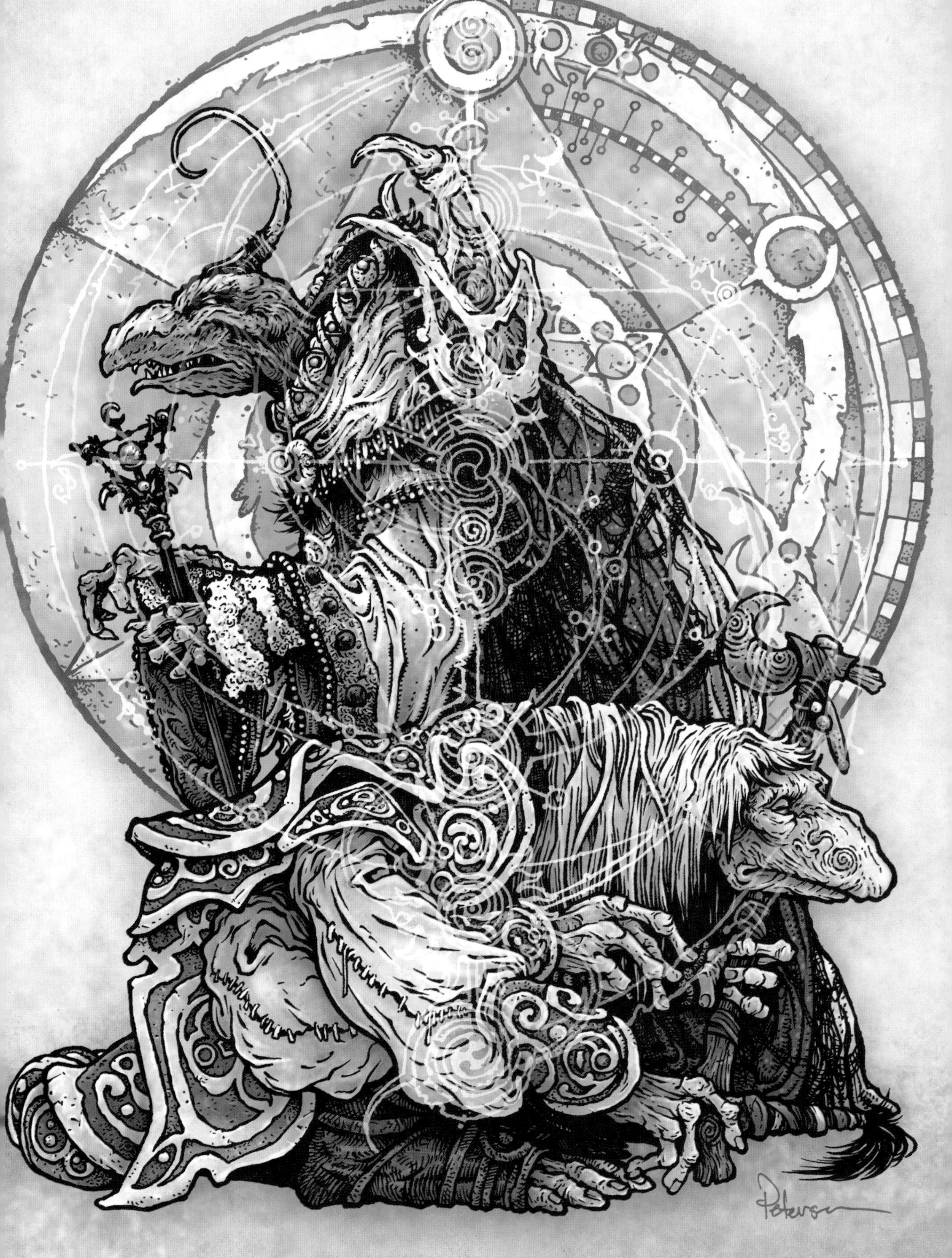

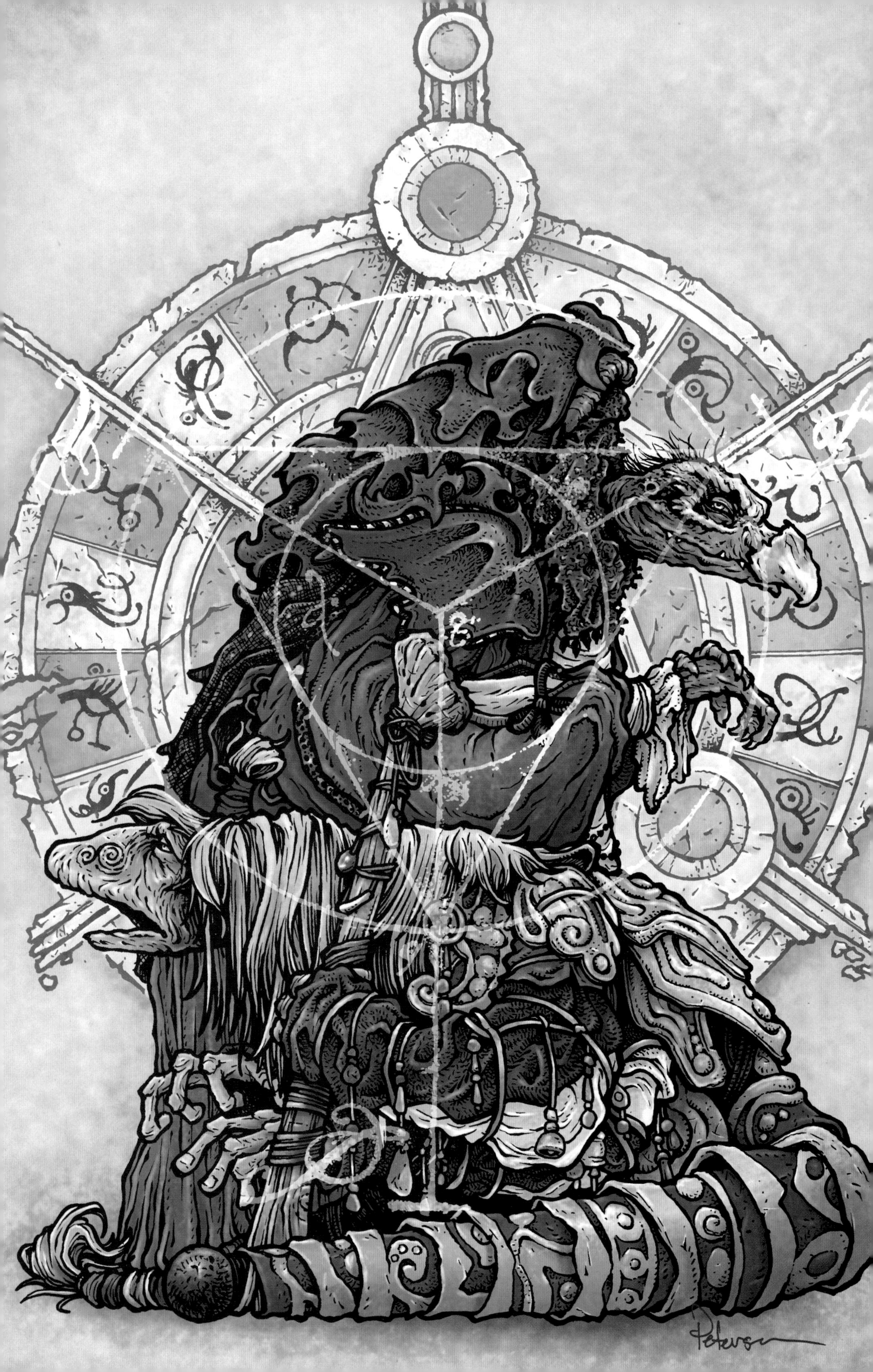

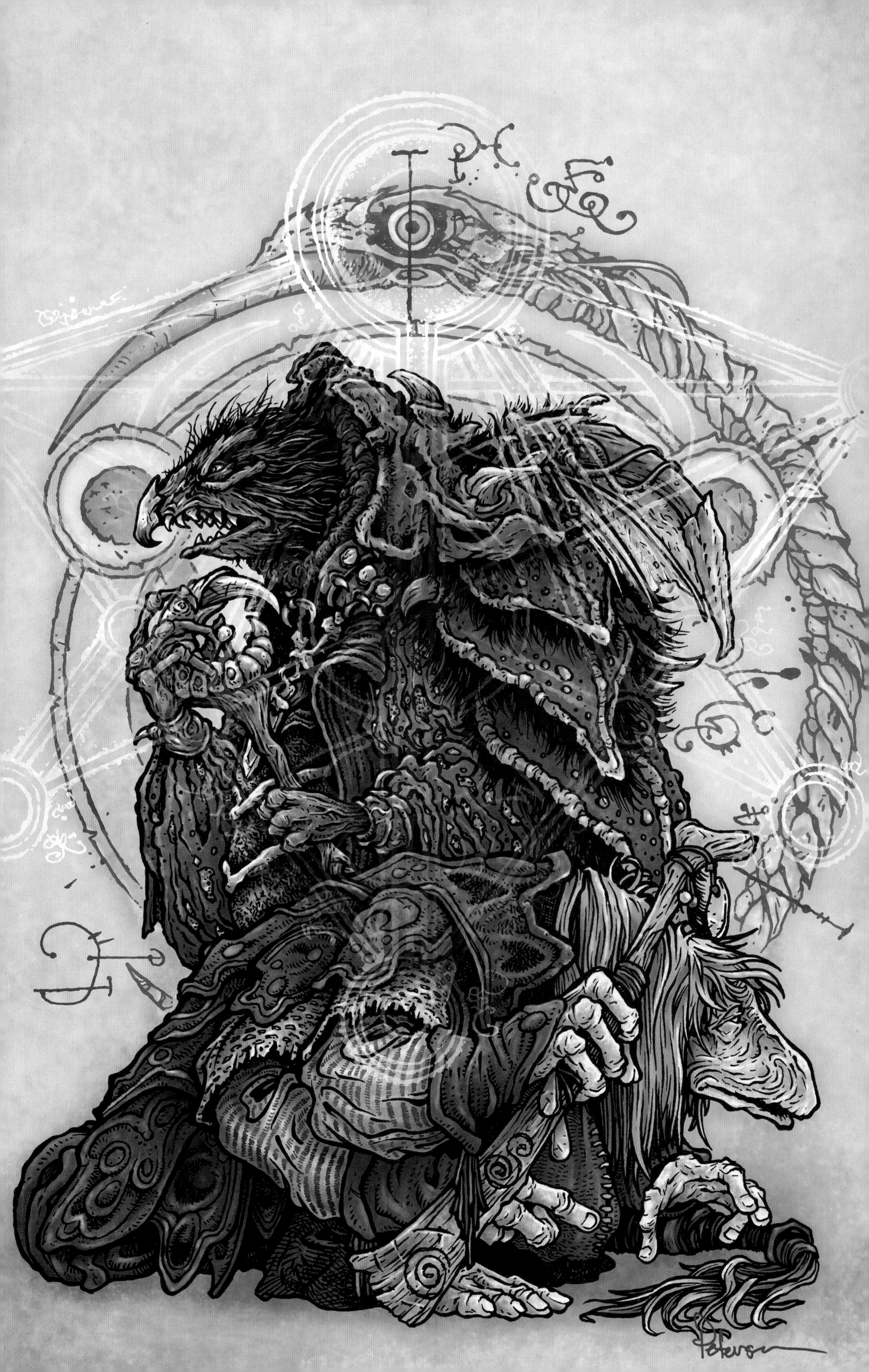

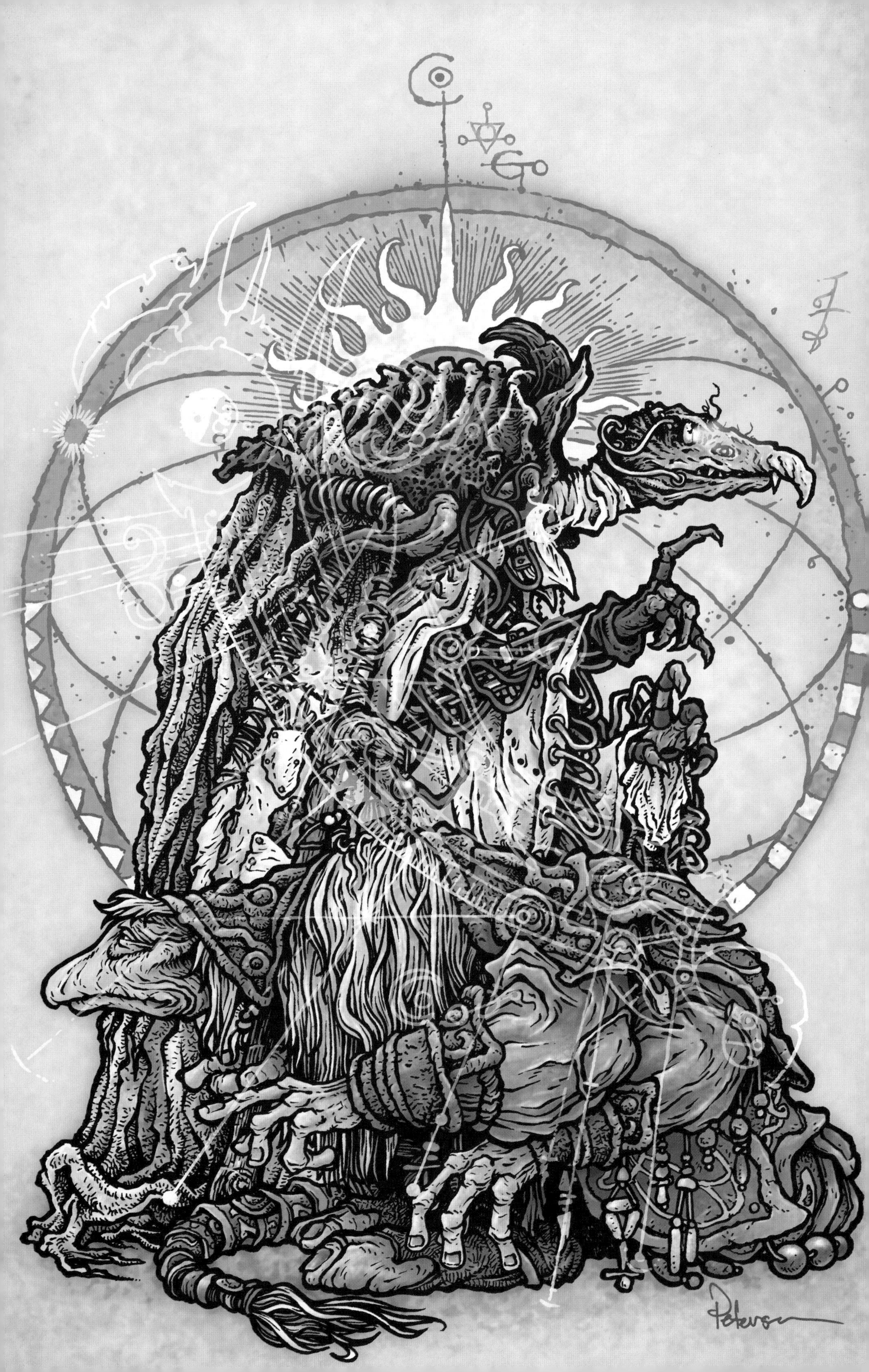
Peterson

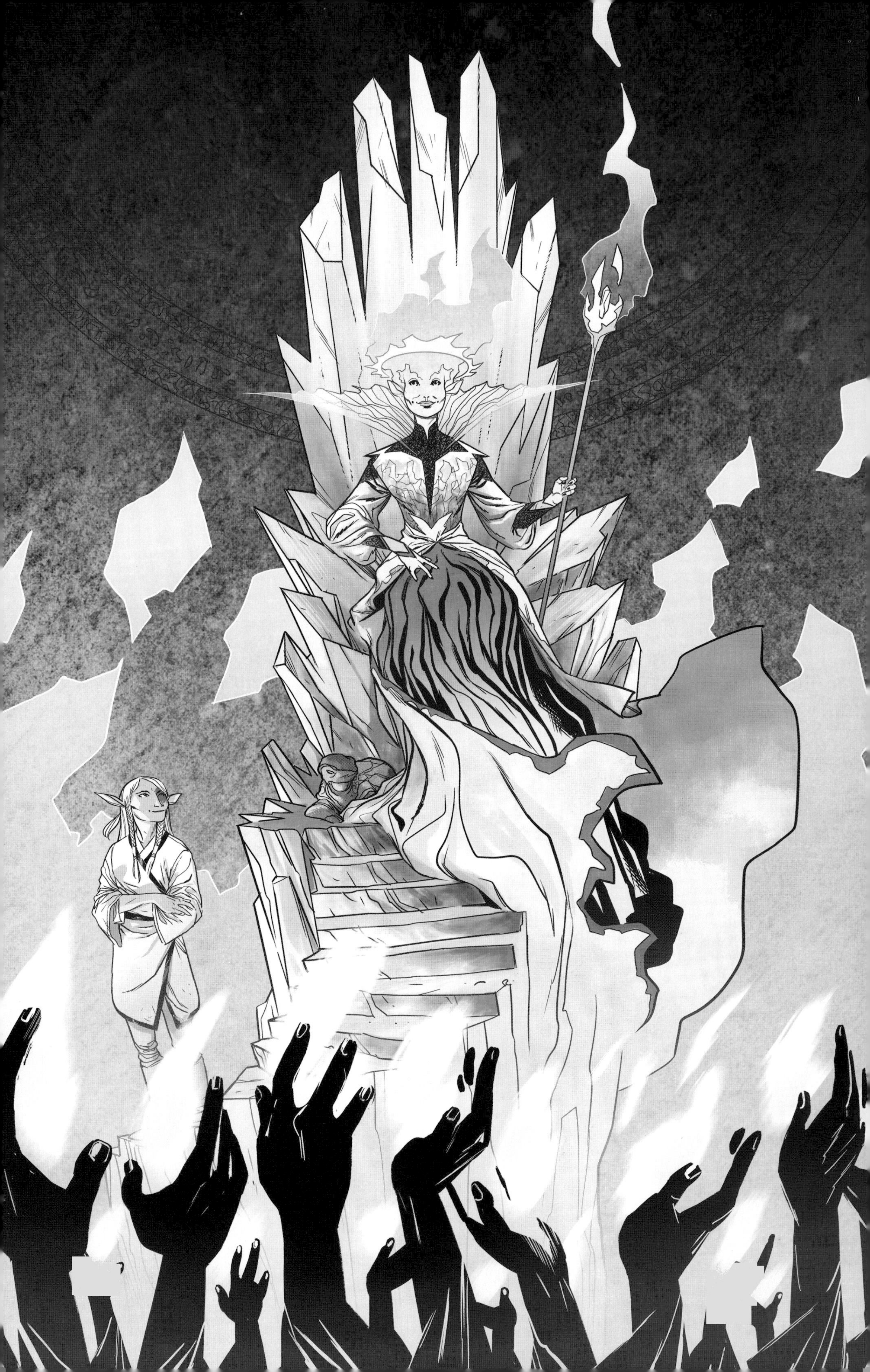

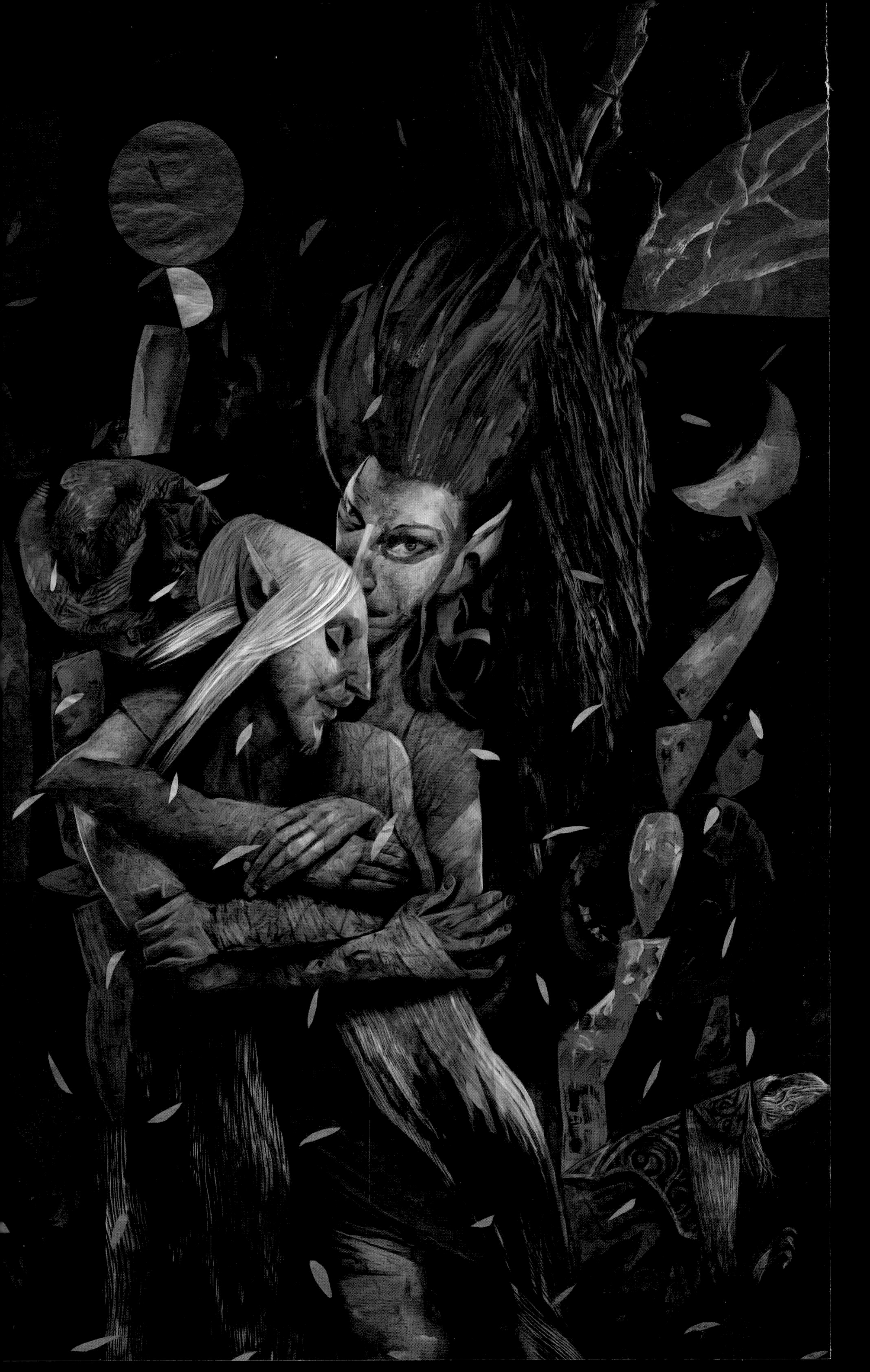

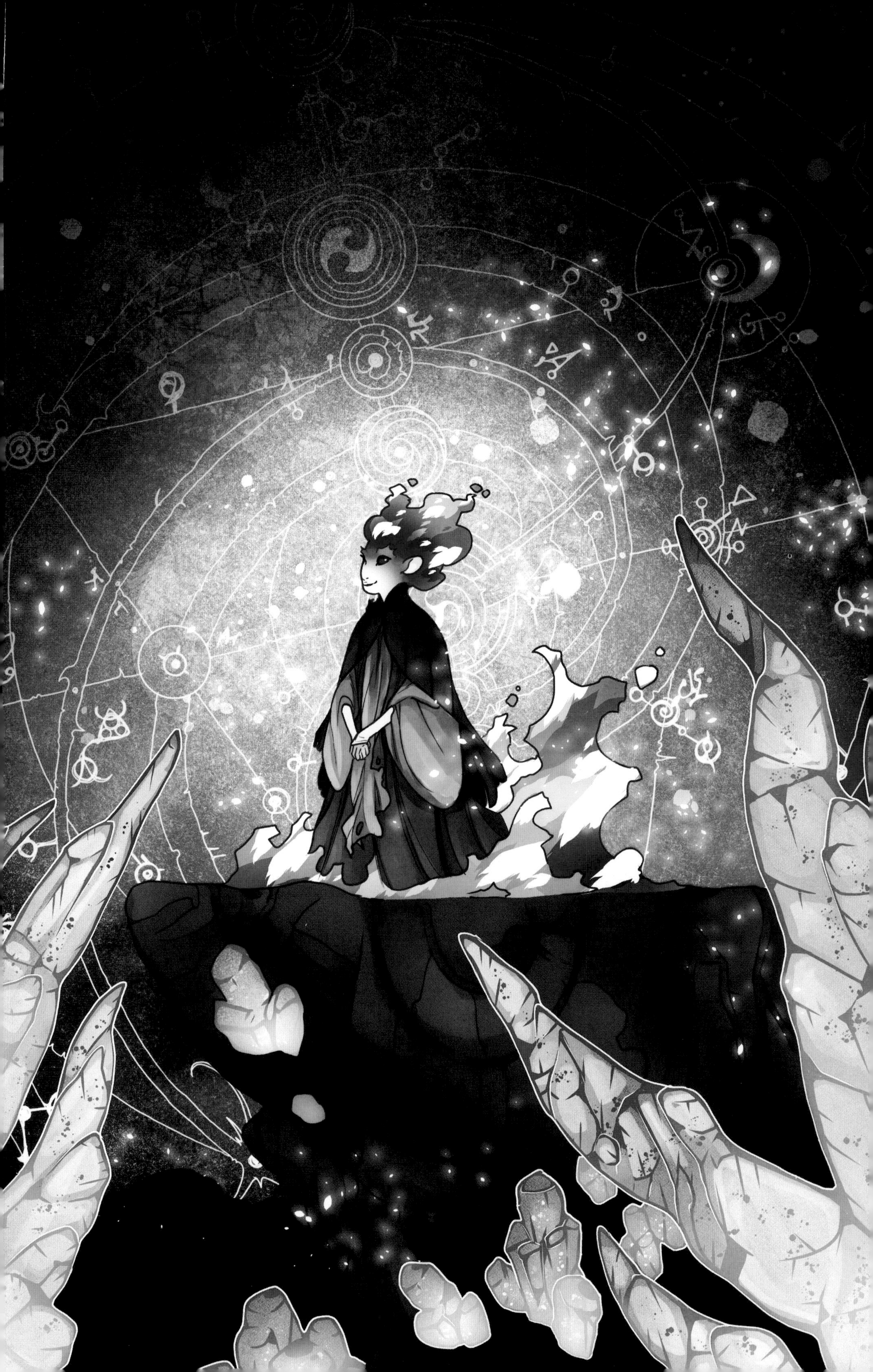

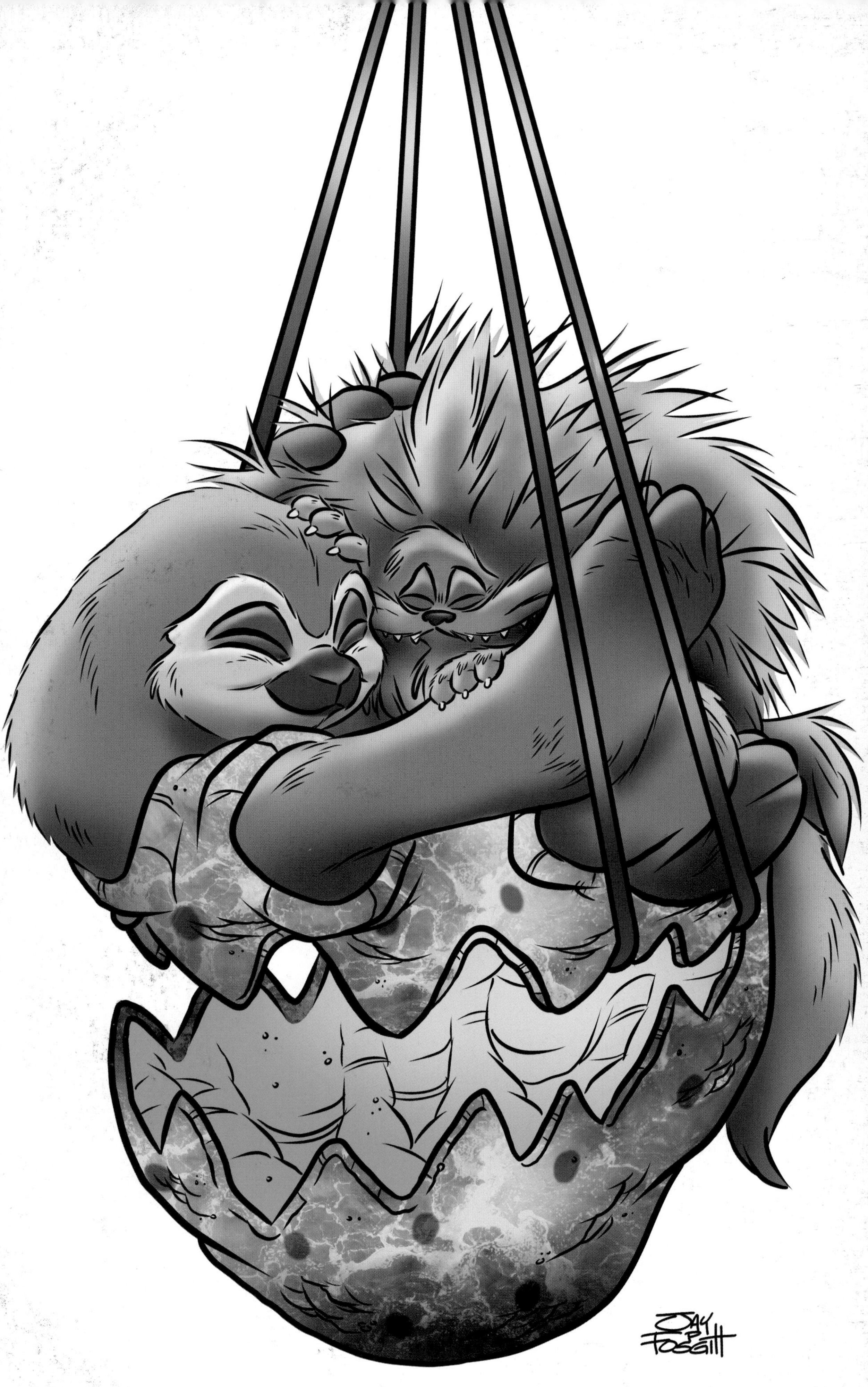
JAY FOSGITT

Previous Page: Issue #1 Previews Exclusive Cover by Kelly and Nichole Matthews.
Current Page: Issue #1 San Diego Comic Con Exclusive Variant Cover by Jay Fosgitt.
Facing Page: Issue #1 Variant Cover by Chris Samnee with colors by Matt Wilson.

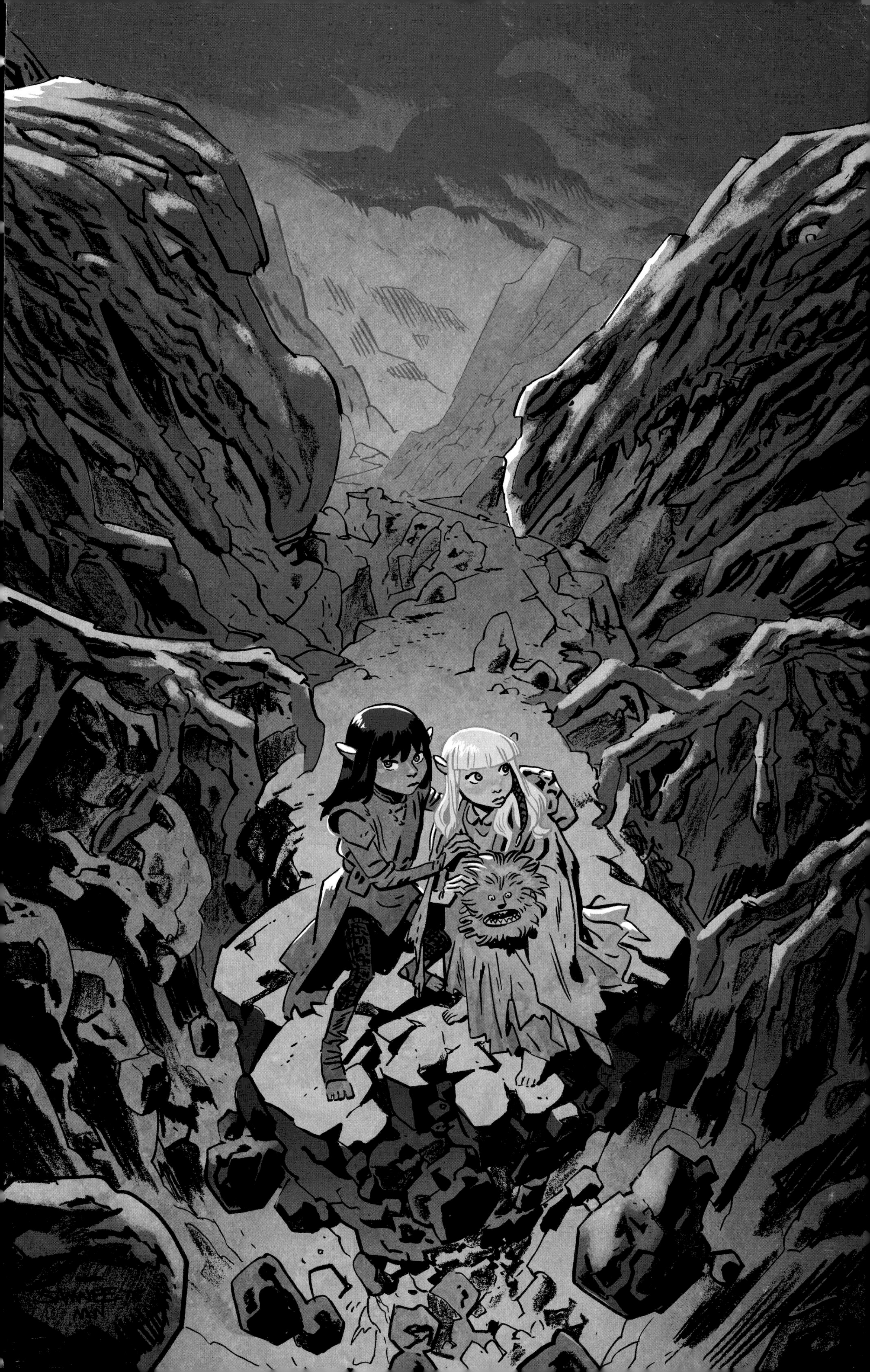

DISCOVER
THE WORLD OF JIM HENSON

Jim Henson's
TALE OF SAND
The lost screenplay
by JIM HENSON
and JERRY JUHL
As realized by
RAMÓN K. PÉREZ

Jim Henson's
LABYRINTH
ARTIST TRIBUTE

Jim Henson's
THE POWER OF THE
DARK CRYSTAL
Simon Spurrier
Kelly Matthews
Nichole Matthews

Jim Henson's
THE
STORYTELLER
Dragons

Jim Henson's
The Dark Crystal
TALES

Jim Henson's
LABYRINTH
ADULT COLORING BOOK

ARCHAIA™

AVAILABLE AT YOUR LOCAL COMICS SHOP AND BOOKSTORE

To find a comics shop in your area, call 1-888-266-4226

WWW.**BOOM-STUDIOS**.COM

Jim Henson's Tale of Sand
Jim Henson, Jerry Juhl, Ramón K. Pérez
ISBN: 978-1-93639-309-1 | $29.95 US

Jim Henson's The Dark Crystal: Creation Myths
Brian Froud, Alex Sheikman, Joshua Dysart, and others
Volume 1
ISBN: 978-1-60886-704-2 | $14.99 US
Volume 2
ISBN: 978-1-60886-887-2 | $14.99 US
Volume 3
ISBN: 978-1-60886-906-0 | $14.99 US

Jim Henson's The Power of the Dark Crystal
Simon Spurrier, Kelly and Nichole Matthews
Volume 1
ISBN: 978-1-60886-992-3 | $24.99 US

Jim Henson's The Dark Crystal Tales
Cory Godbey
ISBN: 978-1-60886-845-2 | $16.99 US

Jim Henson's Labyrinth Artist Tribute
Michael Allred, Dave McKean, Faith Erin Hicks, and others
ISBN: 978-1-60886-897-1 | $24.99 US

Jim Henson's Labyrinth Adult Coloring Book
Jorge Corona, Jay Fosgitt, Phil Murphy
ISBN: 978-1-68415-111-0 | $16.99 US

Jim's Henson's The Musical Monsters of Turkey Hollow
Jim Henson, Jerry Juhl, Roger Langridge
ISBN: 978-1-60886-434-8 | $24.99 US

Jim Henson's The Storyteller: Witches
S.M. Vidaurri, Kyla Vanderklugt, Matthew Dow Smith, Jeff Stokely
ISBN: 978-1-60886-747-9 | $24.99 US

Jim Henson's The Storyteller: Dragons
Daniel Bayliss, Jorge Corona, Hannah Christensen, Nathan Pride
ISBN: 978-1-60886-874-2 | $24.99 US

Jim Henson
THE JIM HENSON COMPANY

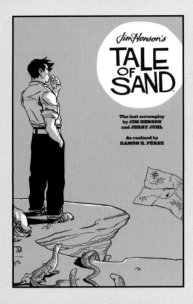